DISTRIBUTED PROCESSING AND DATA COMMUNICATIONS

DISTRIBUTED PROCESSING AND DATA COMMUNICATIONS

DANIEL R. McGLYNN

A Wiley-Interscience Publication

JOHN WILEY & SONS
New York / Chichester / Brisbane / Toronto

Library of Congress Cataloging in Publication Data:
McGlynn, Daniel R.
    Distributed processing and data communications.

    "A Wiley-Interscience publication."
    Bibliography: p.
    Includes index.
    1. Electronic data processing—Distributed processing
2. Computer networks.   I. Title.

QA76.9.D5M3   001.6′4   78-1117
ISBN 0-471-01886-4

To My Wife

preface

The concept of a computer data communications system is rapidly changing due to recent advances in computer hardware and transmission technology. The concept of a single, large-scale, centralized computer and numerous remote terminals, characteristic of computer network design of the late 1960s and early 1970s, is gradually giving way to evolving "distributed processing" designs incorporating more recent technology—microprocessors, satellite transmission systems, and new network architectures and communication protocols.

Distributed processing is the implementation of a data processing task at remote locations connected by a data communication channel under a common network architecture or communication discipline. The term "distributed processing" is used here generically, and includes the concepts of distributed computation, distributed data bases, and distributed control and supervision.

This book is a review of distributed processing and data communications systems and technologies with an emphasis on those systems and designs that are expected to be of significant future importance. Distributed processing systems are only now emerging, and thus it is important to provide the reader with a perspective on not only those technologies currently available, but also future ones.

This book is intended for computer systems analysts, data communication managers, and electronic engineers concerned with the planning, design, and implementation of a data communications/distributed processing network. It gives an overview and survey of data communications and distributed processing facilities, as well as their features, capabilities, and limitations. Examples of IBM systems are primarily used as illustrations throughout the text because of the commercial importance of IBM equipment in the marketplace, but it must be emphasized that similar systems are available from other vendors.

This book is based on professional courses taught by the author and his associates throughout the United States. It may therefore also be useful in college computer science courses, in data communications and distributed processing. The background required for such a course would be introductory courses in computer science, programming, and systems analysis. Data communications is a multidisciplinary subject, and the treatment here is kept on a uniformly introductory level so as to be accessible to students from a wide variety of backgrounds.

Chapter 1 is an overview of data communications systems and, more generally, the information transmission industry. Data communications systems are no longer concerned merely with "data" associated with computers, but also more generally with *information*—including text, speech, and pictures—that is processed and transmitted digitally.

Chapter 2 is a review of data communications system hardware, from the basic computer peripherals such as terminals and printers, to specialized communications equipment such as communication processors and interface devices.

Chapter 3 deals with the software aspects of data communication systems, such as the host operating system, access methods, and applications programs.

The combination of hardware and software into a distributed processing network is the subject of the fourth chapter. The chapter first treats the basic level of terminal and processor configurations, and then analyzes network topology and architecture in more detail. The network control architecture and data communications protocols of various commercial systems—for example, IBM's System Network Architecture (Synchronous Data Link Control) and DEC's Digital Network Architecture (Digital Data Communications Message Protocol)—are considered in Chapter 5.

Chapter 6 is concerned with the final element of the data communication system—the transmission system and technology. The chapter reviews some of the common-carrier and specialized common-carrier transmission services; it also examines new technologies such as optical fiber transmission and satellite technology.

As an illustration of many of the concepts of data communication systems, Chapter 7 surveys some of the important computer networks (e.g., ARPANET) and reports the progress of emerging satellite networks.

Finally, Chapter 8 considers a spectrum of data communications and distributed processing applications, ranging from banking and telephony to the electronic office of the future. Of course, the actual implementation of future distributed processing systems depend not only on technologic realization and feasibility, but also on numerous commercial, administrative, and regulatory issues which are affected by the rapidly changing technologic environment. The Appendix on Technology Forecasting and Assessment is therefore included in order to place the subject of planning a data communications/ distributed processing system in somewhat broader context.

I would like to express my appreciation to those people whose comments and helpful criticisms have contributed to this work: Sy Ratner, Jim Grey, Don Sheppard, and Norman Abramson.

DANIEL R. MCGLYNN

Briarcliff Manor, New York
January 1978

contents

one
DATA COMMUNICATION SYSTEMS— OVERVIEW AND PERSPECTIVE

A s the computer and communications industry evolve with the development of new technology, the architecture and applications of data communications systems are also changing. Data communications can no longer be considered merely a form of remote computing just concerned with data, but is now concerned with additional forms of information transfer and handling, including the processing and transmission of encoded speech and pictures for a variety of applications. The system design and network architecture of such data communications systems for such new and emerging applications is the basis for this book.

The present chapter first places data communications systems within the broader perspective of the information industries, and considers some of the important present and potential applications of such systems. In the second section, the particular application of computer-communications networks is considered in greater detail, and some of the basic issues of distributed data processing are analyzed in view of the rapidly changing technology, architecture, and applications of data communications systems.

THE INFORMATION INDUSTRIES

The information industries are concerned with the collection, processing, and distribution of information in one variety or another. Data communications may be broadly defined as the handling and transfer of information from one location to another. In analyzing the role of data communications in the information industries, consideration can be given to two distinct areas: data processing services and information handling services.

Data processing services are those typically associated with computer processing—i.e., financial services such as payroll, accounts receivable, invoicing, and inventory control; data base services such as file maintenance; and technical services, such as supplying computing services for users.

Information handling services are those associated with the generation, handling, transfer, distribution, and classification of information, either written or spoken. Information handling services are typically associated with office equipment, including dictation machines, telephones, typewriters, copying machines, and file cabinets.

As computer and telecommunications technology matures, the structure and applications of data processing and information handling services are undergoing rapid change. In the subsections that follow, we will consider the structure of the information industries, the role of data communications in the data processing services area, and the potential role of data communications in the information handling services area. Having established such a framework for analysis, subsequent subsections examine the technical and the economic and social impact of data communications in the information industries.

Information Industries Structure

In order to properly analyze the structure of the information industries, the approximate gross revenues as of 1975 of the various individual industries are presented in Table 1.1. Table 1.1 lists and compares the size and scope of the most significant industries performing information handling services. Financial data for the financial services and government services industries are omitted since such services are not immediately comparable with the other types of services listed.

Since government services are one of the most important of the information "industries," Table 1.2 lists some of the important administrative and operational functions performed by the Federal govern-

TABLE 1.1.   The Information Industries

Industry	$ (Billions)
Domestic telephone	37.1
Domestic telegraph	2.2
Broadcast television	4.5
Broadcast radio	1.9
Cable television	0.8
Newspapers	10.9
Book publishing and printing	5.4
Periodicals	4.3
Advertising	12.9
Educational	119.0
Motion pictures	2.5
Financial services	
Banking	
Insurance	
Securities	
Government services	
Postal Service	
Census Bureau	
Other information agencies	

Source: U.S. Department of Commerce.

ment that involve the use of data processing and data communications. State and local government agencies also make extensive use of data processing, and such applications are shown in Figure 1.1. The transfer of information between local agencies, shown on the periphery of Figure 1.1, and state agencies shown in the middle, illustrates the complex information handling and transfer processes which future data communications systems might be called upon to implement.

DATA PROCESSING SERVICES.   The role of data communications in data processing services can best be analyzed by considering the data processing budgets in a variety of industries. Table 1.3 lists the data processing budgets of various industries ranked as a percentage of the gross revenues of the organization. It is not surprising that one of the most extensive users of data processing services as a proportion of total organization revenue are educational institutions. In addition to the usual administrative and financial applications of data processing systems found in every organization, educational institutions also utilize computers for research and instructional purposes.

TABLE 1.2. Federal Government Information Functions

Administrative

Supply Management: procurement
control
maintenance
repair

Operational Management: planning
research and
development
evaluation

Property Management: land
structures
equipment
machinery

Financial Management: budget
accounting
payroll

Personnel Management

Operational

Financial: tax administration
insurance administration
benefits administration
loans and mortgages

Regulatory: securities and commodities
banking
and financial institutions
common carriers
labor organizations

Records: national statistics
military services
intelligence
patents, copyrights,
trademarks
Library of Congress

Services: agricultural
commerce
educational
health care
social services
transportation

Table 1.4 breaks down the data processing budget into itemized components: personnel (salaries, training, etc.), hardware (including maintenance), media (including supplies and accessories), and communications (voice and data lines). Since the relative magnitude of such components varies with the size of the installation, examples of three different size installations are given: small (up to $50,000/year hardware budget), medium (up to $250,000/year hardware budget), and large (over $1 million/year hardware budget). The data given is that for non-IBM installations in order that the design philosophy of any one manufacturer does not influence the sample.

In installations of all categories, Table 1.4 indicates that communications services is a relatively small expense. The hardware expenditures also include communications gear, and it is therefore worthwhile to break down the hardware expenditures in the same manner. This is done in Table 1.5.

Table 1.5 indicates that the largest proportion of hardware expenditures is in computer (i.e., central processing unit) and memory. The communications gear is still a relatively small expense. It must be emphasized, however, that the computer industry is of substantial

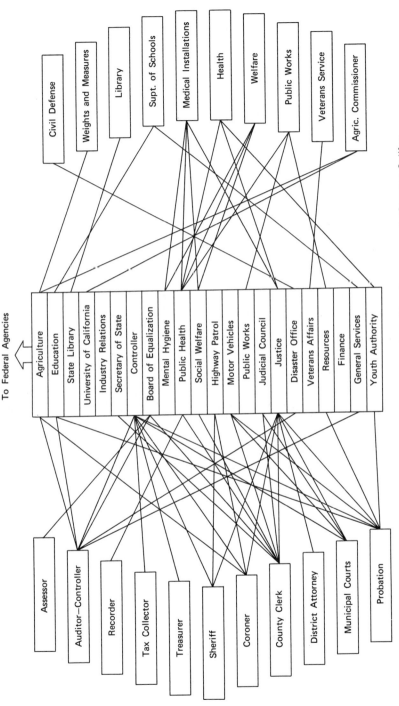

FIGURE 1.1. Information flow between state and local government. (Source: California Statewide Information System Study, Lockheed Missiles and Space Company, Final Report.)

5

TABLE 1.3. Data Processing Budgets

Industry	Gross Revenues (%)
Educational institutions	3.0
Utilities	2.0
Medical	1.8
Insurance	1.6
City and county gov't.	1.4
Transportation	0.8
Construction	0.4

Source: *Datamation,* February 1976.

size: the U.S. Department of Commerce estimates 1976 shipments of computers and related equipment at $12.1 billion, and projects 1985 shipments at $22.6 billion. The communications segment of the industry, though relatively small compared with other segments, is the most rapidly growing and changing segment, and merits our close examination.

As we pointed out above, data communications is not considered part of the usual data processing operations, but with broader applications in information handling and transfer. However, recent studies do show that data processing services are expected to account for the greatest proportion of volume of data traffic. The results of one such study concerned with data traffic volume in Western Europe is reported in Table 1.6. The nine leading applications of data transmission are listed in the order of their anticipated proportion of the total data traffic volume in the year 1985. These nine applications accounted for 60% of the total data traffic volume in 1972, and are anticipated to account for 66% of the total data traffic volume in 1985.

TABLE 1.4. Data Processing Budgets by Installation Size

Category	Small (%)	Medium (%)	Large (%)
Personnel	54	46	42
Hardware	34	39	45
Media	7	7	6
Communications	0.5	2.9	1.4

Source: *Datamation,* February 1976.

TABLE 1.5.   Data Processing Hardware Expenditures by Installation Size

Category	Small (%)	Medium (%)	Large (%)
Central Site			
Computers, memory	44	48	41
Peripherals	40	27	37
Data entry	13	8	3.5
Communications	0.9	3	1.9

Source: *Datamation*, February 1976.

INFORMATION HANDLING SERVICES.   The role of data communications in information handling services is a broad subject. There are various types of "information handling" services, some of which lend themselves to digitizing and data transmission, while others do not. Table 1.7 presents a list of various types of transactional services that could be implemented through a data communications system.

As we suggested above, many of the information handling services noted in Table 1.7 are performed manually. Only recently has the concept of "word" processing, analogous to "data" processing, been developed, and commercial "word processing systems" been introduced.

Word processing is a term that denotes information handling ser-

TABLE 1.6.   Data Transmission Applications

	Data Traffic Volume		Annual Growth (%)
Application	1972	1985	1972–1985
Data processing services			
scientific/engineering	12	18	26
general business	7	18	31
Education and research			
scientific/engineering	10	7	18
Discrete manufacturing	8	6	19
Other data processing services	2	4	28
Process manufacturing			
administrative and financial	6	4	17
Banking and financial	8	4	14
News agencies	3	3	21
Process manufacturing			
sales planning	4	2	19

TABLE 1.7. Services Ranked in Accordance with Magnitude

Service	Transactions/Year, 1990	Conversion Factors		Bits/Year
Telephone	482×10^9 calls	360 sec/call	64000 bits/sec	1.1×10^{19}
Videotelephone	1×10^9 calls	360 sec/call	6.3×10^6 bits/sec	2.3×10^{18}
Mail	100×10^9 letters	3×10^5 bits/letter		3.0×10^{16}
Television	72×10^3 hours	3660 sec/hour	64×10^6 bits/sec	1.7×10^{16}
Remote library browsing	20×10^6 accesses	200 pages/access	3×10^5 bits/page	1.2×10^{15}
Interlibrary loans	100×10^6 books	10^7 bits/book		1.0×10^{15}
Facsimile transmission of "mug shots," etc.	25×10^6 cases	10 pages/case	3×10^6 bits/page	7.5×10^{14}
Remote medical lit. search	200×10^6 searches	30 pages/search	3×10^4 bits/page	1.8×10^{14}
Checks and credit trans.	340×10^9 transactions	50 char./trans.	8 bits/char.	1.4×10^{14}
Patent searches	7×10^6 searches	6 pages/search	3×10^6 bits/page	1.3×10^{14}
Facsimile transmission of newspapers	20 newspapers using service	365 days/year × 50 pages/day	180×10^6 bits/page	6.6×10^{13}
National crime info. ctr.	70×10^6 messages	3×10^5 bits/trans.		2.1×10^{13}
Remote title and abs. search	20×10^6 searches	30 pages/search	3×10^4 bits/page	1.8×10^{13}
Stock transfers	5×10^9 transactions	3000 bits/trans.		1.5×10^{13}
National legal info. ctr.	30×10^6 searches	10 pages/search	3×10^4 bits/page	9.0×10^{12}
Airline reservations	1.4×10^9 passengers	3 trans./pass. × 200 char./trans.	8 bits/char.	6.7×10^{12}

Remote medical diagnosis	200	$\times 10^6$ cases	30000 bits/case	6.0×10^{12}
Electrocardiogram analysis	200	$\times 10^6$ tests	30000 bits/test	6.0×10^{12}
Motor vehicle registration	245	$\times 10^6$	6000 bits/item	1.5×10^{12}
Remote print. of new books	105	$\times 10^3$ books	10^7 bits/book	1.1×10^{12}
Driver's license renewal	90	$\times 10^6$ items	6000 bits/item	5.4×10^{11}
Stock exchange quotations	4	$\times 10^9$ transactions	100 bits/trans.	4.0×10^{11}
Hotel/motel reservations	100	$\times 10^6$ reservations	1000 bits/res.	1.0×10^{11}
Auto rental	40	$\times 10^6$ transactions	1000 bits/trans.	4.0×10^{10}
Sports and cultural event ticketing	200	$\times 10^6$ transactions	200 bits/trans.	4.0×10^{10}
Telegraph	35	$\times 10^6$ messages	20 words/message 50 bits/word	3.5×10^{10}
Stolen property info. trans.	7	$\times 10^6$ cases	3000 bits/case	2.1×10^{10}
Stolen vehicle info. trans.	5	$\times 10^6$ cases	3000 bits/case	1.5×10^{10}

Source: R. W. Hough, "Future Data Traffic Volume," Computer, September–October 1970.

vices that concentrate on text material rather than data. Although the technical problems associated with processing text (i.e., "string processing," to use the correct computer science term) are far more difficult than handling pure numbers, the potential applications are far greater. Although word processing may be performed in a stand-alone mode, the transfer of the processed text to another location through some communications link (mail, telegram, telephone, etc.) is an important aspect of the information handling sequence. The transfer of text from one location to another through a data communications system is often called "electronic mail" and is one of the most rapidly growing uses of such systems.

Returning now to the potential applications of data communication in the information industries, we must first quantify the amount of information that is handled by the various information industry media. The annual information volume in terms of the number of transactions is estimated. The amount of information contained in a typical transaction is also estimated, and a determination made of the total amount of information, as measured in bits, for an annual period. The various information industry services are then ranked in Table 1.7 according to the number of bits/year such services account for.

The data presented in Table 1.7 is not meant to suggest that the transactions shown will actually be handled digitally in the year 1990, but merely to provide a perspective on the potential size and relative importance of the various information industries.

The underlying assumption in presenting the data of Table 1.7, and indeed of our entire consideration of the broad field of the information industries, is that many of the common and well-known information transactions now performed by paper transfer or through analog media may be performed electronically and digitally in the future. The digital transmission of telephone calls, which is listed as the leading service in the table, is perhaps the most important example of "data" communication, and various forms of digital voice communications will be considered in greater detail throughout this book.

Technological Impact

There are two basic technological impacts of data communications in the information industries:

• The impact on computer organization
• The impact on control and access over information

IMPACT ON COMPUTER ORGANIZATION.   The principal technological impact of data communications systems on an organization is on the structure and organization of its data processing and information handling operations. The basic concept made possible by data communications is that of *distributed processing.* The data processing functions of an organization no longer need be centralized in one large installation, but may be distributed geographically to the organization's user locations, and connected by a data communications link.

The data processing functions that may be "distributed" include the following:

• Input/output
• Processing
• Data storage
• Programming and maintenance
• Audit and control

Of course, for reasons of reliability and control, such functions need not exclusively be performed at the remote location, but such operations could be initiated there.

Distributed processing is characterized by three important features:

• Use of small, dedicated computers
• System modularity
• Fault tolerance

The use of small, dedicated minicomputers or microcomputers at the remote location in place of mainframe computers is perhaps the most significant aspect of distributed processing in terms of its technologic impact. Although large mainframe computers are suitable in applications involving large data bases, or requiring high-speed processing, many typical user functions do not need the speed and sophistication of such large computers. The result has been the increasing use of minicomputers at several user locations to replace a single large mainframe computer. In some applications microcomputers (i.e., a computer incorporating a microprocessor as the central processing unit of the computer) have been custom designed by the user to perform specialized functions at the remote location in the most efficient manner.

Another important aspect of distributed processing is the creation of system modules, either in hardware or software, for performing particular functions. System modularity implies greater maintainability, reliability, and control. By organizing a system into discrete modules electrically and functionally separate from other modules, only connected by a communications link, system operation is much more flexible. Individual modules may be replaced, updated, tested, and expanded without interfering with other operating modules or affecting overall system operation.

Fault tolerance, as we use it here, is concerned with the design of computing systems which are able to execute specified tasks correctly, according to some "correctness" criteria, in the presence of hardware and/or software faults. More specifically, fault tolerance is the feature in distributed processing which is concerned with the implementation of fault detection, fault location, and system reconfiguration procedures that can be used to maintain or recover system integrity in the presence of such faults. Although fault tolerance is not the principal design feature of many distributed processing systems, it is an important characterization that distinguishes such systems from centralized systems.

CONTROL AND ACCESS OVER INFORMATION.   The issue of control and access over information handled by a data communications system is perhaps the most basic question to be considered by the system designer. Information is a valuable asset. It represents an investment in gathering, classifying, and processing raw data. It is legally sanctioned by being considered "confidential information," and in some instances even a "trade secret." The disclosure of such information may represent an invasion of privacy or the loss of a significant economic advantage.

The primary objective of the design of a data communications system is to ensure that the information transferred from one station to another station remains secure and is only available to authorized users. One of the important technologic impacts of data communications on the information industries is that control and access of information is just as important as the availability of that information to the authorized users. Stated in other terms, it is generally equally important that certain information be *un*available to certain users as it is to be available to certain other users.

The issue of control and access over information is a technologic question, since it is the hardware and software of the system that determines whether a given user has access or control over particular data files. However, it must be emphasized that it is a management decision as to what degree of security over certain files or processes should be implemented. Such decisions are reflected in the system architecture and security cost and overhead of the system. Therefore, as far as the technologic impact is concerned, we can conclude: (1) data communications systems raises issues of control and access over information that were not present in stand-alone systems and (2) the system design must reflect a management decision concerning the value of providing certain data to designated individuals, as well as preventing other individuals from having access to that data.

Economic and Social Impact

There are two basic economic and social impacts of data communications in the information industries:

- The tradeoff between data communications and other facilities
- The effect of data communications on organization structure

TRADEOFF BETWEEN DATA COMMUNICATIONS AND OTHER FACILITIES.   One broad issue of concern to the system designer is the tradeoff between data communications and other forms of information transfer. Although the business environment or the particular processing task may create a demand for remote computing facilities, it is the task of the system designer and data communications manager to implement the required information transfer.

There are many types of media and communications technologies for implementing information transfer, many of which will be considered in detail in Chapter 5. At this stage we simply wish to mention the noncommunications technologies as a means of information transfer. These include the mail and other means of physically transporting information in the form of written records from one location to another.

Data communications may be considered as a practical replacement of conventional transportation for information transfer in several instances:

- When the need for information at the remote location is required within a relatively short time after it is requested
- When the cost of conventional transportation is prohibitive
- When conventional transportation presents problems of reliability or security of the data

The first instance is the basis for the majority of the applications of data communications systems: in inquiry/response or data collection systems in which the rapidity of the interaction with the host computer is the principal design characteristic of the system.

The second instance—the relatively high cost of conventional transportation—occurs when the amount of information to be transmitted is small relative to its value, or when geographic factors make the cost of physical transportation of data prohibitive. The first case is typified when there is very little information transmitted, as for example in a response to an inquiry. Another point that must be considered is the "value" of the information. In commercial data processing systems it is fairly easy to assign a monetary value to certain information. Such values are determined by the cost of collecting that information, the replacement cost (i.e., duplication from a master file), or its value to a third party. Certain information of a "trade secret" nature may be very valuable and may preferably be transmitted to remote locations by conventional transportation. The second case is typified by remote locations situated in areas that are infrequently served by regularly scheduled carriers, or are physically difficult to reach by ordinary transportation.

The third instance is when conventional transportation presents problems of reliability or security of the data. There are numerous possible reasons for such problems, and data communications offers the reliability and security that might not be available from other facilities.

There is considerable interest in the potential for data communications in replacing other forms of transportation, such as document transportation. Such transaction-related information transfer is now performed by physical documents (invoices, checks, statements of account, etc.), but could well be performed by communications of data in an "electronic funds transfer system." Such systems will be considered in greater detail in Chapter 8.

EFFECT OF DATA COMMUNICATIONS ON ORGANIZATION STRUCTURES. One consequence of the evolving development of data communications systems, and the trade-off and replacement by such systems of conventional transportation tasks, is the effect on organizational structures. Loosely speaking, modern day business is organized by transporting people to the data base (i.e., the office). The rapid evolution of data communications has suggested the feasibility of transporting data to the people.

The replacement of people-transportation by data communications is of course a highly speculative, and highly unlikely, change in the structure of society. However, the technologic feasibility of home-office data processing terminals makes consideration of such alternative futures important in the evaluation of new data processing systems.

The subject of the replacement of the transportation of people and goods with the transportation of data is particularly of interest to rural or suburban regions concerned with the improvement and economic development of their area. Such regions see the extension of tele-communications facilities in their area as opportunities for increased employment, as well as a means for supplying educational or other services. One method suggested for providing such telecommunications services is through a broadcast satellite system, called "Rural-Sat."

On a smaller scale, data communications systems also replace convention transportation of documents within an office. The development of word processing systems, and the capability to transport written text or other documents in the form of digital information from one location to another, has an important effect on organizational structure. More importantly, the actual implementation of such document transportation through telecommunications is far closer to widespread commercial implementation than a broadcast satellite system.

In summary, the most important economic and social impacts of data communications are concerned with its replacement of conventional information transfer facilities, and the possible organizational changes that may be necessary to accommodate such new facilities.

COMPUTER-COMMUNICATIONS NETWORKS

One of the most important types of data communications systems is the computer-communications network. The importance of computer networks is the increased interest in distributed data processing as a means of delivering computing power to the user. Although the concept of computer networks goes back to the early development of time-sharing, the recent revolutionary decrease in the cost of processing units and memory due to advances in semiconductor technology has restructured the way computer power may be implemented and efficiently delivered to the user.

An examination of computer-communications networks must consider the following basic issues:

User population
Evolution of the general-purpose digital computer
Economic basis for computer networking
Network technology

User Population

The concept of distributed data processing and computer networking primarily relates to the processing requirements of the various categories of users that exist in the marketplace. Such categories depend on the type of processing required, the system resources needed to support such processing, and the programming or administrative support needed or available at the user location.

The type of processing required by the user is the first determinant of the type of distributed processor and computer network configuration that should be implemented. The user may require a specialized service, for example an on-line data base inquiry/response service, or a generalized service, for example a time-sharing service. The concept of a distributed processing system is to provide as much processing power at the user location as is feasible for the particular application, considering the constraints of:

The number of users at the remote location
The number and mix of programs being run
The system resources required at the remote location
The support available at the remote location
The economic trade-offs involved

The number of users determines the number of terminals or other facilities that should be provided at the remote location. The number and mix of programs determines the type of terminals (CRT, hardcopy, etc.) that are to be provided. The system resources required at the remote location is directed to the type of processing being done, and whether the user should be able to interact with other network elements.

The support available at the remote location should not be underestimated. Systems analysts, systems programmers, and applications programmers are skilled professionals, and their services are both unnecessary and uneconomic for most routine data processing activities. The goal of the computer network is therefore to provide as much flexibility and processing power at the user location, without the requirement of sophisticated programming capability by the user.

A final point which must be considered with reference to the user population is the economic trade-off between hardware, software, and data processing personnel. Hardware is the least expensive element in the network, and the duplication of hardware—for example, terminals—may be the most efficient way of implementing a network. Software is more expensive, but not as expensive as trained data processing personnel; therefore general software packages are frequently used in computer networks rather than requiring system programmers to interface to the computer network. Therefore, whatever the composition of the user population, the computer network should be accessible to the least experienced user. This means fairly sophisticated hardware at the user location, and simplified network control software.

Evolution of the General-Purpose Digital Computer

During the early development of computer technology, the concept of a "general-purpose" digital computer emerged. Such a computer was able to handle a wide variety of users—commercial and scientific—as well as different operational configurations. What became specialized was the software: software for business applications, software for scientific use, software for interactive computation, and so on.

As hardware technology becomes less and less expensive, the concept of a general-purpose computer operating with specialized software may not be the most practical or cost-effective solution to the processing requirements of a wide variety of users. More specifically, the availability and low cost of "special-purpose" or dedicated processors may be a feasible alternative to general-purpose mainframe computers.

As hardware technology becomes less and less expensive, the general purpose, mainframe computer operating with specialized software may not be the most practical or cost-effective solution to the processing requirements of a wide variety of geographically dispersed users. More specifically, the availability and low cost of special purpose or dedicated processors may be a significant alternative to traditional centralized computers.

A number of such dedicated processors may be implemented in a distributed processing or "computer-communications" network. In such a network not only processing but data, system functions, and control are distributed. The traditional mainframe computer may still be present in such a network, but it functions now as that of a "host" computer supervising the network.

The computer user market has, in the last 20 years of computer technology development, acquired a maturity and sophistication whereby the demand for a general-purpose machine has been redirected. Users now acquire different machines for performing different functions—for example minicomputers for control applications and large-scale business computers for commercial applications. Although the basic elements of such computers are the same, in reality such machines are not general purpose. Once the manufacturers of computer equipment realize that there is no general-purpose computer market, an important step in defining the system architecture of new computer applications will be taken.

Economic Basis for Computer Networking

A computer network is a specialized and sophisticated system for accomplishing an information handling and transfer task. For many applications, particularly commercial applications, the economic basis of computer networking is one of the most important criteria in the organization and technical design of the network. It is therefore important to evaluate some of the economic criteria for establishing a computer network, and some of the alternatives. The economic criteria are:

• Existence of computer facilities adapted to data communications
• Cost/effectiveness compared with alternative information-transfer facilities
• Availabilities and capabilities of suitable transmission media

Computer networks are concerned with the handling of computer-processed data. It is therefore important that the computer facilities incorporate communications capabilities and are compatible with data communications standards. Such requirements are more significant than they normally might seem. Only recently have the major computer manufacturers announced products, both hardware and software, that are oriented to data communications. Furthermore, data communications "standards," such as data-link protocols, are only just being developed.

Another aspect of the computer facilities which should be evaluated is their adaption to data communications—for example, through the use of an interactive data file. If the computer facilities were developed as stand-alone units, the effort and expense of implementing processor or memory sharing at remote locations may not be justified. The first economic criterion is therefore whether the existing or planned computer facilities are data-communications-oriented, as determined by the nature of the processing task, and the availability of hardware with communications capabilities.

The second point is of cost/effectiveness of computer networks compared with alternative information-transfer facilities. Data communications is a very rapid, yet very expensive, method of transferring information from one location to another. The mail, or private transportation, are economically preferable alternatives when the speed of the information transfer is not essential.

Another aspect of cost/effectiveness which must be considered is the economies of scale. A computer network serves to combine several smaller systems into a single large system. It could be expected (and sometimes does indeed occur) that the single large system works as a unit, and offers an economic advantage over the sum total of the smaller systems working alone.

Finally, the availabilities and capabilities of the transmission media is an important economic factor. The transmission media (i.e., telephone switched circuit, private line, microwave link, satellite, etc.), is a regulated facility, and thus is the one aspect of a data communications system that is not controlled by the user. The user is faced with a rather limited choice of facilities at fixed tariffs. In some areas the user may only have one or two choices. The economics, availability, and capability of such media in such cases is a significant factor in the overall economic basis for computer networking.

One alternative to a computer network is the large, centralized mainframe computer. Such systems are still the most practical implementation for performing large scale information handling tasks, such as operations on large data bases, and are expected to remain so for some time in the future. However, more demanding requirements of a heterogenous user population, the improving cost-effectiveness of smaller, dedicated processors for specialized tasks, and the increasing availability of computer networking facilities suggest that more and more user applications may be effectively implemented through distributed processing networks.

Finally, other alternatives to note are essentially compromises between a pure distributed processing network and a pure centralized processing system. Such networks are perhaps the most realistic ones of all, since they are characteristic of a typical user's evolution from an existing centralized mainframe system to an increasingly distributed processing network. Moreover, such evolution seems to be encouraged by many mainframe vendors whose new systems emphasize distributed processing capabilities.

Network Technology

Network technology is the basic subject matter of this book. Computer communications networks are one of the most complex and expensive projects that are undertaken by a corporation or other institution. In order for such corporations to be competitive in their industry, and institutions to be effective in their field, such networks must be designed with the capability of using not only present technology, but also future technologies as they become available.

The chapters that follow will closely analyze the various aspects of network technology: hardware, software, system architecture, and transmission technologies. The objective of such analysis is to enable the system designer to develop working knowledge of the present alternatives in system design, and to explore some of the more recent technology that is expected to be of importance in the future.

It must be emphasized that the changes in network technology make possible new applications of computer-communications networks throughout the information industries, even opening new industries to the use of data communications networks. Once such applications have been implemented, the entire structure of the industry, or even entirely new industries may be possible. The telecommunications industry, the appearance of specialized common carriers, is just one example of this important trend.

In analyzing network technology, a consideration of the impact of computer-communications network on the structure and administration of the organization is equally important as the technical and financial aspects. Although a network may be initially structured on the basis of existing resources in specific locations, once the network has been implemented it then affects all future growth patterns of the organization. Thus the specification of a particular geographic location of a computer center or a communications facility means that future facilities must take the existence of the installed facilities into account. Not only service facilities, but administrative structures are developed around the computer-communications network.

As the computer-communications network becomes effective, it begins displacing other facilities, and the organization comes to depend more upon the network. In short, the network begins to take on numerous functions, and in effect becomes a "management-information system" in addition to merely an administrative facility.

The design of management-information systems through the use of computer-communications networks is one of the most important applications of network technology, and the implementation of such systems in a variety of industries will be considered in detail later in this book.

two
DATA
COMMUNICATION
HARDWARE

A data communications network is a system whereby one user is able to exchange information with a remote, designated second user. Such exchange of information takes place through both hardware and software facilities in the network shared by all users. In this chapter the hardware facilities of a data communications network will be considered. Such facilities include:

Terminals
Host computers
Communication interface devices
Communication processors
Digital filters
Transmission carriers

TERMINALS

The terminal is the user's access to the data communications network. Depending on the particular user's requirements, the terminal's design and capabilities are adapted for the task it is intended to perform. Terminals may therefore be classified into a number of general categories:

Keyboard terminals
Specialized input/output terminals
Remote batch terminals

Autotransaction terminals
Sensor-based terminals
Intelligent terminals

Keyboard Terminals

The keyboard terminal is the basic device for inputting alphanumeric information into the data communications network. Coupled with the keyboard is usually a printer or display which permits the operator to observe and verify the inputted information, as well as alternatively serving as an output device when the terminal is receiving information from the network.

The keyboard terminal, in its simplest and most basic embodiment, may consist merely of numeric keys, such as the Touch-Tone™ keyboard of the Bell System. A specially designed telephone, the Transaction™ Telephone, shown in Figure 2.1, is an example of a numeric data input terminal in a credit verification system that also serves as a telephone. Most keyboard terminals, however, include a full set of alphanumeric keys so that character strings, as well as numeric information, may be transmitted to the remote location. Specialized software systems may even require additional keyboard

FIGURE 2.1.   The Transaction II telephone.

functions to represent certain predetermined operations, such as in the APL high-level computer language. An APL terminal keyboard is shown in Figure 2.2.

The function of the keyboard terminal is to convert the character indicated by the pressed key into a serial bit stream for use by the data communications network. Each character is represented by a seven- or eight-bit code, such as USASCII or EBCDIC. The sequence of characters are thus sent bit by bit over the data link to the receiving terminal, which performs the opposite function of reassembling the characters from the code, and printing or displaying the decoded character for use by the remote user.

The typing speed of a keyboard operator is considerably slower than the transmission capabilities of the terminal, so means are provided in the terminal for storing characters entered on the keyboard until a "carriage return" or "enter" key is pressed. The terminal then transmits the entire block of characters at its designed transmission speed over the data link, and then frees the data link for access by other users.

Another important type of keyboard terminal is the portable terminal, such as shown in Figure 2.3. The portable terminal is designed to be taken to the source for data entry and recording, and is therefore suitable for high-volume data entry operation such as in retailing. The handset is equipped with a display panel for immediate visual verification of the data entered. The handset is connected with a recorder which records the data on a magnetic tape cassette. The entire device is controlled by a microprocessor.

CRT Terminals

The use of terminals incorporating a cathode ray tube (CRT) as a display device is becoming increasingly popular for many applications. Such terminals are sometimes also referred to as VDUs—visual

FIGURE 2.2. APL keyboard.

FIGURE 2.3.   Portable keyboard terminal. (Photograph courtesy Telxon Corp.)

display units. CRT terminals require more circuitry for generating and refreshing character images on the face of the CRT screen, and are therefore somewhat more expensive than hardcopy terminals. However, the advantages of such terminals—silence, speed, appearance—generally outweigh the cost factor in customer environments, such as reservation and financial systems (Figure 2.4).

CRT terminals may be adapted to display alphanumeric characters, special symbols (such as APL characters), or graphic information. Alphanumeric characters are typically generated by an arrangement of a sequence of dots on a matrix field, such as shown in Figure 2.5. The particular sequence of dots corresponding to each character or symbol is stored in a read-only memory (ROM) in the terminal, which automatically supplies the desired sequence of light and dark areas in the character field as the field is scanned on the CRT screen. Figure

FIGURE 2.4. Keyboard CRT terminal: Teletype Dataspeed 40.

2.6 illustrates how a character is formed on the face of the CRT as the character field is scanned.

Graphic terminals, such as the IBM 2250 shown in Figure 2.7, provide a means of representing two- or three-dimensional objects on the screen of the CRT. Two-dimensional objects are represented by a set of vertex points connected by straight-line segments. Such terminals are provided with a light pen for automatically indicating a particular vertex or line segment on the face of the CRT.

Three-dimensional objects may be displayed in perspective on the CRT screen, as shown in Figure 2.8, by internal software. Such

FIGURE 2.5. Dot matrix character generation.

software automatically generates a perspective view from the coordi-
nates of the vertices and surfaces of the object stored in memory.

Both alphanumeric and graphic CRT terminals are best suited for
inquiry/response type applications where the use of a hardcopy or
printout is unnecessary. Applications that specify either a hardcopy
input or output require specialized input/output terminals, discussed
in the next section.

Specialized Input/Output Terminals

There are a wide variety of specialized input/output (I/O) terminals
adapted to handle particular data entry media. On the input side these
include:

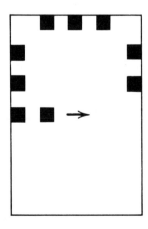

FIGURE 2.6. CRT scanning pattern.

FIGURE 2.7. IBM 2250 graphic terminal. (Photograph courtesy IBM Corp.)

Punch cards
Paper tape
Magnetic media
   magnetic tape (reel, cassette, cartridge)
   magnetic disk (fixed, flexible)
   magnetic cards and strips
   magnetic ink (MICR)
Optical mark, character
Digitized images

On the output side are:

Punch cards
Paper tape
Magnetic media
   magnetic tape (reel, cassette, cartridge)
   magnetic disk (fixed, flexible)
   magnetic cards and strips
   magnetic ink (MICR)

FIGURE 2.8.   Three-dimensional display. (Photograph courtesy IBM Corp.)

Impact printers
  chain
  serial
  drum
  dot matrix
Nonimpact printers
  thermal
  magnetic
  electrostatic
  xerographic
  ink jet
  electronic
  laser
  electrophoretic
Displays
Plotters
Computer-output microfilm

PUNCH CARDS. Punch cards should not be overlooked as an important input/output media. Cards are frequently used for representing simple documents—such as invoices, checks, receipts—which may be punched in appropriate columns and used directly for computer input/output. Even more ambitious financial systems have been proposed, such as securities clearing and transfer operations, which suggest utilizing the punch card as an actual stock or bond certificate.

PAPER TAPE. Paper tape is a very low cost I/O medium. It is generally used in connection with a low cost terminal, such as a Teletype. However, paper tape is relatively slow and inconvenient to use, and is therefore not found in more sophisticated systems.

MAGNETIC MEDIA. Magnetic recording is the standard I/O technique of most modern computer systems, as well as in data communications systems. Although open-reel tape systems offer the highest data transfer rate, cassettes and flexible disks offer more convenience as data entry media, and are frequently used in "key-to-tape" or "key-to-disk" data entry systems. In addition to tape and disk, magnetic media may also be used in the form of magnetic strips, cards, or marks. Because of the importance of magnetic media as an input/output facility, it is worthwhile to consider each of the media in greater detail.

Magnetic Tape. Magnetic tape data storage offers high density, low cost, and portability in a variety of packaging concepts: open reel, cassette, or cartridge.

Data storage on magnetic tape is achieved by recording sequential patterns of magnetization on a linear "track" along the tape, as shown in Figure 2.9. There are several different coding techniques which may be used depending on the overall system design: return-to-zero (RZ), non-return-to-zero (NRZ), non-return-to-zero inverted (NRZI), Miller code, and Manchester or phase encoding (PE), which are compared in Figure 2.10.

The RZ method (Figure 2.10a, and physically represented in Figure 2.9) is based on representing a zero-bit by a zero-level signal, and a one-bit as a pulse that rises to the one-level, and then "returns to zero" within one cycle time. (In reality, the read head of the magnetic tape unit produces a positive signal as it detects a "north" pole, and a negative signal as it detects a "south" pole. We justify these signals to 0–1 levels for simplicity.) Since the RZ method requires two pulses

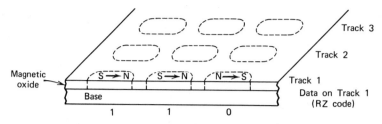

FIGURE 2.9.   Cross-sectional view of magnetic recording medium.

per bit stored, it is not an efficient code and is infrequently used in practice.

There are two variations on the NRZ method (Figures 2.10*b* and *c*): the first variation simply represents a zero-bit by a zero-level signal, and a one-bit by a one-level signal (Figure 2.10*b*); the second variation represents a zero-bit by no signal change, and a one-bit by a signal change, either from the zero-level to the one-level, or the one-level to the zero-level (Figure 2.10*c*). Although NRZ is an efficient code, sophisticated synchronization is required in order to correctly decode long strings of zeros or ones.

The NRZI method (Figure 2.10*d*) is a variation of the NRZ method in which the signal levels are inverted—for example, for the second variation of NRZ, a zero-bit is represented by a signal change, and a one-bit by no signal change.

Miller code (Figure 2.10*d*) represents a one-bit by a pulse transition in the middle of a cycle, and a zero-bit by no transition during the cycle followed by a transition to the one-level at the end of the cycle. If the cycle is already at the one-level, no transition at the end of the cycle is made.

Manchester code or phase encoding (Figure 2.10*e*) utilizes a transition in the middle of each cycle to represent either a zero-bit or a one-bit. A one-bit is represented by a transition from the one-level to the zero-level, while a zero-bit is represented by a transition from the zero-level to the one-level.

As we pointed out above, magnetic tape is packaged in three basic configurations: open reel, cassette, and cartridge.

Open-reel magnetic tape storage is generally used with large mainframe computers. A standard reel contains 2400 feet of $\frac{1}{2}$-inch-wide magnetic tape. Either seven or nine tracks are provided across the width of the tape, with recording at a density from 200 to 1600 bits/inch (bpi). Lower density recording generally uses NRZI coding, while the higher densities (1600 bpi and over) use phase encoding.

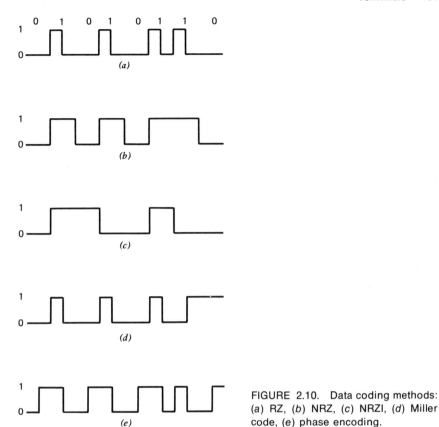

FIGURE 2.10. Data coding methods: (a) RZ, (b) NRZ, (c) NRZI, (d) Miller code, (e) phase encoding.

Typical specifications of open-reel magnetic tape systems are given in Table 2.1.

Group code recording (GCR) is another technique for increasing the data packing density. GCR utilizes a code to avoid recording more than two zeros in succession by translating every four bits of source data into five bits of recorded data. The specific translation is shown in Table 2.2.

In magnetic tape systems, the actual recording of the five-bit GCR code is done through phase encoding (PE), as indicated in Table 2.1. When reading, the five-bit GCR code is translated back into the four-bit source data.

In addition to using GCR code, high-density (6250 bpi) recording systems utilize techniques for interleaving resynchronization signals among sublocks of digital data within a block of recorded data on the

TABLE 2.1. Open-Reel Magnetic Tape Systems

Model (IBM)	Tape Speed (inches/sec)	Data Rate (Kbytes/sec)	Linear Density (bits/inch)	Recording Code
3420-4	75	120	1600	PE
	75	470	6250	PE—GCR
3420-6	125	200	1600	PE
	125	780	6250	PE—GCR
3420-8	200	320	1600	PE
	200	1250	6250	PE—GCR

magnetic tape, enabling reestablishment of self-clocking in a track in which a signal has been lost.

Cassette magnetic tape storage is generally used in simple, low-cost systems where relatively small amounts of data are involved, such as in the remote data entry application illustrated in Figure 2.3 above. The standard Philips cassette contains 300 feet of 0.15-inch magnetic tape. Recording is performed serially on either one or two tracks across the width of the tape in discrete blocks or records which are separated by interrecord gaps much like on open-reel systems.

TABLE 2.2. GCR Code

Four-Bit Source Data	Five-Bit Recorded Data
0000	11001
0001	11011
0010	10010
0011	10011
0100	11101
0101	10101
0110	10110
0111	10111
1000	11010
1001	01001
1010	01010
1011	01011
1100	11110
1101	01101
1110	01110
1111	01111

Recording on cassette drives is either performed continuously or incrementally, depending on the application. Continuous recording, typically used in terminal applications, permits the highest density, with up to 700,000 characters on a 300-foot reel. Incremental recording, such as for the portable data entry operation shown in Figure 2.3, records and reads the tape character by character by starting and stopping the tape. The storage capacity for a cassette using incremental recording is typically 75,000 to 100,000 characters.

A similar low-cost magnetic tape storage device is the 3M cartridge. A comparison of the Philips cassette and the 3M cartridge is found in Table 2.5 on page 38.

A different type of magnetic tape cartridge storage is intended for large, mass-storage systems such as the IBM 3850 shown in Figure 2.11. A magnetic tape cartridge for such a system, shown in the foreground of Figure 2.12, contains a wide web of magnetic tape which is unwound from the cartridge and read.

Disk Storage. There are three basic types of direct-access disk storage systems: moveable-head disks, fixed-head disks, and flexible disks.

The moveable-head disk drive consists of a disk pack (such as the one shown in the background of Figure 2.12), having several disks mounted on a shaft and rotated. Magnetic reading heads are mounted on arms which are moved radially in and out of the disk

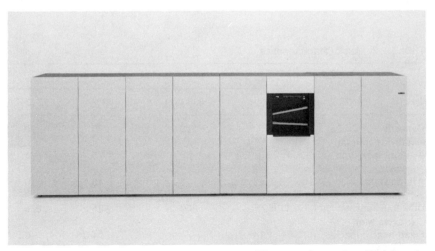

FIGURE 2.11. IBM 3850 mass storage system. (Photograph courtesy IBM Corp.)

FIGURE 2.12.   Data cartridge for IBM 3850. (Photograph courtesy IBM Corp.)

pack, reading information out of an annular track on the surface of the disk. Some typical parameters for storage on a disk are 1000 to 4000 bits/inch linear storage density, and 100 to 200 tracks/inch track density. Some typical characteristics of the most advanced disk drives are given in Table 2.3, and the basic design of the moveable-head disk drive is shown in Figure 2.13*a*.

The fixed-head disk drive also features a disk pack; however, the reading heads are fixed over the tracks on the surface of the disk. Track selection is performed electronically rather than mechanically,

TABLE 2.3.   Disk Characteristics

	IBM Model			
	3350	3330–11	3344	3340–70
Capacity (Mbytes/spindle)	317.5	200	280	70
Average seek time (msec)	25	30	25	25
Average latency (msec)	8.4	8.4	10.1	10.1
Data transfer rate (Kbytes/sec)	1198	806	885	885
Fixed-head capacity (Mbytes/spindle)	1.14	—	1.0	0.5

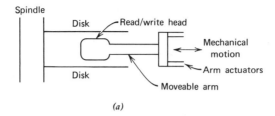

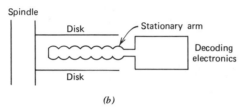

FIGURE 2.13.   (a) Moveable-head disk drive. (b) Fixed-head disk drive.

as shown in Figure 2.13*b*. Moveable-head systems offer higher storage capacities, and offer the convenience of removeable disk packs or data cartridges or modules (e.g., the 3348 Model 70 data module for the IBM 3344). On the other hand, fixed-head disk drive systems have faster access times and greater mechanical reliability. Both the IBM 3350 and 3344 disk drives are available in fixed-head versions with a storage capacity of 1 megabyte/spindle.

The flexible disk or diskette ("floppy disk"), shown in Figure 2.14, is one of the most popular low-cost storage mediums. The floppy disk is a magnetic oxide coated Mylar disk 0.005 inches thick and 7.8 inches in diameter, with a 1.5-inch hole in the center. The floppy disk is packaged in an 8-inch square plastic envelope which protects the oxide layer.

In actual use, the diskette and the plastic envelope are inserted into the disk drive, and the read/write head of the drive is fitted into a slot on one edge of the envelope, thereby coming in contact with the oxide layer. In the standard IBM format, the diskette rotates at 360 rpm.

The diskette was originally developed by IBM for use in a larger disk controller, and later was introduced as part of the IBM 3740 key-to-disk data entry system. The 3740 recording format consists of 77 tracks, each track being divided into 26 sectors. Each sector consists of 128 bytes, so that the total disk capacity is about 243,000 bytes. Some of the characteristics of a typical floppy disk drive are pre-

FIGURE 2.14.   IBM 3740 diskette. (Photograph courtesy IBM Corp.)

sented in Table 2.4. A smaller version of the floppy disk, known as a "minifloppy," is also available and is particularly suited for low-cost, microcomputer applications. A detailed comparison of the floppy disk, the minifloppy, cassette, and cartridge characteristics is presented in Table 2.5.

Floppy disks can utilize several different recording techniques. The most common is called frequency modulation (FM) coding. The storage surface is divided into uniformly sized "bit cells," with a clock pulse placed at the leading edge of each bit cell. A one is represented by an additional pulse in the center of the bit cell, while a zero is represented by no additional pulse. The coding technique is called "frequency modulation" since a sequence of zeros has frequency f while a sequence of ones has a frequency $2f$. FM is illustrated in Figure 2.15a.

One variation of frequency modulation is modified frequency modulation (MFM), which is similar to Miller code described above.

TABLE 2.4.   Floppy Disk Specifications

Storage capacity	
Unformatted	
Per disk	3,208,128 bits
Per track	41,664 bits
Formatted (IBM 3740)	1,943,552 bits
Per disk	1,943,552 bits
Per track	26,624 bits
Sector	1,024 bits
Number of tracks	77
Recommended coding technique	Double frequency (FM)
Bit transfer rate	250,000 bits/sec, nominal
Positioning mechanism	Stepper motor, electrical detent
Head stabilization time	10 msec
Head load time	16 msec
Rotational speed	360 rpm ± 2.5% (167 msec/revolution)
Motor start time (to ready)	2 seconds maximum

MFM eliminates the clock pulses placed at the beginning of each bit cell in FM. A one is represented by a pulse in the center of the bit cell, while a zero is represented by a pulse at the beginning of the bit cell, except when that bit cell is preceded by a bit cell representing a one. MFM is illustrated in Figure 2.15*b*.

Another variation of frequency modulation, derived from MFM, is called modified-modified frequency modulation (M^2FM). In this code, a one is defined as a pulse in the center of a bit cell and a zero as a pulse at the beginning of a bit cell, except where preceded by a cell containing either a zero or a one pulse. M^2FM therefore produces fewer pulses than MFM during a long string of 0s. M^2FM is illustrated in Figure 2.15*c*.

Group code recording (GCR) is another technique for increasing the data packing density. GCR utilizes a code to avoid recording more than two zeros in succession by translating every four bits of source data into five bits of recorded data. The specific translation was shown in Table 2.2.

The actual recording of the five-bit GCR code is done as in NRZ— that is, a one is represented by a flux reversal and a zero is represented by no flux reversal. When reading, the five-bit GCR code is translated back into the four-bit source data.

In order to compare the efficiency of the various recording codes, one must compare the recorded bit density (measured in flux reversals per inch, or frpi), and the phase margin (the allowable shift

TABLE 2.5. Comparison of Popular Low-Cost Mass-Storage Systems

Characteristic	Shugart SA400 Minifloppy	Floppy Disk	Philips Cassette	3M Cartridge
Unformatted capacity (bytes)	110k	400k	720k	2870k
Tracks	35	77	2	4
Heads	1	1	1	4
Transfer rate (bps)	125k	250k	24k	48k
Relative head/medium velocity (ips)	80 max.	120 max.	30	30
Recording density/track (bpi)	2600 max.	3200	800	1600
Average access time (sec)	0.566	0.286	20	20
Typical drive size (in.)	3.25×5.75×8.0	4.62×8.55×14.25	4×6×8	4×6×8
Typical weight (lb)	3	14	5	5
Typical dc power requirements (V)	5, 12	−15, 5, 24	+12, 5	+12, 5
Drive price (quantity 1)	$390	$600	$500	$500
Medium size (in.)	5.25×5.25	8.0×8.0	4×2.5×0.4	4×6×0.67
Medium price (quantity 1)	$4.50	$6.50	$8	$20

Note: Average access time = average seek time + average latency time.

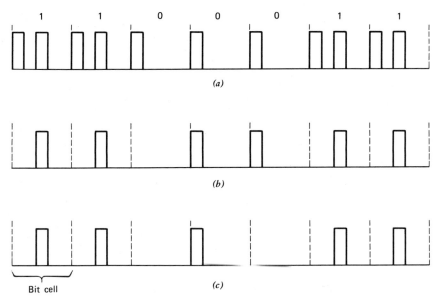

FIGURE 2.15. Floppy disk recording codes: (*a*) frequency or double frequency modulation (FM); (*b*) modified frequency modulation (MFM); (*c*) modified modified frequency modulation (M²FM).

distance between flux changes as a portion of the bit cell size). Modified frequency modulation has a recorded bit density, in standard format, of 6536 frpi, compared to 8170 frpi for GCR code. On the other hand, MFM has a phase margin of 0.125 bit cell time compared with 0.20 for GCR. This would suggest that GCR is intrinsically more reliable than MFM.

However, it must be realized that GCR requires more hardware for performing the encoding and decoding operation, and the greater recording density places a corresponding greater reliability burden on the reading element of the system.

Magnetic Cards and Strips.   The magnetic card is a flat, rectangularly shaped card which stores data along a number of parallel tracks. The typical specifications in presently available commercial systems are shown in Table 2.6.

Magnetic cards are convenient to handle and store a moderate amount of information. They are therefore frequently used in the less sophisticated word-processor systems.

Another method of implementing conveniently handled magnetic

TABLE 2.6.   Magnetic Card Specifications

	Type 1	Type 2
Number of tracks	64	50
Track capacity (characters/line)	160	100
Data density (bits inch)	222	250
Record length (inch)	6.425	6.250

recording media is through the use of magnetic strips adhesively affixed to a carrier, such as a paper record card or a plastic identification card.

Magnetic Ink (MICR).   One of the most widely used magnetic recording media is magnetic marks or characters formed by magnetic ink. Such characters are widely used in banking and finance. Figure 2.16 illustrates a typical MICR (Magnetic Ink Character Recognition) reader/sorter with a handling capacity of 750 documents/minute.

OPTICAL MARK AND CHARACTER READERS.   Optical mark and character readers are specialized input devices for handling relatively large amounts of source data without being transferred to another computer-compatible input such as punch cards or magnetic media. We mention optical mark and character readers here more for completeness in surveying the various computer input media than their relevance to data communications systems.

DIGITIZED IMAGES.   Another important source of computer input is a visual image that is digitized and processed. Perhaps the most publicized image digitizing and processing is that associated with satellite data gathering systems. In addition to the data transmission of the image, host computers perform image analysis and enhancement and the preparation of statistical data for comparative analysis. Applications include natural resource surveying, agricultural analysis, environmental monitoring, and mapping.

A more commercially significant data transmission of digitized images is the transmission of network television throughout certain regions of the country using digital communications links, as well as the transmission of wirephotos.

Output Media

The characteristics of punch cards, paper tape, and magnetic media as output devices are similar to those described above with reference

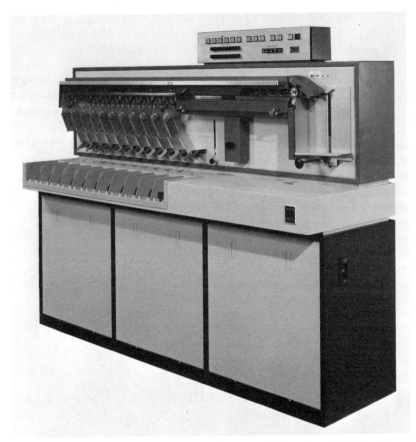

FIGURE 2.16. MICR reader/sorter. (Photograph courtesy NCR Corp.)

to their use as input media. Our analysis of output media will therefore be directed to impact and nonimpact printers, and will conclude with some brief remarks on displays, plotters, and computer-output microfilm (COM).

IMPACT PRINTERS. Impact printers form their image on paper by the impact of an inked character or character elements on the paper. There are four basic types of impact printers: serial, chain, drum, and dot matrix.

Serial. The serial printer uses a character set mounted on a character wheel, petal, or ball. As the desired character is passed on the rotating element, a print hammer strikes it with a predetermined force. The amount of force depends on the character so that a uniform pressure is exerted on the paper. A typical example of a petal or "daisy-wheel" serial printer is shown in Figure 2.17.

Chain. The chain printer uses a character set mounted on a revolving belt. The belt moves in front of a sequence of printing hammers, which are activated as the appropriate character is passed.

Drum. The drum printer is similar in operation to the chain printer, except that the character set is formed on the circumference of a wheel. A sequence of such wheels are mounted next to one another to form a drum. As the desired character is passed, a print hammer strikes it.

Dot Matrix. The dot matrix printer uses an array of pins which form a dot matrix. A character is printed by automatically selecting a group of dots of the array—for example, a 5×7 dot array—and driving such pins to the paper by means of electronically actuated solenoids.

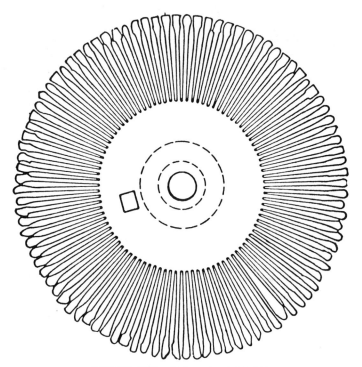

FIGURE 2.17. Daisy wheel printer.

NONIMPACT PRINTERS. Nonimpact printers form their image on paper by the collection and adhesion of a contrast material on specific portions of the paper under external control. Nonimpact printing technology is rapidly developing, and the principal characteristics of the various technologies are summarized in Table 2.7.

Thermal. Thermal printing is a low-cost, slow-printing technique used for terminals. It utilizes heat-sensitive thermal paper that forms images when heated dot-matrix elements are applied. Some of the manufacturers of thermal printers, along with their characteristics, are listed in Table 2.8.

Magnetic. Magnetic printing is a relatively old technology, dating back to 1952, although various improvements have been made since then. One commercial implementation utilizes a dry-ink transfer process on plain paper. Character images are formed magnetically using a 10×10 dot matrix. At a speed of up to 120 characters/second, the magnetic printer is four times faster than most thermal printers. Printing density is 6 lines/inch.

Magnetic printers are small, quiet units suitable for low-cost terminal applications. More sophisticated magnetic printers are presently under development. One design in early development utilizes a rotating drum which is written upon by either a scanning laser or a thin-film magnetic head. Magnetic ink then adheres to the surface, forming the final image. With such technology it would be possible to produce an 8½×11 sheet in as little as 1 second.

Another sophisticated magnetic printer under development is designed for a multicolor printing system. In that system, a magnetizable

TABLE 2.7. Nonimpact Printing Technologies

Technology	Speed	Cost	State-of-the-Art	Application
Thermal	slow	low	commercial	terminals
Magnetic	slow	low	commercial	terminals
Electrostatic	fast	medium	commercial	high-speed graphics
Xerographic	fast	medium	commercial	general purpose
Ink jet	medium	medium	commercial	document printer
Electronic	fast	medium-high	commercial	graphics
Laser	fast	high	commercial	computer output
Electrophoretic	slow-medium	medium	early development	multicolor output

TABLE 2.8. Thermal Printers

Manufacturer	Model	Character Formation	Speed (cps)
Anderson–Jacobson	630	5×8 matrix	30
Computer Devices	1130	5×7 matrix	30
Computer Transceiver	300	5×7 matrix	30
NCR	260-2	5×7 matrix	30
Texas Instruments	732, 733	5×7 matrix	13.3–30

surface is recorded upon by recording heads producing a different recording frequency for each color to be printed. The printing toner is composed of particles of different colors which adhere to areas on the recorded surface having a frequency specific for the particular particle type.

It must be emphasized that products under development have significant technological and economic barriers to cross before they may be commercially realizable, and are discussed here merely to indicate that magnetic printing technology has not been exhausted, but is evolving along with other more widely known reprographic technologies.

Electrostatic. Electrostatic printers operate by the electrostatic attraction of contrast material to specific regions on the record carrier. Xerographic printing, the most well-known implementation of electrostatic printing, will be discussed in the next section.

Some of the important manufacturers of electrostatic printers are listed in Table 2.9, along with the characteristics of such printers.

Electrostatic printing utilizes a row of conductive stylii at a density of 100 to 200 per inch which contacts a nonconductive dielectric paper one line at a time. The paper is then passed through a liquid

TABLE 2.9. Electrostatic Printers

Manufacturer	Model	Type	Speed (lines/minute)
Gould	5000, 5100, 5200	line	650–3600
Varian	3182, etc.	line	275–1000
Versatec	D800, 900, 1100	line	190–1200
Honeywell	PPF 6068, 6032	page	12,000; 18,000

toner, permitting the contrast material to be attracted to the charged regions, which is then fused thereto forming a permanent image.

Due to the high cost of paper for electrostatic printing, most applications have been for high-speed graphics and plotting. The Honeywell printer, on the other hand, is intended for high-speed computer output.

Xerographic. Xerographic printing is a particular type of electrostatic printing in which the image is first formed on an intermediate carrier, and is then transferred to the final copy. Xerographic printing thus prints on plain paper, as opposed to the coated paper required for electrostatic printing.

An example of a xerographic printer is the Xerox 1200, introduced in 1973 and capable of printing 60 pages/minute.

Ink Jet. Ink jet printing produces images on a recoding medium by precisely expelling ink droplets from a jet head which is transported along a print line. The droplets are given an electrostatic charge and passed through deflection plates which direct the droplet to the desired print position on the paper. Actual characters are formed from a dot matrix pattern.

The IBM 46/40 Document Printer is an example of an ink jet printer first delivered in 1976. The IBM 46/40 is a high-quality printer that prints at speeds up to 92 characters per second with three possible pitches: 10 pitch, 12 pitch, or proportional spacing. Three type styles in each pitch are available.

As a medium-speed, medium-cost device, the IBM 46/40 is designed for word-processing rather than data-processing applications. The unit includes a magnetic card reader which accepts up to 200 cards recorded on a magnetic card typewriter, and includes an optional communications interface for transmitting the information on the magnetic cards to a remote IBM 46/40, or a remote computer for storage or further processing. Thus the IBM 46/40 not only serves as a printer but as a communications interface in a data communications system performing word-processing tasks. A more detailed discussion of word-processing data communications networks is presented in Chapter 8.

Electronic. Electronic printing refers to the dynamic (as opposed to static) focussing of charged contrast material on the record carrier. One practical implementation of electronic printing is through the use of ions, which is known as electroionic printing. Electroionic printing utilizes an ion-containing gas stream which is directed at the record carrier.

Another example of electronic printing uses electric discharges. The Centronics Micro 1 is an example of a nonimpact printer using electric-discharge technology. The printer produces 5×8 dot-matrix characters on aluminum-coated paper by discharging a low-voltage electric arc through the styli which melts the 1-micron-thick coating, exposing a black background. The Micro 1 has a printing speed of 180 lines/minute, making it particularly suitable for simple, low-cost applications such as industrial instrumentation and hard copy from a CRT terminal.

Laser.   The laser printer is a very-high-speed printer for computer output, using a laser for character image formation. The IBM 3800, illustrated in Figure 2.18, is a commercial example of a laser printer which was first shipped in 1976.

The IBM 3800 prints at the rate of 13,360 lines/minute (45,000 characters/second), using up to 255 characters in four different character sets. The technology of the IBM 3800, as shown in Figure 2.19, is a combination of laser imaging and electrophotographic reproduction.

Light from a low-powered laser is used to form dot-matrix representations of characters to be printed. A mirror wheel reflects the laser beam horizontally across a rotating photoconductive surface, shown as the drum in Figure 2.19. The drum is first charged by the usual corona-discharging device found in electrophotographic systems. If the printout is to include any forms overlay, such as a design,

FIGURE 2.18.   IBM 3800 laser printer. (Photograph courtesy IBM Corp.)

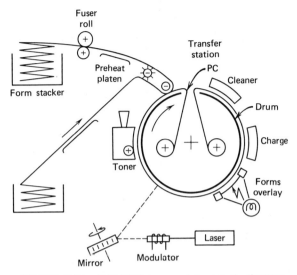

FIGURE 2.19. IBM 3800 laser printer block diagram.

rulings, or the like, it is provided by a strobe light. The character images are then applied to the photoconductive surface by the laser, crossing the surface 144 times per vertical inch.

The photoconductive surface then passes the toner station, where toner, a black thermoplastic powder, is applied to the surface and electrostatically adheres where the characters and other images have been exposed. The surface of the drum next rotates past the transfer station where the toner is transferred to plain paper. The constant paper feed rate is 1840 inches/minute, which produces about 10,000 11-inch forms/hour. The plain paper is fed through a fuser roller where the toner is fused to the paper to form permanent images, and stacked in the form stacker.

Electrophoretic. Electrophoretic printers are based on the principle of electrophoresis—the selective migration of charged particles in a fluid medium upon application of an electric field. Electrophoretic technology is presently in its early development stage, with attention being directed both to displays and printing applications.

One of the more important applications of electrophoretic research is the development of a multicolored output. Since the charged particles may have different colors and may be arranged to selectively migrate to the image surface upon application of specific electric fields, a multicolored image may be formed automatically. Means may be devised for transferring the image to a record carrier, thereby forming a permanent copy of the image.

Electrophoretic printing is relatively slow, and directed to highly specialized applications such as multicolor copiers and printers. Commercial realization of such devices is not expected for another 7 to 15 years.

DISPLAYS.   A display is an output medium for providing a visual readout of relatively small amounts of information, such as a few lines. A display may be implemented in the form of a panel display, or an entire terminal such as shown in Figure 2.20.

The VuSet data terminal shown in Figure 2.20 is worthwhile discussing in greater detail since it is particularly adapted for data communications. The VuSet data terminal is a small CRT display which is used in conjunction with a Touch-Tone telephone to access and display data from a remote computer. The user accesses the computer through the switched telephone network, and requests specific data be displayed by keying a numerical code through the Touch-Tone telephone. Since the user does not enter alphanumeric

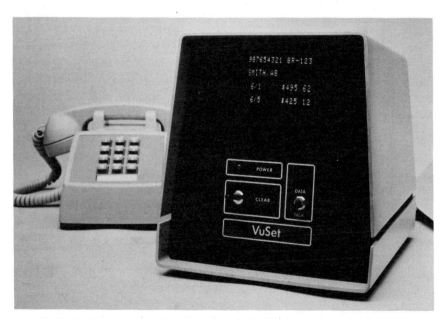

FIGURE 2.20.   VuSet data display terminal. (Photograph courtesy AT&T.)

information, the VuSet is not truly a "keyboard" CRT terminal, but merely a simple, economical desk-top display unit. However, the VuSet is able to display both numeric and alphanumeric information.

In addition to the CRT, other technologies are used for implementing displays. These include light-emitting diodes (LEDs), liquid-crystal devices (LCDs), and gas panel or plasma displays. Electrophoretic image displays (EPIDs) is an important future display technology.

PLOTTERS.   A plotter is an output medium that converts digital information into a hard-copy graphics output. Plotters are important for such applications as computer-aided design, architecture and drafting, and mapping. Plotters are used in a data communications network where frequent output of a hard-copy graphic data is required, such as in providing periodic weather maps to a remote weather facility.

COMPUTER-OUTPUT   MICROFILM.   Computer-output   microfilm (COM) units produce microfilm records of a computer output directly, without going through either hard or soft copies. We mention COM units here for completeness in surveying computer-output media rather than suggesting that such units may be important in a data communications network. Figure 2.21 illustrates the CalComp Alphanumeric COM system.

Remote-Batch Terminals

A remote-batch terminal is any type of specialized I/O terminal configured to operate in a remote location and transmit or receive data from the host computer in batch form. Frequently some type of control unit is provided at the remote-batch terminal to perform simple control over buffering and communications. Such control units may range from relatively simple hard-wired logic, to the actual incorporation of a programmed minicomputer at the remote-batch location for scheduling (e.g., handling several peripherals) and pre-processing.

Remote-batch terminals are distinguished from distributed processor terminals in that no user functions are implemented at the remote-batch terminal. Instead, the remote-batch terminal is merely an extension of the I/O capabilities of the host computer to a remote location. The characteristics of remote-batch terminals are summarized in Table 2.10.

FIGURE 2.21. CalComp 2100 Alphanumeric COM System. (Photograph courtesy California Computer Products, Inc.)

Autotransaction Terminals

An autotransaction terminal is a consumer-oriented terminal which permits the user to perform simple transactions by interacting with the host computer. The most typical examples of such autotransaction terminals are the Transaction™ III telephone, shown in Figure 2.22, and automatic teller terminals for performing banking transactions.

As consumer-oriented terminals, autotransaction terminals are characterized by highly simplified program keys and displays. The Transaction™ III telephone is a good example of such a terminal, and can be considered in greater detail.

The Transaction™ III telephone is designed for use in credit-verification systems for retail establishments. After being presented with a credit card, the retail establishment makes a local call to the credit-validation computer center of the credit card company. This may be done by manually dialling the number using the Touch-Tone

TABLE 2.10. Remote-Batch Terminal
Characteristics

Input
    Card reader: 200–1500 cards/minute
    Keyboard
    Magnetic media: tape, disk, diskette

Output
    Card punch: 100–200 cards/minute
    Serial printer: 10–60 characters/second
    Line printer: 50–1250 lines/minute
    Magnetic media: tape, disk, diskette
    CRT

---

keyboard on the Transaction™ telephone, or by using an automatic dialling card. When contact with the computer is established, a signal is sent back to the Transaction™ telephone to indicate that the computer is ready to receive the customer's card number for validation purposes. A microprocessor (the Rockwell PPS-4) within the Transaction™ telephone interprets the encoded computer signal and actuates the appropriate indicator lamp on the front panel to instruct the user to proceed to the next step—that is, "Insert customer card or manually enter information," as shown in Figure 2.23.

The user now passes the credit card with a magnetic stripe containing the customer card number through a slot on the Transaction™ telephone. Magnetic heads sense the data contained in encoded form on the magnetic stripe on the credit card and convert the data into digital signals. The microprocessor determines whether the card has been read correctly by performing a parity check of the read information. If the card has been read correctly, the microprocessor decodes the encoded data and operates the touch-tone oscillators in the Transaction™ telephone to send the data over the telephone lines to the validation computer at the other end. If the computer receives the data correctly, another signal is sent back to the Transaction™ telephone to indicate that the computer is ready to receive the dollar amount of the transaction for recording. The microprocessor in the Transaction™ telephone interprets this second signal and actuates the indicator lamp on the front panel instructing the user to "enter dollar amount (other information), press END."

The user now enters the dollar amount of the transaction on the touch-tone keyboard. The entered digits also appear on the display for visual verification of the data. If the user should make a mistake in

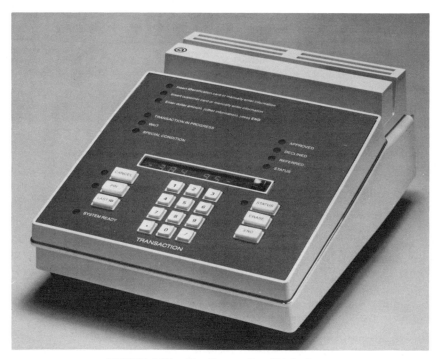

FIGURE 2.22.   The Transaction III telephone.

entering the data, the ERASE key may be pressed and the data reentered. After the user is satisfied that the data has been entered correctly, the END key is pressed, and the data transmitted to the validation computer.

The validation computer performs a validity check of the card number, expiration data, and authorized credit from its centralized files. An encoded signal is then sent back to the Transaction™ telephone indicating whether the credit is approved, declined, or some other condition (card has expired, authorized credit has been slightly exceeded, etc.). The microprocessor in the Transaction™ telephone interprets the encoded signal and actuates the appropriate indicator lamp on the front panel to indicate whether the transaction is APPROVED, DECLINED, or REFERRED.

Sensor-Based Terminals

A sensor-based terminal is an input device adapted to receive information in some form from a "sensor," convert such information into

FIGURE 2.23. The Transaction III telephone: front panel features.

encoded digital form, and transfer it to the host processor for processing. The host computer transmits appropriate responses back to the sensor-based terminal for actuating some elements or displaying some processed information.

An example of a simple sensor-based terminal is a controlled access lock shown in Figure 2.24. As suggested in the illustration, the user inserts an ID card into the sensor-based terminal. The ID number is transferred to the computer where it is checked against the authorized ID numbers. Once verification of access authorization is determined, a signal is sent back to the remote station for opening a gate or other access. The computer may also record the ID number and time of entry for control purposes.

More sophisticated sensor-based terminals may be used in an industrial process-control environment where they may perform periodic monitoring and control functions. One simple implementation of such a system, shown in Figure 2.25, uses a punch card input as part of an extension telephone for digitally transmitting process

FIGURE 2.24. IBM 3223 entry/exit reporter. (Photograph courtesy IBM World Trade Corp.)

information to a remote computer. More sophisticated systems utilize transducers which continuously monitor process conditions. A sample-and-hold digital circuit is connected to such transducers for periodically registering the process conditions, and means are provided for transmitting such information to a remote host computer for processing.

Intelligent Terminals

An "intelligent" terminal is an I/O device which incorporates processing capability within the terminal itself. Such processing is frequently limited to text-editing, character checking, encoding/decoding, and communications handling functions, although significantly more sophisticated processing may be implemented in an intelligent terminal. Such processing may include user programmable functions, such as performing simple arithmetic processing on information entered on the terminal, or similar specialized functions.

FIGURE 2.25. IBM 3221 numeric multifunction device. (Photograph courtesy IBM World Trade Corp.)

The stand-alone small-business computer or word-processing system (typified by IBM's System/32, Burroughs B700, DEC's Datasystem 300, Basic Four, and others) is also evolving into potential use as an intelligent terminal in a data processing network. Such systems may process text or data in a stand-alone mode, and then operate in a communications mode to transmit portions of the processed text or data to a remote computer for further handling. Another mode of operation is for the system to act in a distributed-intelligence mode: the host computer transmits information to the system where it performs additional processing—for example, it may utilize programs or parameters supplied by the host computer with data or text entered by the user at the remote location.

HOST COMPUTERS

The host computer is a central processing unit (CPU) used to implement the specialized data processing operation for which the data communications system was designed. There are five basic types of data processing applications performed by the host computer:

1. Message switching
2. Inquiry/response
3. File management
4. Data collection
5. Remote batch

Message switching refers to the processing and communication of messages between remote terminals by a central computer. The computer does not modify the message but merely performs the administrative functions of routing the destination request and queuing the message, if necessary, before releasing access to the destination channel or data link. Message switching is therefore also referred to as "store-and-forward" operation, and should be distinguished from circuit switching in which such message storage does not take place.

Inquiry/response systems are the simplest access systems. The central computer maintains centralized data files and the remote terminals have the capability of making inquiries of such files. If the inquiry is a valid one, the central computer transmits the appropriate response back to the remote terminal.

File management systems are more sophisticated centralized data file access systems. The remote terminals have the capability of file updating, entry, and similar file handling and processing functions.

Data collection systems collect data from remote stations and store it for further use or processing. The system may be arranged so that the remote terminal stores the data until polled by the host computer or, alternatively, the remote terminal may forward the data immediately to the host computer as soon as a predetermined quantity of data is "collected."

Remote-batch systems utilize remote terminals to batch process data on the host computer, and return the processed data to the remote terminal.

The host computer may be arranged in several different computer configurations for performing the above applications. These configurations are:

• Stand-alone
• Clustered
• Distributed

The stand-alone configuration is shown in Figure 2.26. It simply means a single processor in a given location which handles the processing of data originating from remotely located terminals.

The clustered configuration, as shown in Figure 2.27, refers to the use of a cluster of more than one processor in a given location. There are in turn several different variations of the cluster configuration. The connection of the remote terminals to the processors in the cluster may be done in at least the two different manners shown in Figures 2.27*a* and *b*.

In the first variation (Figure 2.27*a*) each of the processors in the cluster is associated with a group of terminals. Each of the processors are connected with adjacent processors.

In the second variation of the cluster configuration (Figure 2.27*b*) only some of the processors are associated with terminals. Such processors are not connected with one another but with a second group of processors in the cluster. The processors within this second group are connected with adjacent processors.

The "connections" shown in Figure 2.27 are meant to represent data and control lines so that two processors in the cluster so connected are able to interact, share memory and processing facilities, and therefore operate with load-sharing, greater reliability, and throughput.

There are many administrative, privacy, or applications-oriented reasons for configuring clustered computers in different manners as suggested in the two examples shown in Figure 2.27. In a university application using a single host computer, the terminals used by students are associated with one preprocessor, while those used by the administration are associated with another, as illustrated in Figure 2.27*b*. In other applications where the users have similar applications

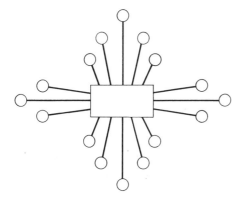

FIGURE 2.26. Stand-alone processor configuration.

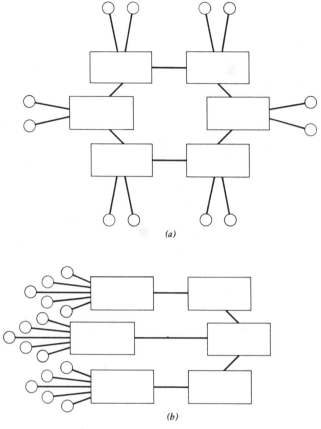

FIGURE 2.27. (a) Clustered processor configuration: general-purpose; (b) clustered processor configuration: dedicated.

and equal priority of authorization, the configuration shown in Figure 2.27a may be more effective.

Finally, the distributed configuration is shown in Figure 2.28. The processors are "distributed" among remote locations, and each processor has associated terminals at that location.

COMMUNICATION INTERFACE DEVICES

The term "communication interface device" refers to any hardware component that interfaces or couples the user access device (e.g.,

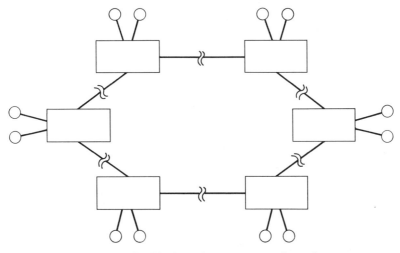

FIGURE 2.28. Distributed processor configuration.

terminal) with the transmission carrier. Such interface devices include:

- Modems
- Conditioning/equalization
- Multiplexing/concentration
- Switching processors
- Encoders/decoders

In addition, communications processors and digital filters may also be associated with such interface devices, and later sections will be devoted to such important hardware elements.

Modems

The use of the analog, voice telephone network for the transmission of digital information has led to the demand for devices for modulating and demodulating a voice-frequency carrier signal with digital information. Such devices are known as modems (from *mo*dulate-*dem*odulate).

Modems are usually classified according to the data rate or speed at which they operate, which ranges from under 100 bits/second (bps) to 9600 bps. The most common data rates used in data communication systems are 1200, 2400, and 4800 bps. Figure 2.29 illustrates a

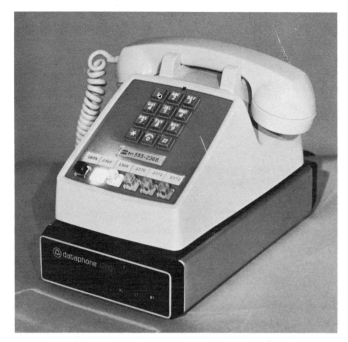

FIGURE 2.29.   Dataphone 1200, a 1200-bps modem.

typical 1200-bps modem, Figure 2.30 a 4800-bps modem, and Figure 2.31 a 9600-bps modem.

At this point it is worthwhile to point out the distinction between bps and baud. Baud is defined as a unit of signaling speed as measured by the number of signal events per second. The bps unit measures the number of information bits transmitted in 1 second. If the transmission of one signal event represents one bit, then the baud rate is equal to the bps rate. If, however, the number of signal events is not equal to a single bit of information, through some type of coding scheme or redundancy check, then the baud rate would be different from the bps rate.

Another means for classifying modems is whether the modem operates synchronously or asynchronously. Synchronous modems operate by transmitting a continuous, synchronous stream of data, and thus are usually associated with data-entry devices which produce a continuous data entry stream—for example, a magnetic tape facility. Asynchronous modems operate by transmitting bursts of data at random intervals (i.e., asynchronously), and thus are usually associated with data-entry devices that generate an intermittent data-entry stream—for example, keyboards.

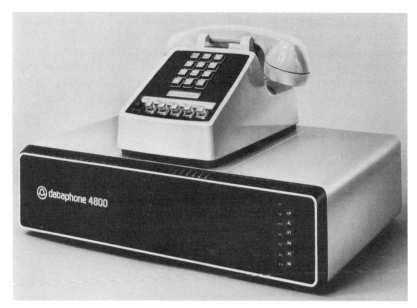

FIGURE 2.30.   Dataphone 4800, a 4800-bps modem.

As the name "modem" implies, the principal function of the device is modulation. Various types of modulation may be used in modems: frequency-shift keying (FSK), phase-shift keying (PSK), differential phase-shift keying (DPSK), vestigial-sideband amplitude modulation (VSB), quadrature amplitude modulation (QAM), or a combination of PSK and amplitude modulation.

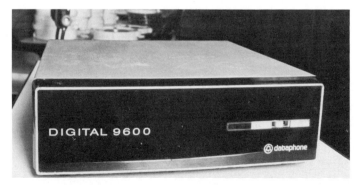

FIGURE 2.31.   9600 data service unit (DSU), a 9600-bps modem. (Photographs courtesy AT&T.)

In order to clarify the various types of modulation that are applicable to data communications, Figure 2.32 illustrates the most common types of modulation. Figure 2.32*a* represents the carrier in the form of a sine wave, while Figure 2.32*b* represents the digital signal which is to modulate the carrier wave. Amplitude modulation (AM) of the carrier with the digital signal of Figure 2.32*b* is shown in Figure 2.32*c*.

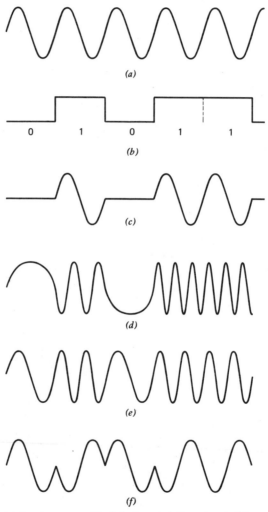

FIGURE 2.32.   (*a*) Carrier wave; (*b*) digital modulating signal; (*c*) amplitude modulation; (*d*) frequency modulation; (*e*) frequency shift keying; (*f*) phase shift keying.

The one-bit corresponds to full AM, while the zero-bit corresponds to zero modulation.

Frequency modulation (FM), in which the one-bit and the zero-bit correspond to different frequencies, is shown in Figure 2.32*d*. A variation of FM, frequency-shift keying (FSK), is shown in Figure 2.32*e*. In FSK, one of the frequencies used is the carrier frequency (e.g., corresponding to the zero-bit), while the other frequency is another "shifted" frequency with respect to the carrier.

In phase modulation (PM), the phase of the carrier is varied so that the one-bit and the zero-bit correspond to different phases. A variation of PM, phase-shift keying (PSK), similar to FSK, is shown in Figure 2.32*f*. In PSK, one of the frequencies used is the carrier frequency, while the other region utilizes a phase shift of the same frequency.

One common technique of representing the particular type of phase modulation is to use a phase diagram, in which each data sample takes on a value represented by one of a set of complex numbers. These complex numbers are in turn represented by M points even spaced around a circle in the complex plane so that one can pictorially represent the signal structure. Figure 2.33*a*, 2.33*b*, and 2.33*c* illustrate 4-, 8-, and 16-phase PSK modulation, respectively.

The same technique is also useful for representing quadrature amplitude modulation (QAM). In QAM, the real and imaginary parts of the signal may take on independent values, which are typically equally spaced. Figures 2.33*d* and 2.33*e* illustrate the phase diagrams of 4-level and 16-level QAM, respectively.

Combined amplitude and phase modulation is another important modulation technique in which both the amplitude and phase variables may be independently varied. Figure 2.33*f* illustrates a 4-phase, 2-amplitude structure; Figure 2.33*g* a 4-phase, 4-amplitude structure; and Figure 2.33*h* an 8-phase, 2-amplitude structure.

Finally, double-side-band quadrature carrier (DSB-QC) should also be noted. DSB-QC is a variation of QAM and combined phase-and-amplitude modulation which is particularly useful for high-speed data communication. Figures 2.33*i* and 2.33*j* illustrate two DSB-QC modulation structures. In Figure 2.33*i*, the input data samples are 3-bit words and take on one of the eight values represented on the diagram. In Figure 2.33*j*, the input data samples are 4-bit words and take on one of the sixteen values represented on the diagram.

Another form of modulation frequently used in digital communications systems is pulse modulation. Various types of pulse modulation are shown in Figure 2.34. Pulse modulation is based upon sampling

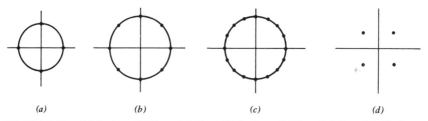

(a)   *(b)*   *(c)*   *(d)*

FIGURE 2.33. (a) 4-phase PSK modulation; (b) 8-phase PSK modulation; (c) 16-phase PSK modulation; (d) 4-level QAM.

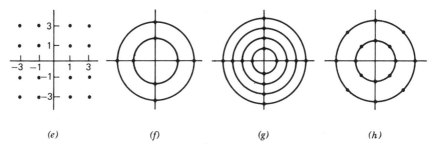

(e)   *(f)*   *(g)*   *(h)*

FIGURE 2.33 (continued). (e) 16-level QAM; (f) 4-phase 2-amplitude modulation; (g) 4-phase 4-amplitude modulation; (h) 8-phase 2-amplitude modulation.

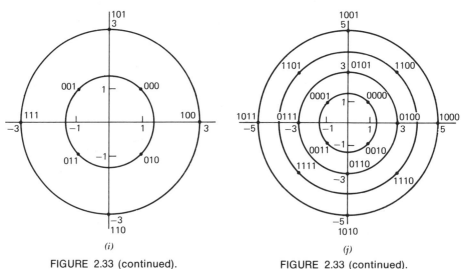

(i)

FIGURE 2.33 (continued).
(i) 3-bit DSB-QC modulation.

(j)

FIGURE 2.33 (continued).
(j) 4-bit DSB-QC modulation.

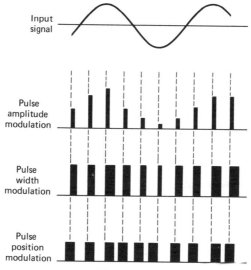

FIGURE 2.34.   Pulse modulation.

the input signal at predetermined intervals and converting the sample into a signal pulse. It is typically used in the digitizing and digital transmission of voice signals.

The transmission of digital data at high rates over existing limited bandwidth communication networks is becoming increasingly important. The basic requirement of any transmission system is that data be transmitted and received at a given data rate with a minimum number of errors. As the data rate increases, problems such as amplitude and delay distortion, frequency shift, and noise become more and more troublesome, causing the error rate to become excessive unless special, and often elaborate, means of reducing these problems are employed. In a well-designed transmitter-receiver system the primary cause of errors is impulse, or transient noise, and the type of modulation used is not a significant factor in reducing the effect of this noise on the error rate. It is worthwhile to consider the various types of carrier modulation that may be used. The AM system has advantages over other types with respect to cost, complexity, and size. In this connection we consider a high-speed synchronous quaternary, suppressed-carrier, vestigial-sideband transmission system employing both amplitude and phase modulation.

The primary characteristics that must be overcome by the system are:

1. Amplitude distortion
2. Delay distortion
3. Frequency shift
4. Background or broadband noise
5. Impulse noise

The first four items can be handled by a well-designed system. However, the last is much more difficult since an impulse can appear equal in duration and shape to a data bit or to many data bits. Thus the receiver cannot tell the difference between signal and noise.

By virtue of the suppressed carrier transmission, a 4800-bit/second quaternary code system has about the same signal-to-noise ratio as a two-level 2400-bit/second unsuppressed carrier systems. The reason for this is that by using suppressed carrier modulation only two actual voltage levels are transmitted, each with two phases. Thus, there are four signal conditions after modulation, but only two voltage amplitudes. As stated previously, impulse noise affects every type of transmission approximately the same. The complexity, size, and cost of this method of transmission, however, are considerably less than any other form.

The advantages of vestigial-sideband transmission over double-sideband AM for high-speed data transmission arises from the bandwidth limitations of conventional wire line circuits. At present, most lines have bandwidths from approximately 300 to 3000 cps. Vestigial-sideband transmission almost doubles the transmission rate over double-sideband transmission. This is so because both sidebands contain all the data information and the carrier can then be set so that one sideband and a portion (or vestige) of the other sideband is transmitted. As the data rate approaches the carrier frequency, distortion effects become more and more severe. When the data rate equals the carrier rate, there is one cycle of the carrier for each bit of information. As the data rate is further increased, the distortion becomes intolerable. If a conversion is made from binary code to quaternary code, the information rate can be doubled. Each state of quaternary signal corresponds to two states of the binary signal. A data stream coming into the transmitter at 4800 bits/second is converted to a data stream of 2400 quaternary digits/second. The carrier and all the other systems parameters remain the same.

The transmitter is provided with serial binary information from a synchronized data source connected to a clock pulse generator. A given constant voltage represents a binary one and another constant voltage represents a binary zero of the data. The binary data is limited to a given voltage level by limiter. The data is then supplied to data converter, which changes the input data so that transitions form one voltage level to another represent a binary one, and the absence of transitions represents a binary zero.

For modest data rates, modulation schemes such as 4-phase PSK modulation provide good margins against both gaussian noise and phase jitter. At higher data rates, more bits of information must be sent per signaling interval, so multilevel signaling structures of greater complexity must be used. The standard schemes mentioned above begin to degrade rapidly against either gaussian noise or phase jitter when more signal points are required.

In high-speed data transmission across narrow-bandwidth channels such as the typical voice grade telephone channel, DSB-QC modulation has certain inherent advantages over SSB and VSB techniques, such as are used in the majority of high-speed modems today. Against gaussian noise, it is inherently as efficient as SSB or VSB techniques in terms of the signal-to-noise ratios required to support a certain speed of transmission at a certain error rate in a given bandwidth. In addition, a coherent local demodulation carrier can be derived directly from the received data, without requiring transmission of a carrier or pilot tone. Furthermore, DSB-QC systems can be designed to have a much greater insensitivity to phase jitter on the line, or to phase error in the recovered carrier, than is possible with SSB or VSB signals.

Table 2.11 below gives required signal-to-noise ratios and minimum phase separations of points of the same amplitude for the signal structures of Figures 2.33a–2.33h. (The 2.33a–h minimum phase separation criterion below is an oversimplified, but still qualitatively indicative, measure of phase jitter immunity, since errors will actually be caused by the combined effects of noise and phase jitter.)

TABLE 2.11. Modem Signal Structure Comparison

Signal structure:	a	b	c	d	e	f	g	h
Required signal-to-noise ratio (dB)	3	8.3	14.1	3	10	8.4	13.9	11.5
Phase separation	90°	45°	22.5°	90°	37°	90°	90°	45°

Source: Codex Corporation.

On telephone lines a minimum phase separation of 45° may be insufficient to guarantee low error rates when phase jitter is severe. For $M = 8$ or 16, this means that only the 4-phase, 2- or 4-amplitude structures of Figures 2.33 f and g can be used. But these structures are rather inefficient in their use of power, as is shown by their values of required signal-to-noise margin in Table 2.11.

The signal structures of DSB-QC modulation retain the full 90° phase separations of the 4-phase structures, as well as their 4-phase symmetry, while substantially reducing the required signal-to-noise margin over the structures of Figures 2.33f and 2.33g.

Table 2.12 gives required signal-to-noise ratios and minimum phase separations over the structure of Figures 2.33i and 2.33j. The savings over Figures 2.33f and 2.33g are 1 and 2.6 dB, respectively. In fact, Figure 2.33j is only 1.3 dB worse than the optimal Figure 2.33c for $M = 16$, but has greatly enhanced protection against phase errors.

Conditioning/Equalization

Conditioning and equalization refer to improvements in voice grade data communications lines which effect a more reliable transmission of data. Line conditioning is a service provided by the common carrier on leased lines under special tariffs. The effect of conditioning is to adjust the amplitude attenuation and envelope delay to within specified ranges. Low speed modems (1200 bps and less) generally do not require conditioning, while increasingly higher speed modems require conditioning at increasing higher (and more expensive) levels.

Equalization refers to the selective amplification of certain frequencies which are attenuated by line characteristics, or subject to envelope delay. Figure 2.35 shows graphically how the process of selective frequency amplification "equalizes" the characteristics of the data signal over a predetermined frequency range.

TABLE 2.12.   Modem Signal Structure Comparison

Signal structure:	i	j
Required signal-to-noise ratio (dB)	7.4	11.3
Phase separation	90°	90°

Source: Codex Corporation.

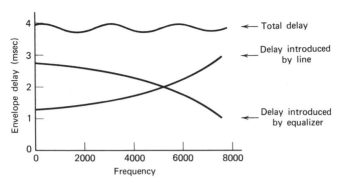

FIGURE 2.35. Equalization of envelope delay.

Multiplexing/Concentration

Multiplexing and concentration refer to the process of dividing a communications link into slots, each capable of carrying information from a separate source. The "slots" may be separated from each other by either time or frequency, thus defining either time-division multiplexing (TDM), or frequency-division multiplexing (FDM).

Frequency-division multiplexing is the simplest and lowest cost type of multiplexing, and is generally utilized on modems with a data rate of 1800 bps or lower. One of the limitations of FDM equipment is the necessity of using guard bands between adjacent frequency slots to prevent overlapping of signals. Such guard bands significantly decrease the efficiency of the FDM technique.

TDM falls into two categories: synchronous time-division multiplexing (STDM), and asynchronous time-division multiplexing (ATDM). STDM equipment allocates each data source into a permanent time slot. ATDM equipment performs the allocation process dynamically as required by those terminals actually transmitting data. Since the allocation process in ATDM equipment is statistical, asynchronous TDM is also called statistical TDM. Because of the simplicity and lower cost of STDM equipment, most commercial applications utilize the STDM technique.

Concentration is a process similar to standard multiplexing. Whereas multiplexing refers to a process where a fixed number of data sources share the same number of channels, concentration refers to a fixed number of data sources sharing a smaller number of channels. Through storage, queuing, and statistical allocation of the available channels, the data sources are "concentrated" along the communication channel. The process of ATDM is therefore a process of "concentration" rather than simply multiplexing. As is pointed out in the next section, the process of concentration is often performed by a communication processor.

Switching Processors

A switching processor is used to interface various types of communications lines, and to "switch" messages between them. An important characteristic of a switching processor is that it be able to handle various terminals, line speeds, codes, and line protocols. In addition, a switching processor may be able to handle routine administrative functions, such as message logging, control, and reporting. Since it is central to all stations, it is able to produce status reports on terminal and line usage and other characteristics.

Encoders/Decoders

Another important communications interface device is the encoder/decoder. Encoding may be done for security purposes, or for achieving a more efficient code for increasing transmission efficiency. Such encoding may be done through either hardware or software facilities. Commercial encoding systems are available which permit the user to change the code at periodic intervals to decrease the probability that it could be broken.

COMMUNICATION PROCESSORS

A communication processor is a special purpose computer which handles communication functions for the host computer in a communications network. Communication processors typically perform the following functions:

- Character assembly
- Protocol handling
- Network interface (polling, handshaking)
- Message queuing
- Error detection and recovery
- Code conversion

Character assembly and protocol handling are the basic functions of the communication processor. As will be described in greater detail in Chapter 3, messages are transmitted along a communications link according to a specific line control procedure or "protocol." The communication processor interprets the incoming bit stream according to the rules of the protocol, synchronizes itself with respect to the data stream, and decodes the message into character units.

Network interface is concerned with the coupling of the remote station with the communications processor with another remote station so that communication can occur between the two stations. The communications processor can achieve this coupling by, for example, polling the remote stations. The communications processor sends out an individual poll or query to each of the remote stations, requesting a response if that remote station has a message to transmit to the polling station. If not, the poll is not acknowledged and the communication processor polls another station. If the poll is acknowledged, then a communication link between the two stations is established. The establishment of this link is a process known as handshaking, in which one station sends out a query and another station acknowledges it.

Another important function of the communication processor is message queuing. While the host processor is engaged in processing applications programs and managing its own main memory, an incoming data stream is being supplied over the communication link. The communication processor has its own buffer memory available to temporarily store the incoming data and queue the messages until the host processor is able to process the messages. The communication processor thus serves as a means of processor and main memory offloading, thereby increasing the efficiency of the system with a given size processor and main memory.

Error detection and recovery is performed by the communication processor as one consequence of the protocol-handling function. The protocol provides a block of check bits which characterizes the message transmitted according to some algorithm. Examples include a vertical redundancy check (VRC), longitudinal redundancy check (LRC), or cyclic redundancy check (CRC), which will be described in greater detail in Chapter 3. By performing the algorithm on the data contained in the message and comparing it to the check bits, the communication processor determines if the message (and/or the check bits) were correctly transmitted. Recovery from error is achieved by identifying the message block or blocks where the error has occurred, and retransmitting such blocks.

Code conversion is also performed by the communication processor when the character coding format (ASCII, EBCDIC, etc.) is different in the remote station associated with the communication processor from other stations in the network. Such code conversion in the communication processor is performed by software.

The most widely known communication processors are the IBM 2701, 2702, and 2703 family (collectively referred to as 270X). These models have recently been replaced by the 370X family, which will be described in greater detail in Chapter 5. Many of the independently manufactured communication processors on the market are operable with IBM equipment, and act as emulators of the 270X and 370X series. In addition to the controller functions performed by the 270X and 370X, some communication processors also perform functions of remote concentration, message switching, and store and forward processing.

The remote concentration function of a communication processor permits the multiplexing or "concentration" of data messages to be more closely associated with the immediate communications task than would an ordinary hardwared multiplexer. Some of the important features made possible by the programmable nature of a communication processor include adjustment of each channel to a particular interface, code format, and data rate.

The message-switching function performed by a communication processor is similar to that performed by a switching processor, discussed in the previous section. Again the communication processor is able to more closely associate the particular switching task to be performed based upon current conditions. If, for example, the load at a particular terminal was known to be high at a particular moment, incoming messages destined for that terminal may be switched to an alternative terminal.

Similar remarks pertain to the store-and-forward function of the communication processor. The storing or buffering capability of the processor may be programmably adjusted to adapt to current communication conditions.

Some of the important features of communication processors which must be considered in analyzing and comparing such products are:

- Internal specifications
- Transmission specifications
- Functions performed
- Error-checking and recovery techniques
- Host computer compatibility

The internal specifications that must be considered include the type (core, semiconductor) and size of the memory, cycle time, and internal hardware features such as buffering technique, microprogrammability, and so on.

The transmission specification refers to the block size of the data structure, the capacity of the buffers in the communication processor, the various types of transmission codes that can be used (ASCII, EBCDIC, etc.).

The functions performed refers to the different types of data handling and network management tasks performed by the processor. These include:

Data packing/unpacking
Formatting
Routing
Scheduling
Line-speed sensing
Line monitoring
Automatic calling
Automatic answering
Terminal recognition
Polling

The error-checking and recovery technique of the communications process refers to the type of error checking implemented—whether hardware or software, and the use of CRCs, LRCs, and/or polynomial checks—and the recovery method—redundancy, retransmission, multiple cpus, mass storage, or through some software technique.

Finally, host computer compatibility refers to the type of computer that the process can interface—for example: IBM 360, 370; Burroughs; Univac; and so on. Another area of compatibility that must be noted is the type of interface channel: direct memory access (DMA), selector channel, character multiplexer channel, or block multiplexer channel. (A channel is an I/O controller associated with a main-frame computer for performing the transfer of data between the main memory and various selected external devices.)

Another aspect of host computer compatibility is software and device interfacing. Some communications processors can be used with IBM access methods such as BTAM, QTAM, and VTAM (such access methods will be discussed in greater detail in Chapter 3). Others must be interfaced with special programs. Finally, the actual hardware interface, including the path width in bits and the maximum data transfer rate, must be compatible between the communications processor and the host computer.

DIGITAL FILTERS

A digital filter is a device or process for converting an input signal, defined by a sequence of input words, into an output signal, defined by a sequence of output words, according to a predetermined transformation function.

This compact definition merits some analysis. Digital filters are a means of implementing a filtering operation on an analog signal. The analog input signal is sampled at a predetermined rate, and converted into digital form in the form of a sequence of input words. The digital filter itself may be implemented either in hardware devices or as a process in a general-purpose digital computer. Because of the specialized nature of digital signal processing, the use of special-purpose, dedicated hardware is more efficient, and is the more typical implementation.

The dedicated hardware operates to perform a predetermined transformation function on the input data. The "transformation function" is not a simple arithmetic operation but is a time-dependent

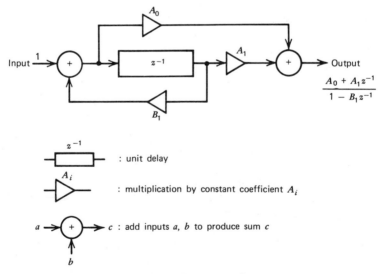

FIGURE 2.36. Digital filter.

"filtering" function. An example of filtering is the selection of only a given band of frequencies for transmission, and rejection or suppression of all other frequencies.

The hardware elements of a digital filter consist typically of an adding element, a multiplication element, and a delay element, as shown in Figure 2.36.

Digital filters are typically incorporated in the data communications hardware, such as in a modem or communications processor for performing the function of equalization. In more advanced applications, such as speech and image processing, digital filtering is considerably important for signal analysis.

TRANSMISSION CARRIERS

The last "hardware" element of a data communications network considered here is the transmission carrier, the means for transferring data from one remote location to another. A complete discussion of the various transmission systems and technologies is presented in Chapter 6.

three
DATA
COMMUNICATION
SOFTWARE

A data communications network is organized and managed by software facilities. As we noted in Chapter 2, the host computer implements the specialized data-processing operation by means of an application program, such as a file-management program. In addition to the basic application program, communications software must be provided somewhere throughout the network for interfacing the terminals to the host computer's application program as well as organizing and managing the network. Finally, the operating system of the host computer must supervise all operations with the host computer.

In analyzing data communications software one must therefore consider three different levels or "layers" of software: the host operating system, the communication-based access software, and the application program. It is important to view such software as a "layered" structure rather than as a localized facility since modern system architecture distributes aspects of each layer throughout network facilities. The specific implementation of such layering will be presented in the chapters to follow. In this chapter we consider the role of the host operating system and the communication-based access methods.

HOST OPERATING SYSTEM

The host operating system is those programs within a computer system that are concerned with the overall job, task, and system resource management. The supervisory and control functions of the host operating system are concerned with the following functions:

- Operating facility management
- System administration
- Network control
- Program and job control
- Data management

The host operating system programs are often referred to as systems programs, as distinguished from the applications programs that are run for the user. Depending on the software architecture of the host machine, the system programs may be centralized in the memory of the host processor or distributed throughout the system.

Operating facility management is concerned with the management of basic hardware facilities, such as memories, peripherals, communication channels, and power distribution.

System administration is concerned with the control and scheduling of system resources, including processors, memories, I/O devices, transfer channels such as busses, and communications links.

Network control is concerned with the management of the communications network associated with the host computer, including the remote stations and communication links.

Program and job control is concerned with the handling of user programs and jobs within the computer system, along with program monitoring and accounting.

Data management is concerned with the handling of data throughout the computer system, including the creation of various data structures and data files.

Operating systems may vary in scope from large-scale systems for general-purpose mainframe computers to specialized systems for minicomputers. Table 3.1 lists various types of operating systems associated with some well-known general-purpose mainframe computers.

Operating systems for minicomputers offer considerably fewer facilities than those for mainframe computers. Most minicomputer operating systems (which are often called *executive programs* or *monitors*) are concerned with management and control of a particular type of facility, such as a storage device or communications link. As an example of the types of operating systems implemented on a

TABLE 3.1.   Operating Systems for Mainframe Computers

IBM:		
	BOS/360	(basic operating system)
	TOS/360	(tape operating system)
	DOS/360	(disk operating system)
	OS/360—PCP	(primary control program)
	OS/360—MFT	(multiprogramming with fixed tasks)
	OS/360—MVT	(multiprogramming with variable tasks)
	CP-67/CMS	(control program and Cambridge monitor system for the System/360 model 67)
	TSS/360	(time sharing system for the System/360 model 67)
	DOS/VS	(virtual system)
	OS/VS-1	
	OS/VS-2	
	OS/VS-2 Release 2	
	VM/370 (virtual machine)	

minicomputer system, Table 3.2 lists the Datapoint computer operating systems.

In addition to the operating systems, various utility programs are available which enhance the user's access to the storage facility and provide typical user functions such as list, dump, file-protection, sorting, and file-manipulation routines.

COMMUNICATION-BASED ACCESS METHODS

A communication-based access method is a software module used in connection with the data management facilities of a particular operating system for interfacing to the actual teleprocessing equipment. IBM's communication-based access methods are probably of greatest interest, and therefore are reviewed here.

TABLE 3.2.   Datapoint Operating
Systems

Cartridge disk operating system
Mass storage disk operating system
Diskette operating system
5500 dual partition system
Cassette tape operating system
Magnetic tape operating system

There are three IBM access methods to consider:

BTAM (basic telecommunications access method)
TCAM (telecommunication access method)
VTAM (virtual telecommunication access method)

BTAM

BTAM is the simplest access method for use with either IBM's DOS or OS operating systems. BTAM is a software facility that permits the system programmer to communicate with terminals throughout the system on a macro level. The facility includes instructions for polling terminals, addressing specified terminals, dialing services in a switched network, and coding and error-correction functions.

BTAM provides a very low level of communications support, and additional programming is required to provide for more extensive data-handling capabilities such as scheduling, queuing, and message processing. The lines and devices controlled by a BTAM application are dedicated to that application.

TCAM

TCAM is a more sophisticated access method that provides the facility for the system programmer to create a message-control program for handling message traffic throughout the network. Some of the more important features of the facility include queuing capabilities, message control and editing, operator control functions, and debugging, checkpoint, and restart services.

TCAM is implemented by means of a message-control program (MCP) which is coded by a user in assembler macro instructions. The MCP enables the user to specify the particular equipment configuration being implemented—in particular, the buffers used for temporary storage of message data which are transmitted throughout the network. Furthermore, the MCP macros provide functions for message routing, editing, and error-checking.

TCAM operates under control of System/370 under OS/VS-1, OS/VS-2 SVS, and OS/VS-2 MVS. Applications programs operate concurrently with the MCP under OS scheduling. The basic function of TCAM is to control efficiently the flow of data within the computer-based teleprocessing network while concurrently performing processing of such transferred data or user batch programs. Since messages flow into the system at random times and from random user locations, the function of TCAM is to organize such data flow into storage regions and process the information at the higher computer speeds. The MCP itself may perform certain limited processing functions—for example, examining the header of a message to determine routing operations.

As we pointed out above, TCAM operates under control of System/370 under OS/VS-1, OS/VS-2 SVS, and OS/VS-2 MVS. Partitions or regions should be provided so that the MCP is executed in the partition with highest priority, while concurrent batch-processing jobs are executed in partitions having a lower priority. In analyzing the general concepts and facilities of TCAM, the following features should be particularly noted:

- Message-control program
- Macro capabilities
- Data Set definition
- Message format

MESSAGE-CONTROL PROGRAM.   The MCP enables the user to control the flow of data through the teleprocessing system. TCAM support is provided in two separate categories: message control in the MCP, and message processing in the applications programs. Applications programs are able to run in the other partitions of memory.

The MCP basically functions as an intermediary between stations in the teleprocessing network as well as with the various applications programs in memory. The MCP operates by means of executing user commands expressed as macro instructions.

MACRO CAPABILITIES.   The macro capabilities of TCAM refer to the ability of the programmer to select specific TCAM routines and parameters suitable for a particular network. The primary macro capabilities provide message-handling instructions such as designating which stations are to transmit messages and which stations are to receive messages; message editing; queuing and rerouting; and error control and recovery.

DATA SET DEFINITION.   A data set is a separately identifiable collection of information which is filed and handled by the processor as a unit. Each data set handled by the MCP is identified by a data control block (DCB). There are various types of data sets associated with the data network: those referring to communication line groups, message queues, and checkpoint data sets stored on a secondary storage device. The programmer uses DCB macro instructions for each of these data sets, thus enabling data to be transferred to and from the application programs.

MESSAGE FORMAT.   The message format in the MCP consists of a header portion followed by a text portion. The header portion indicates the destination, the origin, and control information such as the input sequence number. The text portion contains the message data. The system programmer defines the exact message format according to his requirements. Operations on the header fields are performed by message-handling functions within the MCP, again defined by appropriate macros.

VTAM

VTAM is the latest and most sophisticated access method for use with IBM's System/370 computers, utilizing programmable hardware controllers together with a powerful macro language for the system programmer. The hardware includes the IBM 3704/3705 programmable communications controllers, while the software includes the network control program (NCP). NCP resides in the communications controller and performs network management functions as well as interfacing to the application program in the host computer.

VTAM operates under control of System/370 DOS/VS, OS/VS1, OS/VS2 SVS, or OS/VS2 MVS. The latest release of VTAM, at the time of this writing, is referred to as Level 3, which contains certain macro instructions that were not present in releases of VTAM prior to Level 3.

The importance of VTAM is that it interfaces with Systems Network Architecture (SNA), which is considered in greater detail in Chapter 5.

VTAM is basically a facility for controlling communications between terminals and user application programs. The system programmer defines the VTAM system by means of VTAM application programs. Some of the functions that the VTAM application program performs are:

- Associating and disassociating a program from VTAM
- Communicating with or terminating logical units to which the program is connected

VTAM is typically run together with CICS, IMS, or related IBM software product. The functions of controlling, scheduling, and polling communications lines are not the function of host computer software, but are implemented in a communications controller with a network control program (NCP). VTAM interfaces with the NCP in the IBM 3704 or 3705 Communications Controller. While VTAM handles such tasks as input/output buffering, scheduling of exit routines, and sequence numbering of outbound messages, the NCP schedules line activity, error correction, and error data analysis.

VTAM can best be visualized from the simplified block diagram of Figure 3.1. Two VTAM applications programs, each including a processing part and a telecommunications part, are shown resident within the host CPU. The two application programs connect to the VTAM interface module, designated simply as "VTAM," which connects with external devices attached to the CPU.

VTAM connects directly with the NCP, which is resident in the 3704 or 3705 Communications Controller. The NCP is connected along a SDLC link to one or more logical units, which may be either devices or other application programs. Each logical unit may be connected to one or more terminals or other physical devices.

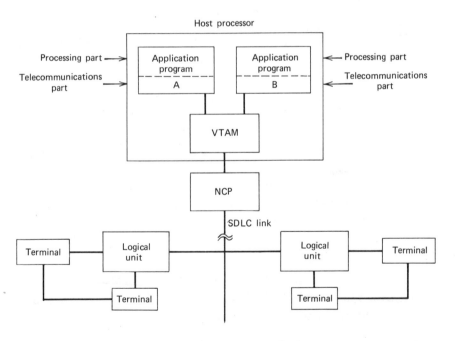

FIGURE 3.1.   VTAM telecommunication system.

Advanced Communications Function

The Advanced Communication Function (ACF) was a 1976 IBM software announcement implementing multicomputer networking. Multicomputer networking refers to the interconnection of several System/370's through their corresponding 3705 communication processors. All message handling is then performed by the 3705's.

The 3705's may act as nodes in the system and, together with the Network Job Entry (NJE) facility, may either execute a job or forward the job to the next node for execution or forwarding.

A listing of the ACF program products and the operating systems is presented in Table 3.3 below.

TABLE 3.3. ACF Program Products

Program Product	Operating System
ACF/NCP/VS	DOS/VS; OS/VS
SSP	DOS/VS; OS/VS
ACF/TCAM	OS/VS1
	OS/VS2 SVS
	OS/VS2 MVS
ACF/VTAM	DOS/VS
	OS/VS1
	OS/VS2 SVS
	OS/VS2 MVS
NOSP	DOS/VS
	OS/VS1
	OS/VS2 SVS
	OS/VS2 MVS
NJE/JES2—	
Release 1	OS/VS2 MVS
Release 2	OS/VS2 MVS
Release 3	OS/VS2 MVS

COMMUNICATIONS CONTROL SOFTWARE

In addition to the IBM communications control software noted above, similar facilities are provided from other hardware and software vendors. In the area of network control, intelligent network processors such as the Codex 6000 shown in Figure 3.2 provide a wide variety of functions, such as:

- Network management
- Automatic port assignment
- Configuration control
- Support for an intermix of terminals (e.g., asynchronous, synchronous)
- Data compression and security
- Statistical multiplexing

It would be worthwhile to explore one of these functions, data compression, in greater detail.

Data Compression

Data compression is the technique of reducing the number of bits sent along a communication channel by performing some type of

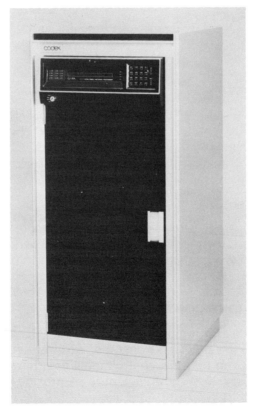

FIGURE 3.2.   Codex 6000 Intelligent Network Processor (92 port configuration).

analysis or processing on the bit stream and transmitting a modified or encoded bit stream to the final destination, where it is decoded. Reducing the number of bits transmitted increases the net data throughput through the channel.

There are two types of data compression that are presently used in commercial products: repeated character suppression and Huffman coding.

Repeated character suppression, the simplest technique, analyzes the data stream for strings of repeated characters and, instead of sending such strings over the transmission channel, sends the repeated character together with a code indicating how many times the character is sent.

Huffman coding is a more sophisticated technique, based on making a transformation between fixed-length source characters and variable-length coded characters. The most common characters in the source-data stream would be represented by coded characters having the shortest length. Similarly, the characters least frequently used in the source-data stream would be represented by coded characters having relatively longer lengths.

Error Control

Error control is one of the most important roles of communications control software in a data communications system. Errors arise from the basic nature of the long-distance communication link, including such effects as thermal noise in the transmission circuit, quantizing noise, and impulse noise (often called "hits" or "dropouts").

There are two basic methods of error control in a data communication system: automatic repeat request (ARQ) and forward error correction (FEC).

ARQ is the technique of having the receiver of the data send back to the transmitter a positive acknowledgment (ACK) when the block of data received is found to be correct. It is assumed that the block of data received incorporates some redundancy of information so that the receiver may in fact determine if the data that were received were the same data that were transmitted. (The various redundancy schemes for error-control purposes are described below.) If the data were received incorrectly a "negative acknowledgment" (NAK) is sent back to the transmitter, which then functions to request automatically retransmission of the block of data that were received incorrectly.

FEC is an even more redundant technique in which sufficient information is present within the transmitted message block so that not only is an error detected but the original data can be reconstructed as well.

The most frequently used error-checking schemes are vertical redundancy checking (or "parity"), horizontal or longitudinal redundancy checking, and cyclic redundancy checking.

VERTICAL REDUNDANCY CHECKING.   Vertical redundancy checking (VRC) or parity checking introduces a single bit (1 or 0) added to each character. For an odd parity-checking scheme, a 1 bit is added if the number of remaining 1 bits in the character is even, thus making in total an odd number of 1 bits in the character. For even parity checking, a 1 bit is added to make the total number of 1 bits in the character even. (The VRC scheme is called "vertical" since a paper-tape representation of the characters arranges them vertically across the width of the tape.)

It is clear that there are basic limitations to VRC. Although a single-bit error in a character can be detected, a 2-bit error (or, more generally, a $2n$-bit error) cannot be detected with such a scheme. This is a significant limitation, since in data communication systems noise frequently occurs in bursts and not one bit at a time.

LONGITUDINAL REDUNDANCY CHECKING.   Horizontal or longitudinal redundancy checking (LRC) is similar to VRC except that a parity bit is used for each bit position in a sequence of characters. The LRC character is sent as a single character after the sequence of characters is transmitted.

It is also possible to use LRC in combination with VRC. However, it must still be noted that the same basic limitations applicable to VRC are applicable to LRC.

CYCLIC REDUNDANCY CHECKING.   Cyclic redundancy checking (CRC) utilizes a check character that represents the remainder of a division of a "generating polynomial" into the message block. Because of the importance of CRC, it would be worthwhile to elaborate on the technique.

First, a remark must be made about notation. Coding theory treats data not as numbers but as mathematical functions—more specifically, as polynomials such as

$$a_n x^n + a_{n-1} x^{n-1} + \cdots + a_1 x + a_0$$

The nth power of x represents the nth binary digit; for example, the number

$$1\ 0\ 0\ 1\ 1$$

is represented by the polynomial

$$x^4 + x + 1$$

In that case, the coefficients a_i ($i = 1, 2, \cdots n$) are

$$a_4 = 1$$
$$a_3 = 0$$
$$a_2 = 0$$
$$a_1 = 1$$
$$a_0 = 1$$

The next concept to introduce is that of congruence. Two numbers are said to be "congruent modulo m" if they leave the same remainder when divided by m. If one polynomial, the data polynomial $D(x)$, is divided by the generator polynomial $G(x)$, the result is a quotient polynomial $Q(x)$ and a remainder polynomial $R(x)$:

$$\frac{D(x)}{G(x)} = Q(x) + \frac{R(x)}{G(x)}$$

Thus $D(x) - R(x) = Q(x)G(x)$.

The CRC character is the remainder $R(x)$. Since most applications require high accuracy, a two-byte or 16-bit CRC character is used. The generating polynomial is therefore of sixteenth order, that is, beginning with an x^{16} term. The choice of the generating polynomial is important so that there are not a large number of data polynomials that are congruent modulo the generating polynomial (i.e., have the same CRC character). There are several standard generating polynomials:

CRC-CCITT:	$x^{16} + x^{12} + x^5 + 1$
CRC-16:	$x^{16} + x^{15} + x^5 + 1$
CRC-12:	$x^{12} + x^{11} + x^3 + x^2 + x + 1$

CRC-CCITT is the European standard; CRC-16 is used in United States systems; and CRC-12 is used in systems that have 6-bit characters.

Telecommunications Monitors

There are a number of software packages for use with host operating systems in a telecommunications environment. Some of these software packages from various vendors are listed in Table 3.4.

As an example of a telecommunications monitor, we now consider TASK/MASTER in more detail. TASK/MASTER manages the resources of an on-line system and provides application programs with a simple interface to them. TASK/MASTER consists of a set of function managers that operate under control of a central dispatching module. The function managers provide TASK/MASTER support for storage management, database access, network control, message queuing, and application program control.

The TASK/MASTER system performs several basic functions:

Dynamic storage management
Task management
Message queuing
System control
Start-up and cycle-down
System statistics
Error recovery
System restart

Dynamic storage management is concerned with defining either reentrant program areas or temporary storage areas where intermediate results can be saved while waiting for a reply from a terminal.

Task management segments application programs, passes control to subroutines, initiates various asynchronous tasks, and performs looping operations.

TABLE 3.4. Telecommunications Monitors

Package Name	Vendor
CICS	IBM
DATACOM/DC	Insyte Datacom Corp.
ENVIRON/1	Cincom Systems, Inc.
INTERCOMM	Informatics, Inc.
MINICOMM	Informatics, Inc.
ROSCOE	Applied Data Research, Inc.
TASK/MASTER	Turnkey Systems, Inc.

Message queuing provides input, output, switched, and priority message queues which are managed on a station-by-station basis. Request codes allow application programs to access queued information directly.

System control includes such functions as adding and deleting terminals, opening and closing files and communication lines, flushing message queues, sending messages, initiating applications, starting and stopping system statistics, displaying and altering main storage, and displaying user files or temporary stored information.

Start-up and cycle-down provides for the start-up of an on-line system, including such parameters as the configuration of the network, polling sequences, message-queue characteristics, and passwords.

System statistics refers to the task of monitoring and maintaining operational statistics on the activity of all lines, stations, application programs, and files.

Error recovery refers to techniques for diagnosing the type of error occurring, logging it, notifying the system operator, and performing corrective action.

System restart allows the system to automatically resume processing after a machine, power, operator, network, or file failure. The restart procedures utilize queue-, file-, and task-protection facilities.

APPLICATION PROGRAMS

The application programs refer to the programs resident in the host computer for performing the basic processing task for which the data communications system was implemented. Some typical application programs perform one or more of the following tasks:

Remote batch
Time-sharing
Inquiry/response systems
Data collection
File management
Message switching

Remote batch refers to the use of the host computer for batch processing of jobs that have been entered from a remote terminal.

Time-sharing refers to the simultaneous processing of several jobs (i.e., by each job "sharing" a portion of the processor's time) by the host computer.

Inquiry/response systems are those in which the remote terminal is able to make inquiries of a centralized file or "data base" maintained in the host computer.

Data collection refers to the host computer's collecting current or updated file information from remote terminals.

File management refers to the file handling and processing of the centralized file in the host computer; in a data communications system, certain specified handling and processing functions may be performed from designated remote locations.

Message switching refers to the processing of messages to specified destinations (i.e., "switching") over limited-channel-capacity systems.

The tasks are performed within the overall management of the host computer operating system. However, the complexity of many of the tasks has led to the development of specialized systems programs—time-sharing systems, data base management systems, and telecommunications control systems—offered as software packages by the mainframe computer manufacturers and by independent software and systems firms. These systems programs, in addition to user-written application programs, perform the data-handling, arithmetic, and logical operations required by the user.

More specific information on the various categories of user applications—banking and financial, insurance, retailing, distribution, and reservation systems—is discussed in Chapter 8.

One important attribute of application programs in a distributed processing environment is that they provide the means by which several users can access the same programs concurrently. Such a technique is often called reentrant programming or using reentrant code. Reentrant programs and any constant data associated with such programs must be kept in a read-only area of the memory so that no user can modify such programs or data during execution. Each user of the application program has its own read-write area of memory wherein current data pertaining to the executing application program are stored and kept inaccessible to other concurrent users.

four
NETWORK ARCHITECTURE AND DESIGN

A data communications system is implemented as an integrated hardware/software "computer network." A number of considerations must be analyzed in developing the network structure and architecture:

User requirements
Technologic cost/performance measurement
Communications systems

An analysis of user requirements is the first step to be performed in designing a computer network. The user population should be categorized in terms of usage and utility value, and basic technologic criteria be established for each type of user. The available hardware and software technology must then be compared to such requirements. More importantly, some cost/performance measurement of such technology must be made relative to such requirements. Finally, the availability of various communications systems options must be considered.

In designing a computer network, the communications system designer must therefore analyze the following issues:

Terminal configurations
Processor configurations
Network architecture
Network design
Supervisory design
Computer system and network security

TERMINAL CONFIGURATIONS

The basic user requirements may generally be specified in terms of the number, type, and locations of user terminals. In specifying a terminal, the following administrative factors must be considered:

- User characteristics
- Media used
- Language used
- Terminal availability
- Communications security

These "administrative" issues should dictate the number and type of terminals and thus the basic data communications network architecture, rather than cost/performance attributes of certain processor or network architectures dictating the type of terminal configurations. In short, the computer network should adapt to the requirements of the user, rather than the user be required to adapt to the typical configurations of commercially available computer network architecture.

User Characteristics

The first requirement, the user characteristics, is a particularly important one. Most commercial computer networks are data-base-orientated systems, in which the typical user is merely required to enter or access information from the data base.

It is not necessary, or desirable, in such applications that *each* user be provided with sophisticated editing or other interactive facilities, or even communications facilities. In such cases it is advantageous to use a cluster configuration, shown in Figure 4.1.

The use of a cluster configuration of terminals is an example of the implementation of the concept of "dispersed data processing." This concept means the dispersal of facilities, such as a terminal, to those locations where data is generated, and where the results of data processing are needed.

In the cluster configuration, the remote terminals perform simple input/output processing, while the host terminals monitor and control the clustered terminals, and interface the cluster to the communications network.

Alternative forms of terminal configurations include loop configurations, shown in Figure 4.2, or hierarchical configurations, shown

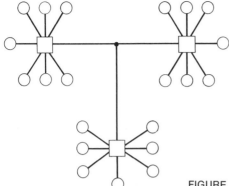

FIGURE 4.1.   Cluster terminal configuration.

in Figure 4.3. The loop configuration is directed at saving communications line cost by minimizing the amount of interconnection between the terminals. Hierarchical configurations are applicable to
situations where there are different classes or types of terminals, or
different control or supervisory levels and functions that must be
implemented.

Some of the important user characteristics that must be considered
in planning the terminal configuration are

Skill of the operator
Type of messages handled
Traffic volume
Location of the terminals

Such characteristics determine not only the type of terminal to be
used but also the terminal configuration and, ultimately, the network
architecture.

Media Used

The choice of media for a terminal configuration is essentially a
matter of the intended application. The minimum requirements of
some type of data input and output may be supplied by a unit as
simple as a Transaction Telephone. The more sophisticated type

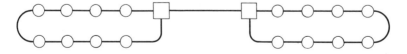

FIGURE 4.2.   Loop terminal configuration.

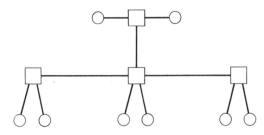

FIGURE 4.3.   Hierarchical terminal configuration.

terminal would provide both hard-copy and soft-copy output, together with a variety of data input options.

The media considerations should be distinguished from the specification of user characteristics described in the preceding section. The media considerations are administrative issues of form specifications, auditing, and documentation, rather than technical issues of operation skill, and message format or volume. Thus the "media" would be different for a management information center, a data input preparation center, and an operation center.

Language Used

The choice of language at a particular user terminal, like the choice of media, depends on the application. Most of the "dispersed data processing system" manufacturers have developed their own simple language for providing means for the average user to access the data base—or perform other simple operations such as data entry, verification, and editing—without knowledge of a "programming" language.

Such user languages are designed with the primary objective of protecting the integrity of the data base or network, rather than giving an arbitrary remote user free access to the entire system. These languages have such facilities as field-protection options, in which certain data fields may be displayed to the user, but not changed by that user.

Similar languages have been developed for networks, in which the network user can define logical links between network components by means of macroinstructions. The macroinstructions are interpreted by a control program which builds an object program from the user's macroinstructions. This object program is then stored at the user locations until the network is activated. Once the network is activated, the object program is transported to the appropriate communications controllers for implementation.

Terminal Availability

The concept of terminal availability is really concerned with several different issues:

Fault tolerance
Multiple-usage options
Nonblocking communications

Fault tolerance is the ability of a terminal to be operative in spite of the occurrence of an error, and is important in high-reliability and high-priority data communications applications.

Multiple-usage options enables a single terminal to perform a variety of user functions. This enables a terminal normally used for one type of operation to be "available" for an alternative operation if necessary. A data terminal may alternatively serve as a facsimile terminal, for example, or as a stand-alone unit for in-house processing. In fact, the word "terminal" may be somewhat inappropriate when the remote processing station being referred to is an IBM System/32.

Nonblocking communications is a way of specifying that communications will not "block" the creation of other communications links.

Communications Security

The type of communications security is an increasingly important one for modern data communications systems. Communications systems—whether data or voice, by radio, satellite, or wire—carry the most current, and therefore most sensitive and valuable, information. Although most data communications systems today are consumer transaction systems, carrying information on reservations or credit purchases that could not really be characterized as competitively "valuable information," more and more facilities are being used for management, financial, and other control functions that do carry competitively important information.

Some of the important information that could be compromised by an intelligence effort directed at an active or passive penetration of the communications system includes:

Financial information: sales, profits, budgets, financial projections
Vendor and customer information: purchase orders, bids, market analysis and projections, service information

Production and inventory information: raw materials, work in process, finished products, inventory, shipments, returns

Corporate development: new product development, expansion plans, personnel changes

Since it is the communications link that is the most vulnerable segment of the network, communications security measures are directed to data encryption. Encryption is the technique of converting a data stream into an encoded data stream by means of a "key" data stream. The "key" is also possessed by the authorized receiver of the message, thus enabling him to decode it back to the original data stream.

Data encryption units may be either off-line or on-line units. Off-line units enable the preparation of message tapes which are transmitted over the usual Telex or other message carriers. One typical commercially available unit for connection to an off-line teleprinter utilizes a high-level key generator. The key generator is a multiregister device with multistop programming for each bit of generated key. The device is also arranged to select a starting point of the key sequence at random, and produce a nonlinear bit stream.

Commercial data encryption units are customized by each user by means of selection of an individual code. This selection is done by means of rotary switches which are secured both inside the unit itself and on the front panel behind a locked door. Thus a two-level code administration hierarchy may be maintained.

One method of achieving data security is by encoding the transmitted message according to some type of general encryption operation or algorithm. The specific operation or algorithm depends on a "key" which is specified by the user. The "key" is a sequence of bits that is provided to both the sender and receiver locations.

There are numerous cryptographic techniques, but the one adopted by the National Bureau of Standards is a recirculating block-product cipher originally proposed by IBM. The specific algorithm utilizes a recirculating block-product cipher with a 64-bit key (which includes eight error-check bits). Details of the algorithm are specified in the NBS standard reprinted in Appendix Two.

Encryption may be performed by either hardware or software, although hardware is generally preferred. The standard NBS algorithm is implemented on a data-security integrated circuit using NMOS technology developed by Motorola, and other manufacturers have announced similar single-board implementations.

PROCESSOR CONFIGURATIONS

The next network level the communications system designer must consider is that of processor configurations. At the terminal configuration level the designer is concerned with matching hardware capabilities with user requirements. At the processor level the designer is concerned with matching hardware capabilities with network requirements.

There are a number of types of processors in a computer network to consider:

Communications processors
Switching-node processors
Host processors

Communications processors are relatively small and simple processors designed to interface the terminals with the communications network. The communications processor performs tasks such as network monitoring and control, interrupt handling, polling, protocol handling, and administrative functions.

Switching-node processors serve to transfer and route data messages to predetermined destinations along the network. Such processors can range in scope from simple data PABX systems for handling less than 100 terminals, to digital central offices, such as the Bell System ESS No. 4, with a capacity of 107,000 trunks, and switching capability of 500,000 calls/hour.

Host processors are concerned with the basic data processing application implemented by the computer network. Depending on the architecture of the computer network, there can be one or more "host processors" in the network. Some networks are designed with a single "primary" host processor and one or more "secondary" processors, while others do not make such a distinction.

The subject of processor configurations may therefore be specified by the number, type, and locations of processors. In determining the processor configuration, the computer network designer is concerned with the following factors:

• Data distribution in the network
• Network management

Data Distribution in the Network

The principal task of the processors in a communications network is the handling of data. The number, type, and location of processors should therefore be directly related to where the data to be processed are located in the network. If the system is organized around a central data base, then a primary host processor at the location of the data base would be the most effective processor configuration. On the other hand, in a data collection system the data are dispersed at remote locations, and depending on the ultimate destination of such data, a number of different processor configurations could be implemented.

The type of processor is also specified by the type of data-handling task to be performed. Whereas most communications processors, for example, are minicomputers today, the use of microcomputers (i.e., a data processing systems using a microprocessor as the central processing unit) for such tasks are expected to be more widely used in the next 5 years. Microcomputers are fully capable of handling the tasks associated with a communications processor.

The location of the processors depend on the type and function of the processor in the network. Communications processors are located most closely to those facilities that interface with the communications network—that is, with the terminals or with clusters of terminals. The switching-node processors are located at intersections or "nodes" in the communications network where switching from one network segment to other network segments can be most efficiently performed. Host processors are located near the data base upon which this processing is performed.

The topic of distributed data bases is a complex one that can only be briefly outlined in this work. A data base is an organized collection of data that is stored for use for given applications. A data base may be either centralized at one location or distributed. Distributed data bases may be classified into two basic categories:

Partitioned
Replicated

A partitioned data base is one in which the information is partitioned into distinct entities, which are stored in remote locations. Customer files for customers in a given region that are stored in a regional computer center are an example of a partitioned data base. A replicated data base is one in which a duplicate copy of the data base exists in more than one location.

The data in a data base are described or defined by some *schema*. Associated with the schema is a *directory* for indicating the physical location of the desired data in the data base. In considering distributed data bases, the second-order issue of distributed directories must be considered as well. Like the data base itself, the directories may be either partitioned or replicated.

In analyzing the distributed data-base system, one can develop a matrix of different possibilities: partitioned or replicated data bases, centralized or distributed directories, partitioned or replicated directories.

The software that supports a data-base system is known as a data-base management system (DBMS). Software, like the data base itself, may also be implemented either centrally or distributed, leading to even more system design possibilities.

Network Management

Another factor that must be considered in planning processor configurations is the subject of network management. We consider this issue here rather than in the section below on network architecture because the network is in fact managed by the processors.

Network management may be simply defined as that process that determines through what facilities a message will travel from its source to its destination. Network management is therefore concerned with the management of network resources—communications links, switching nodes, and communications processors. It should also be distinguished from supervisory design of a data communications network, which is concerned with more general monitoring and control functions, and will be described in a later section.

There are two basic types of network management systems:

- Master-slave or "hierarchical"
- Distributed or "horizontal"

Master-slave network management refers to the use of one or more master stations or processors that control a plurality of slave processors or nodes. The routing of a particular message is directly controlled by the slave processors, but general management is controlled by the master station or processor.

Distributed network management refers to the use of decision-making facilities at each processor or node, with no one processor or node given control over another processor or node.

Depending on the type of network and the number of processors and nodes, data communications networks are typically designed using one of these two types of network management systems.

Some of the issues that must be considered in determining the type of network management system for a given application are:

- Management accountability
- Hardware availability
- Software availability
- Flexibility
- Reconfigurability
- Susceptibility to communications faults
- Security/integrity
- Database administration

Although these issues are not fully discussed at this point, it can be pointed out that master-slave or hierarchical systems are much more structured and accountable, more available and in widespread use, and often more flexible than distributed configurations. Distributed networks are more reconfigurable and may offer less susceptibility to communications faults.

NETWORK ARCHITECTURE

Network architecture may be defined as the topology and function of network components. Topology refers essentially to the interconnection structure between the components, while the function refers to the role of the system component in the network.

The basic task of system network architecture is to optimize the distribution of system resources (hardware, software, data processing personnel) over the network in accordance with predetermined criteria. The predetermined criteria depend on the specific application, and may involve such factors as cost, availability, reliability, security, compatibility with existing resources, and similar considerations.

The system resources may be distributed at a variety of levels:

Terminal-user level
Terminal control unit level
Processor level
Processor control unit level

The distribution of resources depends, of course, on the terminal and processor configurations considered in the sections above. However, within such predetermined configurations, attention must be given to the architectural considerations.

Network topology is concerned with the physical layout of the system components, data and control routing, and technical characteristics such as capacity, throughput, delay, reliability, and cost. Although user requirements may suggest that a particular network node have a certain terminal or processor configuration, network topological considerations may dictate another function on the basis of, say, network reliability criteria.

The technique of determining a network architecture subject to predetermined criteria is known as network analysis. Network analysis is a well-developed discipline of operations research or mathematical control theory, and is presented in full detail in the references.

In this section, we wish to emphasize three important features of network architecture that are important in planning computer communication networks:

- System resource distribution
- Modularity
- Communications structures

System Resource Distribution

A data communications network may be considered an arrangement for distributing and managing system resources over dispersed locations. System resources is a catch-all phase that includes user terminals, programming support, concentrators, and other data communications hardware, switching centers, host computers, and communications links. Such resources are dispersed for reasons related to the business of the user or the particular application, and it is the task of the network designer to integrate the dispersed resources into a functioning network.

It is useful to consider system resources as being distributed over levels or layers rather than just in a physical or geographic sense, not only from the point of view of software but also from the viewpoint of network supervisory design.

Thus any one physical location will comprise several layers, each layer having a specific functional responsibility. Each layer communicates with the adjoining layer as well as with corresponding layers in other physical locations. System resource distribution defines which layers are present at each location and their functional responsibility. Further details on the layered structure of several specific network architectures are presented in the next chapter.

The distribution of system resources over different physical or geographic locations is another important aspect of network architecture. The interconnection of different resources defines different network architectures. A simple example can be used here to illustrate the point.

Figure 4.4*a* shows a hypothetical point-of-sale (POS) network in which the switching center is interposed between clusters of terminals, and various banks. Figure 4.4*b* shows an alternative POS network in which the terminal cluster interfaces directly with the processor level ("Bank") and the switching center also interfaces with

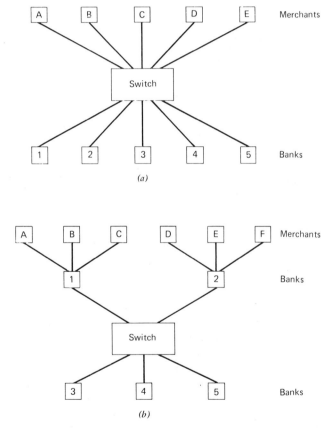

FIGURE 4.4.   (a) Point-of-sale network; (b) alternative point-of-sale network.

the bank. The different distribution of resources in Figures 4.4*a* and *b* depends on the supervisory design of the network, which will be discussed in more detail in a later section. It is important here to note that, although the networks in Figures 4.4*a* and *b* perform essentially the same function, the network architectures are very different.

Another important distinction that should be made concerning system resource distribution is the difference between centralized and distributed networks, both in terms of topology and in terms of communications structures.

In terms of topology, system resources may be distributed in a variety of different configurations similar to the types of terminal configurations shown in Figures 4.1 through 4.3. Although hardware may be physically distributed, certain system resources such as data bases or supervisory software may still remain centralized. Thus in describing a network architecture it is important to specify the relative degree of centralization or distribution of each functional layer of each processing location in the network.

In terms of communications structures, centralized networks may be classified as either circuit switched or message switched. Distributed networks may be classified as either packet switched or ring. Further details and a comparison between these types of communications structures are presented in a later section.

Modularity

Modularity refers to the ability to substitute one network component for another and still achieve the network design objectives. Modularity should be distinguished from redundancy, which refers to a duplication of network components so that if one component should fail, a corresponding component would be activated. Modularity implies that the network components act in an equivalent manner, so that if one component should fail, the message could be rerouted through alternative components and still reach its destination. The network components are thus "modular," rather than dedicated or special-purpose units.

Modularity may be implemented at any level of the system: the terminal-user level, the terminal-control-unit level, the processor level, the processor-control-unit level, and even the communications-link level. Modularity may also be implemented in either hardware or software.

If any network component should fail, that failure is detected, and corrective action taken at the component level. If, for example, in a processor certain routines cannot be executed because of a memory read/write error, other routines will be executed. Such a process is sometimes called "graceful degradation." A neighboring process is informed of the degradation and begins picking up the load from the defective processor; message handling along the communication link continues.

Communications Structures

System resources are linked together by communications structures. The generic term communications structures is an aspect of network architecture that goes beyond a mere description of the transmission system or type of communications link, but describes what happens to the message as it is transmitted through the network.

There are two basic types of data communications structures:

Direct data transmission
Concentrated data transmission

Direct data transmission refers to the use of a single line or communication channel for the transmission of data. Such a technique is the simplest kind and most suitable for handling a predictable, predetermined volume of message traffic. More than one user may be able to simultaneously use the communication channel through some form of multiplexing, such as frequency-division multiplexing (FDM) or time-division multiplexing (TDM).

The type of switching associated with a direct data transmission network is referred to as circuit switching. In circuit switching an electrical connection path is established between the sending and receiving stations and is used exclusively by those stations until communications are discontinued.

Concentrated data transmission refers to the use of a store-and-forward technique for handling messages. Unlike direct data transmission, such a message is not transmitted directly, but is temporarily stored in a buffer prior to transmission. There are essentially two concentrated data transmission techniques: message switching and packet switching.

Message switching refers to the accumulation of a message in a store until a complete message has been assembled, and then transmitting it to the next destination when the communication channel becomes available. Message switching is therefore distinguished from circuit switching in which no intermediate storage takes place.

Packet switching refers to the accumulation of a message in a store, and breaking down the message into fixed-length segments for separate transmission over the communication channel. ARPANET was the first large-scale packet-switching network, and is described in more detail in Chapter 7.

The different types of network architectures, classified according to their communications structures, may be qualitatively compared with reference to the following parameters:

Setup delay
Switching delay
Line utilization efficiency (long messages)
Line utilization efficiency (short messages)
Expandability
Reliability

The network architectures are compared in Table 4.1.

NETWORK DESIGN

Network design is the implementation of a network architecture with specifically defined locations and performance criteria. Once such criteria have been determined, the network design task is one of determining the network topology—the number and type of connections between specific network nodes.

TABLE 4.1.   Network Architecture Communications Structures

	Network Type			
Feature	Circuit Switched	Message Switched	Packet Switched	Ring
Setup delay	high	low (hop-by-hop) high (end-to-end)	low	low
Switching delay	very low	high	low	low
Line utilization Efficiency (long messages)	very high	high	fair	poor
Line utilization Efficiency (short messages)	low	high	high	very low
Expandability	poor	poor	good	good
Reliability	low	low	high	very low

Network design is initially performed manually, based on the experience and intuition of the designer. Basic assumptions are made concerning the type and volume of messages, and a computerized simulation model of the network may be implemented. If graphics capability is available, the simulated network illustrating nodes of various types and the interconnections between them may be generated and displayed, as suggested in Figure 4.5. The basic technique is to use algorithmic search procedures that attempt to optimize the network structure by changing small segments of the network until a "local optimum" is found. Larger segments of the network are then changed, and a cost comparison is made between the new network and the previous "local optimum" network. If the new network is lower-cost, then the local optimization algorithm is applied to it in turn, generating a new "local optimum." The process continues using different starting networks or different "exchange operators" applied in different sequences until a globally optimum network is achieved.

Network design of a packet-switched network is similar, further employing the concept of "cut saturation." The noun "cut" is defined here as any set of lines whose removal (or "cutting") will disconnect the network. A cut will become saturated if the traffic in each component of the cut equals the capacity of that component.

FIGURE 4.5.   Network design generated by computer graphics.

SUPERVISORY DESIGN

The supervisory design of a data communications network consists of providing means for monitoring network usage and enforcing the network design objectives.

Supervisory design may be implemented in either hardware or software. The hardware may consist of line and system performance monitors that carry out continuous network surveillance, or auditing and analysis procedures for administrative or billing purposes. Software may include general operating systems associated with the host processor, or specialized communications software associated with a communications processor.

Another aspect of supervisory design is fault diagnostics. Unlike the passive monitoring function, fault diagnostics is concerned with active network intervention. Either hardware or software determines the specific network component that has failed, and predetermined criteria are applied to specify appropriate corrective action. The particular corrective action that is selected depends on the design objectives of the network.

The actual location and control over supervisory design features of a data communications network is an important feature of network architecture. Although it is important from an administrative viewpoint to provide indications of network component failures or error rates at the primary station for review by the data communications manager, it is equally worthwhile to provide indications of operational performance of equipment at each station. Such local performance indication may be measured by the local communication controller, and a simple visual display may be used to present performance parameters.

Some of the local parameters that may be monitored include signal quality, error rate, response time, and equipment usage. Local personnel may determine the relative performance of communication equipment on a daily basis, and request appropriate maintenance when conditions so warrant.

Fault diagnosis and testing procedures are technically more complex issues than monitoring, and international organizations like the International Telephone and Telegraph Consultative Committee (CCITT) are studying proposed testing standards.

Equipment for fault diagnosis and testing is available from such data communication equipment vendors as Codex, General Data-Comm, Intertel, and Racal–Milgo. Such systems monitor the status of the network and diagnose and pinpoint the location of faults.

COMPUTER SYSTEM AND NETWORK SECURITY

The subject of computer system and network security is a much broader one than communications security noted above. The present section discusses the various types of threats to which computer systems and networks may be subject, the philosophy and strategy of computer security strategies, and finally the types of control mechanisms that can be implemented.

System Threats

Computer system threats are usually divided into the categories of accidental, passive, and active.

Accidental system threats refer to those that occur independently of the intervention of a third party, and include:

1. Software faults
2. Component or other physical hardware failures
3. Communication system malfunction

Passive threats include those that are due to the passive interception of information as it is normally handled by the information processing system. Passive threats include:

1. Leakage of system information and codes through improperly discarded print-out or other I/O media
2. Physical exposure of some system element (network terminal, communication link) to external interception

Active threats are those in which a party attempts to penetrate the information processing by the system and divert the system to its own ends. The party may be an insider (from a computer operator to a corporate officer), or an outsider who through some manner has "logged on" the system.

The type of penetration itself may have several forms and objectives:

1. Unauthorized system usage—the user simply wishes to make use of CPU time without proper billing or accounting;
2. File penetration—access to confidential files and browsing for desired data;
3. File modification—unauthorized creation, modification, or deletion of confidential files;

4. Program modification—unauthorized changes to specific applications programs;
5. System modification—unauthorized changes to the operating system program for handling applications programs and jobs in an unauthorized manner;
6. System subversion—unauthorized changes in system hardware or software for causing the system to operate in error.

Computer Security Strategies

The fundamental issue in planning computer system and network security is cost: what percentage of total system cost should be expended to attain a predetermined degree of security? For most purposes, a security cost of 5% of the total system cost may be appropriate, whereas certain government, military, or defense applications may require 10%. There are a number of different strategies for implementing a security system:

1. Isolation—physically isolating the computer system and its terminals, documentation, etc., from unauthorized users, and monitoring usage by authorized users. Different levels of security classification of documents and access may also be provided (e.g., "for internal use," "confidential," "secret").
2. Encipherment—interposing a code or cipher between the system and the unauthorized user, so that the unauthorized user must first decipher the code before he is able to penetrate the system. The complexity of the code is chosen such that it would require a sufficiently long time and great expense (man-hours or CPU time) to decipher the message, in order to discourage the attempted system penetration.
3. Deterrence—persuading the prospective system penetrator that detection of his unauthorized actions would lead to criminal sanctions.
4. Insurance—the technique of limiting the liability of responsible parties in special circumstances should penetration of the system occur. An example of such insurance is professional liability insurance for attorneys and accountants who give a formal opinion of the financial status of the organization based on computerized records.
5. Delegation of responsibility—the most common technique of implementing a computer security system by an organization is to delegate that responsibility to someone else, be it an internal

security officer or an external facilities management organization. The user must therefore ascertain from the responsible security personnel the security strategies in use.

Control Mechanisms

There are three basic types of control mechanisms that may be implemented in computer system or network to protect against penetration:

• Access control
• Memory control
• Integrity control

   Access control refers to techniques for preventing unauthorized access to the computer system, applications programs, memory, or operating systems. Access control may be implemented by:

• Designation of certain terminals for only certain types of processing and access
• User identification, passwords
• Designation of access privileges for certain users
• Monitoring and logging of user access and processing

   Memory control refers to techniques for setting predetermined criteria as to who can read or write what from system files or memory. In effect, memory control is access control not for just the system, but for specific areas of memory. In addition to the techniques for access control noted above, specialized techniques such as internal usage codes or memory encipherment may be implemented to deter an unauthorized penetration or produce inaccurate information should a detected penetration occur.

   Integrity control refers to techniques for determining the "integrity" of the computer system or network, that is, that it is operating as it was intended to operate. At the most basic level, all system operations—jobs, applications programs, operating systems, communications, and so forth—are given security codes and checks to ascertain whether such operations are occurring when they should be. More sophisticated mechanisms include internal auditing mechanisms, system configuration testing, fail-secure and graceful degradation systems, and security officer surveillance of system operations.

five
NETWORK
CONTROL
ARCHITECTURE

T he network control architecture is a functional description of the components of a data communications system, including hardware, software, and communications links. It is useful to first describe these network architectures in terms of the data link control or protocol, and then describe some of the other ancillary network structures.

A protocol is essentially a set of rules for defining the communications system. There are several discrete "levels" of a protocol that must be defined:

Physical interface
Electrical interface
Link control
Message handling

The physical interface refers to the mechanical characteristics of the connection between two components in the data communications system. The number of signal lines and the shape and size of the connector are specified by the physical interface standard. An example of a physical interface standard is found in the Electrical Industries Association (EIA) RS-232C standard for connections between data terminal equipment (DTE) and data communication equipment (DCE).

The electrical interface refers to the electrical signals that are applied to the signal lines of the connection between two components of the data communications system. An example would be the

20-mA current loop in which the line current is switched on and off to represent bits. The RS-232C standard also defines electrical interface requirements. More recent EIA standards, RS-422 and RS-423, are expected to replace the RS-232C standard eventually.

In countries outside the United States, telecommunications standards are promulgated by the Consultative Committee on International Telephone and Telegraph (CCITT) and the International Organization for Standardization (ISO). The CCITT is part of the International Telecommunications Union (ITU), a United Nations agency. There are certain CCITT codes and recommendations that are important in data communications, and it would be worthwhile to list them here.

The CCITT codes are designated by a "V" number, the recommendations by an "X" number. Some of the important CCITT codes concerned with electrical interface standards are:

CCITT V.10 (X.26)   Electrical characteristics for unbalanced double-current interchange circuits
CCITT V.11 (X.27)   Electrical characteristics for balanced double-current interchange circuits
CCITT V.28   Electrical characteristics for unbalanced double-circuit interchange circuits

The next protocol level is that of link control. Data-link control protocols are the rules for transferring data and control information over the data communications link to remote stations. It is useful to classify such protocols into two basic groups: asynchronous protocols and synchronous protocols.

An asynchronous protocol is one in which data are transferred at nonuniform rates. The beginning of each character is marked by a start bit, the end of each character by a stop bit. (Such protocols are, therefore, sometimes called start-stop protocols.) Of course, the use of start and stop bits associated with each character is not efficient, and such protocols are not useful for high data rate applications. The two asynchronous protocols we examine in the present chapter are the Teletype and IBM 2740 protocols.

Synchronous protocols provide for the transfer of data at a fixed rate with the transmitter and receiver operating in synchronization. Synchronous modems are typically used so that a clock signal is transmitted along with the data stream to ensure that the transmitter and receiver stay in synchronization. Synchronous protocols may be classified into three types, depending on the message-framing format used:

Character-oriented protocols
Bit-oriented protocols
Byte-oriented protocols

In the present chapter we consider the Bi-sync character-oriented protocol; the SDLC, ADCCP, HDLC, X.25, BDLC, BOLD, and CDCCP bit-oriented protocols; and the DDCMP byte-oriented protocol.

In analyzing and comparing data-link protocols, the following features must be noted:

Framing
Line control
Error control
Sequence control
Transparency
Synchronization
Time-out and start-up

Framing refers to the rules used for determining (1) which bits constitute characters and (2) the message portion of the data transmitted. As pointed out above, protocols may be either character, bit, or byte oriented, depending on the framing technique.

Line control refers to the rules for determining which station transmits and which station receives on a half-duplex or multipoint line.

Error control refers to the error-checking code used and the ARQ retransmission procedures.

Sequence control refers to the numbering of messages in sequence as they are transmitted in the network so that the entire message may be properly reconstructed. In this connection two different types of packetization should be noted: datagram service and virtual call service. In datagram service, packets are transmitted independently through the network and arrive at the destination in arbitrary order. Sequence control is thus necessary for such service. In virtual call service the stream of packets is delivered to the destination in the order sent. Such a circuit therefore resembles a physical circuit.

Transparency refers to the ability to transmit data in a message that has the same bit pattern as the control characters. Character-oriented protocols use a special character to designate the beginning and end of the message portion. Bit-oriented protocols utilize a special flag character to identify the message. If the bit pattern of the flag character appears in the message itself, special "bit-stuffing" routines are used to change that bit pattern in a predetermined manner. After receipt of the message, bit-deleting routines are used to reconstruct the original message. Finally, byte-oriented protocols utilize a header that includes a "count" parameter which indicates the number of data characters in the message.

Synchronization refers to the technique used so that the receiving and transmitting stations can maintain synchronous clocks. The transmission of a special synchronization idle character (SYN) is one such technique.

Time-out and start-up refer to a procedure for providing a fixed time during which a given message must be received, after which alternative action is taken, such as starting up for new transmissions.

Data-link control protocols may also be analyzed in terms of at least three different "levels," corresponding to the levels or layers in the network architecture. The level-0 data-link control protocol refers to controlling transmission between adjacent communication nodes, that is, at the level of the "transmission subsystem" layer. In terms of the format of the transmitted packet, the level-0 protocol refers to the initial or outermost data fields in the packet, including for example the SYN characters. The level-1 data-link control protocol refers to transmission control between the source and destination nodes and includes the packet header and other control information. The level-1 protocol thus operates at the "function management" layer and is defined in terms of those fields in the packet adjacent the level-0 fields. Finally, the level-2 data-link control protocol refers to host/host message handling and operates at the "application layer" of the network architecture. In terms of the format of the transmitted packet, the level-2 protocol refers to the innermost fields of the packet, including the message text itself. When used generically, the term "protocol" is typically understood to mean all three levels, although it must be realized that such a single protocol is in fact composed of several subprotocols.

In the present chapter the following protocols for data communication are considered:

Asynchronous Protocols
  Teletype
  IBM 2740

Synchronous Character-oriented Protocol
  Binary Synchronous

Synchronous Bit-oriented Protocols
  SDLC
  ADCCP
  HDLC
  X.25
  BDLC
  BOLD
  CDCCP

Synchronous/Asynchronous Byte-oriented Protocol
  DDCMP

TELETYPE

The teletype interface is typically a 20-mA current loop represented by the block diagram in Figure 5.1. The RS 232C serial interface (Figure 5.2) may also be provided. Actual communication is performed asynchronously, with a message "header" defined by a START bit (space), followed by one or more STOP bits (mark).

A teletype-to-telephone communications link may be suitable for the transmission of text, but its lack of polling capability or error-detection makes it application for data transmission less useful or reliable than other techniques.

Teletypewriters fall into one of three general types: automatic send receive (ASR), keyboard send receive (KSR), and read only (RO). The type of lines that may be used with teletypewriters include simplex (send only or receive only), half-duplex (send and receive alternately), or full-duplex (send and receive simultaneously). Data rates generally range from 45 to 150 bits/second.

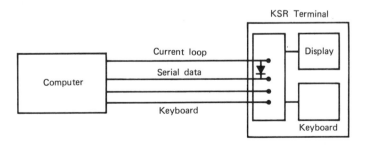

FIGURE 5.1. Teletype interface: current loop.

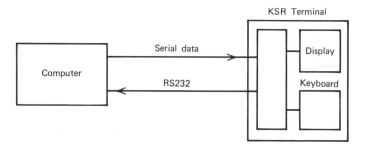

FIGURE 5.2.   Teletype interface: RS 232C.

IBM 2740

The 2740-type protocol is a start-stop half-duplex technique designed for use with the IBM 2740/2741 communication terminals. The sophistication of a protocol can be initially assessed by examining its error-control procedures. The 2740 protocol offers the more basic error-checking procedure, which is a single-bit parity check on each character. Such single-bit parity checking, called vertical redundancy checking (VRC), is generally adequate for simple applications where high reliability is not essential.

The error-recovery technique used in the 2740 protocol is a simple retransmission based on the reception of a negative acknowledgment (NAK) signal. Since such a technique is basic to many other protocols, it would be worthwhile to review the error-detection and correction technique at this point.

Once a message is received by a receiving station, it is checked for errors using the error-checking technique designed in the protocol. If an error is detected in the message, the receiving station sends a signal back to the sending station requesting a retransmission. Such a retransmission request consists simply of the characters NAK. In order to further increase the reliability of the system, if a message is received correctly by the receiving station, the receiving station also sends a signal back to the sending station requesting transmission of subsequent messages. Such a transmission request consists of the characters ACK (acknowledgment). Once the sending station receives an ACK signal, it will transmit the next message in sequence. If a NAK signal is received instead, it will transmit the previous message, corresponding to the NAK signal, and await an ACK signal. Of course, if neither an ACK nor NAK signal is received, the system may become deadlocked, and other techniques must be used to get the system started again.

The limitations and complexity of data link control operations are apparent even from the simple 2740 protocol. In examining the network control architecture of a data communications system, it is therefore expedient to first examine the characteristics of the protocol before describing the other network structures.

As we suggested above, the 2740 protocol is associated with the IBM 2740 communication terminal, which resembles a SELECTRIC typewriter. The IBM 2740 is a general-purpose terminal effective for internal communication among company departments, as well as remote-batch processing and inquiry type use. The 2740 is part of the IBM 2770 communication system, which is a media-oriented terminal system. The various types of media available with the 2770 communication system include card readers/punches, paper tape readers/ punches, magnetic card readers/inscribers, and printers.

It is also worthwhile to point out that certain common carrier teletype systems use essentially the same type of data link protocol as the 2740. For example, in the AT&T 83B-type teletypewriter equipment, a positive acknowledgment signal consists of the letter V, rather than the ACK signal.

BINARY SYNCHRONOUS (BI-SYNC)

The IBM bi-sync (or BSC) protocol is a somewhat more sophisticated data link control for half-duplex operations. It uses a larger number of control characters and permits synchronous operation. Furthermore, more reliability is achieved through better error-checking techniques.

Cyclic redundancy checking (CRC) using 16 bits (CRC-16) is the method of error detection. CRC uses a mathematical algorithm to calculate a block check character (bcc). The value of this bcc is sent from the sending station to the receiving station along with the message. The receiving station also performs the same mathematical algorithm on the message, and computes its own bcc. The calculated bcc and the received bcc are then compared to determine if there has been an error in transmission.

Some of the additional control characters found in BSC are as follows:

SYN: synchronous idle. A control character used on synchronous channels for the purpose of initiating or maintaining synchronism between stations. Some systems perform automatic hardware insertion/deletion of SYN characters.

EOT: end of transmission. A character that indicates the end of a particular transmission.

ENQ: enquiry. A control character used to solicit some type of response from the receiving station.

STX: start-of-text. A character that indicates the beginning of the text or message.

DLE: data link escape. A control character used to extend the set of control characters.

The various types of control characters are concerned with the following operational facilities:

Transmission codes
Synchronization
Initialization
Framing and blocking of text
Error detection and correction
Acknowledgment
End-of-transmission signaling

Such facilities may be applied on point-to-point, as well as multipoint operations.

The transmission format for sending a message in BSC thus might appear as follows:

```
S  S  S  S              E    B  B
Y  Y  Y  T  T   E   X   T  T   C  C
N  N  N  X              X    C  C
```

It is generally customary to write the control characters vertically. The B C C characters refer to the block check characters.

SNA—SDLC

SDLC (synchronous data link control) is the data link control protocol implemented in IBM's systems network architecture (SNA). Because of the importance of IBM's installed base, and therefore the expected widespread implementation of these concepts and facilities, we will review SNA and SDLC in considerable detail. The following basic concepts will be considered:

Systems Network Architecture (SNA)
   Layered structure
   Network addressable units
   Transmission subsystem
   Path control element
   Data link control element

Synchronous Data Link Control (SDLC)
   SDLC format
   Primary station operation
   Secondary station modes
   Command codes
   Function management services
   System services control point
   Network configuration
   Communications system protocol

Systems Network Architecture

Systems network architecture (SNA) is a functional description and definition of all components in a data communications system, including hardware, software, and communications links. Previous data communications systems and networks used a combination of several different computer access methods, different data-link communications protocols, and specialized terminals and lines which were dedicated to particular applications. SNA aims at providing an integrating network structure that is broad enough to satisfy the diverse requirements of various customer communications system configurations, as well as flexible enough to be adaptable to particular dedicated applications.

From the point of view of software or program control, there are three basic structures in SNA:

   Access method interface
   Communications protocol
   Communications control program

The access method interface is VTAM (virtual telecommunications access method), which replaces a variety of previously used access method interfaces, including IMS/VS, CIC/VS, TCAM/VS, BTAM, and so on. The access method interface couples the communication system to the host computer system.

The new communications protocol is SDLC (synchronous data link control), which replaces bisynchronous start/stop (bisync) or other protocol techniques. The protocol is the procedure for defining connection, synchronization, control, and message information over a data link.

A new communications control program, network control program (NCP), is also provided. The NCP interfaces with VTAM on one side and with other SNA components, including other network control programs, on the other.

LAYERED STRUCTURE. One of the essential features of SNA, as well as many other similar network architectures, is its "layered" structure. Each network node, regardless of whether it is a host processor or a simple terminal, has the same layered structure, described in greater detail below (see Figure 5.3).

SNA may be analyzed, on a functional basis, in three fundamental "layers":

Application layer
Function management layer
Transmission subsystem layer

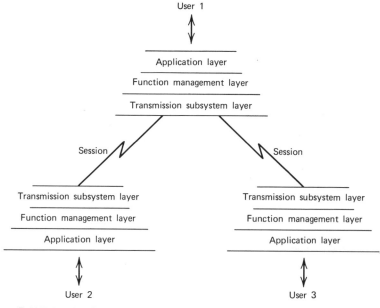

FIGURE 5.3.   Systems network architecture (SNA): layered structure.

The application layer defines the customer's particular application, and includes the hardware and software functions for implementing the application programs.

The function management layer is one level higher than the application layer, and manages the transfer of information between the layers defined by discrete devices distributed throughout the system network.

The transmission system layer is one level higher than the function management layer, and describes the generalized routing and transfer of information between systems nodal points. The transmission subsystem layer comprises three types of hardware elements (Figure 5.4):

Data-link control elements
Path control elements
Transmission control elements

As noted above, the system network is comprised of a number of transmission links extending between discrete points. The purpose of

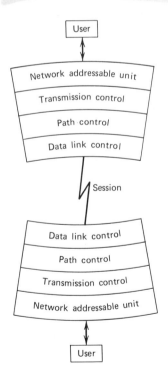

FIGURE 5.4.   SNA: transmission subsystem.

the data-link control element is to manage these data transmissions links. Path control elements are concerned with the routing of data over particular interconnecting network addresses. Finally, transmission control elements control the linkages or *sessions* and manage the data flow in the network.

An important feature of the layered architecture is that each layer is able to communicate with adjoining layers as well as with corresponding layers in another node. The layers basically serve as a hierarchical interface to the user at the node, which is referred to as the network addressable unit.

NETWORK ADDRESSABLE UNITS (NAU).   Each device in the data network that provides the user input or output linkage is known as a network addressable unit (NAU). Each NAU is provided with both a name and an address. The network name is a string of characters by which the users specify the particular NAU in question. The network address is a string of bits by which the data communications system addresses the NAU. A linkage between two discrete NAUs is called a session. A session is defined as a particular communications service over a specified link between two NAUs. A session is implemented by means of a presentation service (PS), a function management element which is part of the NAU. It is possible that a NAU may connect with several discrete NAUs (Figure 5.5). There are three types of NAUs defined by SNA:

System services control point (SSCP)
Physical unit (PU)
Logical unit (LU)

There are three possible kinds of sessions between NAUs:

LU to LU
LU to SSCP
PU to SSCP

Examples of these sessions are illustrated in Figure 5.5.

TRANSMISSION SUBSYSTEM.   The transmission subsystem, as noted above, consists of the following elements: transmission control element, path control element, and data link control element.

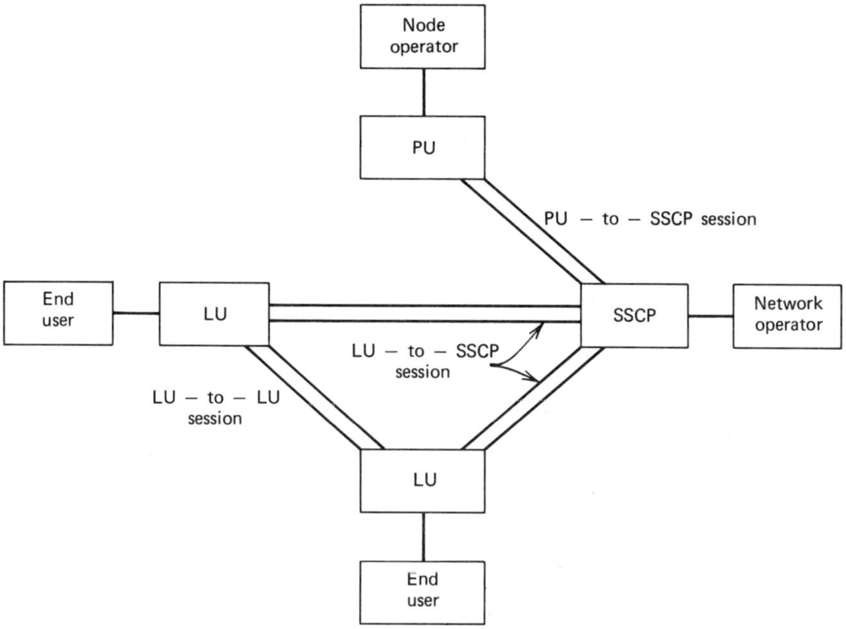

FIGURE 5.5.   SNA: sessions between network addressable units (NAU).

Transmission Control Element.   The transmission control element consists of:

Connection point manager
Session control
Network control component

The connection point manager provides the means of communication between NAUs with corresponding elements throughout the common network by means of an information unit known as a request response unit (RU), symbolized by the data field or block shown in Figure 5.6. A message is defined in SNA as a RU.

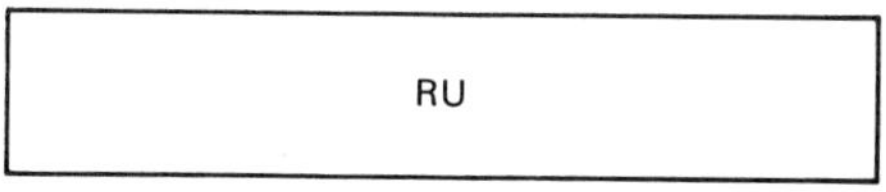

RU

FIGURE 5.6.   Request response unit (RU).

The actual data frame which is transmitted over the communication link is built up from the RU by adding a sequence of header fields and finally a trailer field. The header fields describe the destination as well as the type of information to which the header is prefixed. The trailer fields indicate the end of the frame, possibly also containing error control information.

The sequence of header fields appended to the RU correspond to the basic layers of the network architecture:

Transmission control
Path control
Data link control

As is described shortly, the transmission control element appends a function management header and a request/response header to the RU. The patch control element appends a transmission header, and the data link control element appends the data link control header (e.g., the SDLC header).

As the transmitted data frame travels from node to node, the frame penetrates only those layers of each node as required. Each layer strips the corresponding header from the frame and processes the information contained therein. Thus, for example, the path control element in a receiving node will check the address to see if the data were originally intended for that node. If not, the frame will not penetrate any further layers of that node, but rather will be reconstructed and routed to another node along a path toward its ultimate destination.

The processor adds a request response header (RH) to the beginning of the request unit of Figure 5.6 for identification. The RH–RU combination is defined as a basic information unit (BIU), as shown in Figure 5.7.

The session control component provides a means of implementing a session between NAUs, and coordinating the system resources required to maintain the session. The component also includes

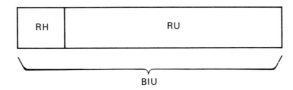

FIGURE 5.7. Basic information unit (BIU).

means for resynchronizing the information flow if a transmission error occurs.

The network control component provides a control communication path through the systems network using the same sessions that have been already established between NAUs.

Path Control Element. The path control element routes the BIUs through the system network. The path control unit thus formats a BIU for transmission of an information unit which is defined as a path information unit (PIU). The first step in this first implementation is the fragmenting of a large BIU into shorter uniform segments (Figure 5.8). Each PIU segment is then supplied with another header, a transmission header (TH) (Figure 5.9). The TH includes data bits that specify the destination address, mapping or segment indicator, sequencing, and related transmission information.

A sequence of these PIUs, each having a possibly different transmission header, may then be grouped together by the path control element into a single basic transmission unit (BTU), as shown in Figure 5.10.

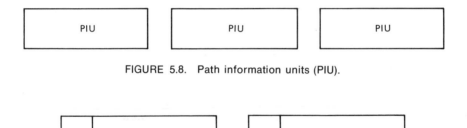

FIGURE 5.8. Path information units (PIU).

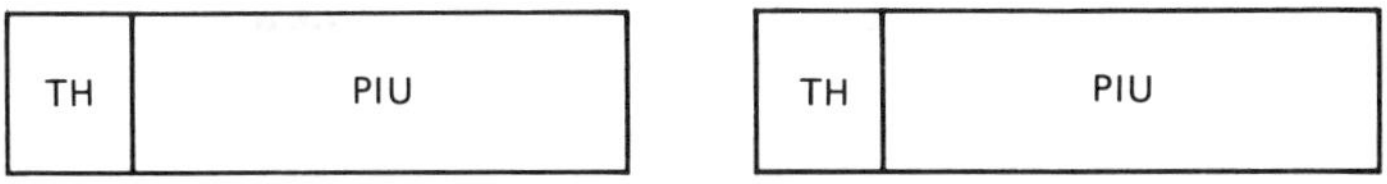

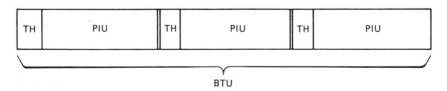

FIGURE 5.9. PIU with transmission header (TH).

FIGURE 5.10. Basic transmission unit (BTU).

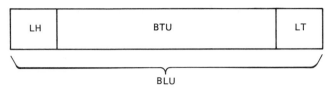

FIGURE 5.11.   Basic link unit (BLU).

Data Link Control Element.   The data link control (DLC) element manages a particular data link. A header (LH) and a trailer (LT) is added to the BTU to form yet another new information unit defined as a basic link unit (BLU), as shown in Figure 5.11. It is the BLU that is actually transmitted over the data link transmission facility. The BLU is transmitted to the next node, a NAU, where it is decoded and utilized at that node, or transferred to another node. The first element in the NAU that is encounted at the node is the DLC element. The DLC element strips the link control information (the LH header and LU trailer) from the BLU and transfers the remaining information unit, a BTU to the adjacent path control element. The path control element breaks the BTU into individual PIUs and examines the particular destination transmission control bits contained in the TH. If after examining the THs it is determined that the BTUs are destined for a different node, the BTU will be reformed and passed on to an adjacent DLC element, which then reassembles the BLU and retransmits the BLU along the transmission facility to the next node.

Synchronous Data Link Control

Synchronous data link control (SDLC) is a data link control protocol particularly adapted for implementation on SNA. SDLC is characterized by a number of basic architectural features:

- The use of a common grammar
- Increased reliance on the data link facility for error detection and recovery
- Two-level hierarchy consisting of primary stations and secondary stations
- Specific format for each data transmission block called a frame

SDLC FORMAT.   The basic structure of an SDLC frame is shown in Figure 5.12. The frame is divided into six fields: an eight-bit flag field (F), an eight-bit address field (A), an eight-bit control field (C), a

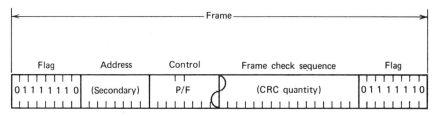

FIGURE 5.12. Synchronous data link control (SDLC): frame.

variable-length data or information field, a 16-bit block check sequence (BC), and an eight-bit ending flag field (F).

The flag field is a unique bit sequence used to designate the beginning and end of each frame. The actual eight-bit sequence used is
01111110. Provisions are made in the system architecture so that this
particular sequence is prevented from appearing in any other position other than the flag field. The actual technique used is a test for
five contiguous ones, after which a binary zero-bit is automatically
inserted. In a received bit stream, after the flag has been detected, the
inserted zeros are automatically deleted.

The address field serves to designate the particular secondary
station to which the frame is addressed. Of course, one address may
designate more than one station.

The control field is shown in Figure 5.13. There are three basic
formats which may be utilized in the control field for different pur-

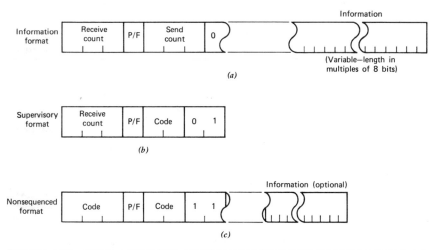

FIGURE 5.13. SDLC: control field. (a) Information format; (b) supervisory format; (c)
nonsequenced format.

poses, as shown in the figure: an information transfer format, a supervisory format, and a nonsequenced format. The control field contains frame sequence information and a poll/final (P/F) bit which acts as a send/receiver control signal.

Frame sequence information is defined by two counts which may be incorporated in the control field. The transmitting station counts each frame transmitted and numbers them sequentially. These numbers are designated Ns, and are inserted in the fourth, fifth, and sixth bit-positions in the control field in the information transfer format (Figure 5.13a). The receiving station also counts the frames it receives, and sequentially numbers them. Then numbers are designated Nr, and are inserted in the zero-, one-, and two-bit positions of the control field.

The frame sequence information is used as a means of identifying the occurrence of an error, as well as acknowledging correctly received frames to the transmitting station. An important aspect of this procedure is that up to seven frames may be received before acknowledgment is necessary. A single frame is then sent back to the transmitting station in which the Nr field specifies the sequence number of the next frame that is expected to be received by the receiving station. The transmitting station then checks the Nr and, if incorrect, concludes that an error must have been made at the receiving station. The transmitting station then terminates its current transmission, and returns to the frame sequence number specified by Nr. This specified frame, and subsequent frames, are then transmitted again to the receiving station.

The P/F bit is used to signify whether a "sending" or "receiving" operation is taking place. A poll bit is sent to a secondary station to indicate that a transmission is requested. A final bit is sent from a secondary station in response to a poll bit-containing frame.

A distinction must be made here between half-duplex and full-duplex communications networks. In a half-duplex system, the line must "turn around" and let the secondary station respond to the poll. In a full-duplex system, the response may be transmitted simultaneously with the polling signals.

The supervisory format (Figure 5.13b) is used to designate ready or busy conditions or for special purposes. For example, it may be used to check the operability of a secondary station even though no data are to be transmitted to the secondary station.

The nonsequenced format (Figure 5.13c) is used for data link management, such as initialization of secondary stations, and various control functions. This particular format is called "nonsequenced" since frames including a nonsequenced format control field are not counted in the Nr or Ns counts.

The actual designation of the information transfer, supervisory, and nonsequenced format is made in the six- and seven-bit positions of the control field, as shown in Figure 5.13.

The information field is any multiple of eight bits in length and contains the data for a message that is to be transferred from station to station in the communications network.

The frame check sequence (FCS) field, or the block check field, is 16 bits in length. The FCS field serves as an error check field by representing a mathematical transformation of all the bits in a given frame. This representation is inserted into the FCS field by the transmitter, while the receiver performs a similar computation on all of the bits of the frame at the secondary station, and compares the computed value with the value found in the FCS field. If the computed value and the value of the FCS field does not match, the secondary station rejects the frame as being erroneous.

The particular mathematical transformation performed on the bits of the frame is known as cyclic redundancy checking, which has been described in Chapter 3.

PRIMARY STATION OPERATION.   The primary station includes two time-out functions used as control operations: idle detect and nonproductive receive.

Idle detect gives a means of detecting a nonresponse condition from a secondary station when a response should have been received. A number of factors must be considered to determine an appropriate time period in which a response should be received: the propagation time to the secondary station, the processing time at the secondary station, the operational characteristics of the secondary station modem, and the propagation time from the secondary station. The timing factor required for various modes of transmission is shown in Figure 5.14. Once the set time period is exceeded, the idle detect function in the primary station assumes that a transmission failure has occurred, and initiates appropriate recovery or retransmission by the primary station.

The second time-out function is the nonproductive receive function. In this case a return signal may be received from the secondary station, but that signal may not be intelligible. Such a situation is known as a nonproductive receive, which is again detected by the primary station and recovery or retransmission measure initiated.

An abort condition is also a function of the primary station. An

Communications Channel	*Secondary Station Modem Clear-to-Send*	*Approx. Two-Way Propagation Time*
Switched (through local exchange only) or very short (distance) private line	0 msec to 25 msec	2 msec/15 miles (X)
Long (distance) duplex private line	0 msec to 25 msec	2 msec/150 miles + 24 msec (Y)
Long (distance) half-duplex (switched or nonswitched)	75 msec to 250 msec	2 msec/150 miles + 24 msec (Y)
Satellite duplex (switched or nonswitched)	0 msec to 250 msec	600 msec + 24 msec (Z)

FIGURE 5.14.   Transmission timing factors.

abort consists of a transmission of eight consecutive binary ones by the transmitting primary or secondary station. The data link is shut down and returns to the idle state.

SECONDARY STATION MODES. A secondary station is characterized by one of three possible modes: a normal response mode (NRM), a normal disconnect mode (NDM), and an initialization mode.

A normal response mode is one in which the secondary station does not initiate any unsolicited transmissions, and transmits only in response to a poll from a primary station. The normal disconnect mode is one in which the secondary station is off-line, and only responds to a test or other supervisory command from the primary station.

The initialization mode is one in which transmission to the primary or secondary station is initiated by a specific routine in the respective stations.

COMMAND CODES. Specific supervisory commands that are possible using the nonsequenced format of the control field are defined by specific bit patterns placed within the control field. These bit patterns and there corresponding control functions are shown in Figure 5.15.

FUNCTION MANAGEMENT SERVICES. As noted above, there are four types of function management services that are provided within the different NAU types. These are presentation services, logical-unit services, physical-unit services, and network services.

The first important element of the function management service is the data flow control protocol support. The protocol is implemented

Format*	Sent Last	Binary Configuration P/F	Sent First	Acronym	Command	Response	I-Field Prohibited	Resets Nr and Ns	Confirms Frames through Nr-1	Defining Characteristics
NS	000	P/F	0011	NSI	X	X				command or response that requires nonsequenced information
	000	F	0111	RQI		X	X			initialization needed; expect SIM
	000	P	0111	SIM	X		X	X		set initialization mode; the using system prescribes the procedures
	100	P	0011	SNRM	X		X	X		set normal response mode; transmit on command
	000	F	1111	ROL		X	X			this station is off-line
	010	P	0011	DISC	X		X			do not transmit or receive information
	011	F	0011	NSA		X	X			Acknowledge NS commands
	100	F	0111	CMDR		X	X			nonvalid command received; must receive SNRM, DISC, or SIM
	101	P/F	1111	XID	X	X				system identification in I field
	001	0/1	0011	NSP	X	X				response optional if no P bit.
	111	P/F	0011	TEST	X	X				check pattern in I field.
S	Nr	P/F	0001	RR	X	X	X		X	ready to receive
	Nr	P/F	0101	RNR	X	X	X		X	not ready to receive
	Nr	P/F	1001	REJ	X	X	X		X	transmit or retransmit, starting with frame Nr
I	Nr	P/F	Ns 0	I	X	X			X	sequenced I-frame

*NS: nonsequenced, S: supervisory, I: information.

FIGURE 5.15. SDLC: control field command codes.

by means of a discrete set of encoded requests, called data flow control (DFC) requests. These data flow requests are exchanged between DFC elements for managing the structures and states of the data flow.

The presentation services provide communication support between users communicating along a session.

SYSTEM SERVICES CONTROL POINT.   The system services control point (SSCP) is operable with logical-unit sessions, physical-unit sessions, and the network itself.

The SSCP logical-unit sessions are engaged in supporting the logical-unit control and use of the communications network. The logical-unit services enable the user to engage in SSCP control functions. SSCP commands and replies may be either field formatted ("formatted") or character coded ("unformatted"). Character coded commands are translated by the SSCP into field formatted commands for execution. The SSCP then routes the instruction to an associated command preprocessor for transmission to the designated network services command processor for execution.

For example, the user may desire to create or destroy sessions between logical units. The user may initiate a program—suppose it is designated LOG ON. The LOG ON character string is sent to the LU–SSCP session. The LOG ON character string is then decoded by a syntax scanner to a field formatted "initiate" request. The initiate request contains the name of the logical unit to which a communications link is desired. Other information is also provided within the request format. The SSCP functions to transform the logical unit into a network address. A control initiate command is then generated by the SSCP which is transferred to the primary logical unit in control of the particular network position desired by the user.

The primary logical unit then either accepts or rejects the session request. If the request is accepted, the logical unit transfers the control initiate command into a "bind" command and transfers it to the secondary logical unit in the terminal. The bind command serves to establish a session between the two logical units.

Once indication is received that the session circuit is established, the primary logic unit sends a "clear" signal, followed by a "unbind" signal.

The SSCP physical unit (PU) provides services for each physical unit in the system network configuration. Sessions exist between the SSCP and the PU.

The SSCP essentially performs a network administrative function in processing commands and acknowledgments used in the creation and destruction of a particular physical network linkage, as well as for recovery and resynchronization after a network failure.

The network services provided by the SSCP include:

• Configuration services for the activation and the deactivation of logical units and data links
• Maintenance services for testing of network facilities
• Session services by providing means for establishing or terminating sessions between logical units

NETWORK CONFIGURATION. The physical configuration of the network is defined in terms of four specific node types:

Host
Communication controller
Cluster controller
Terminal

A host node is a multipurpose facility that is engaged in general systems operation, such as the execution of application programs or management of data bases. An example of a host node is a System/370 computer operating under VTAM.

A communications controller node is concerned with the control of the communications lines. An example of a communications controller node is an IBM 3704 or 3705 operating under NCP/VS.

A cluster controller is a node that services a wide variety of peripheral devices operated by specific users. Examples of cluster controller nodes are the IBM 3601 and 3791.

A terminal node is a specific user device, such as an IBM 3767 or other data terminal.

370X Communications Controllers. The 370X communications controllers (e.g., the 3704 and 3705) perform both the basic and more complex network management functions, including:

Data link control
Dynamic buffering
Control character insertion and deletion

Character codes translation
Error recording and line statistics
Line control
On-line diagnostics

The controllers operate under the following operating systems and access methods: OS/TCAM (except remote), OS/VS TCAM (except remote), OS/VS VTAM, and DOS/VS VTAM. A network control program (NCP) resides in the 370X system and performs in software the hardware function previously performed by the IBM 2701 data adapter, and 2702–2703 transmission control units.

The IBM 3704 communications controller is a programmable unit that improves CPU processing throughput by performing various message control program functions previously performed by the CPU, including: addressing, polling, interrupt serving, error recovery, editing, and code translation. The 3704, shown in Figure 5.16, and in close-up in Figure 5.17, is able to handle up to 32 low-speed start-stop type lines, eight synchronous type lines, and up to two wide-band lines.

The IBM 3705 is similar in function and application to the 3704, but is able to handle up to 352 low-speed start-stop lines, and is able to perform some of the teleprocessing functions previously executed by the processor. The 3705 is shown in Figure 5.18, and in close-up in Figure 5.19.

COMMUNICATIONS SYSTEM PROTOCOL. Information that is transferred between users and defined physical facilities make use of requests and responses which take place between paired function interpreters. Four particular types of function interpreter pairs are recognized and processed:

Function management pair
Data flow control pair
Session control pair
Network control pair

The function management protocol defines a number of different operational modes. These include delayed-control modes, and immediate- and delayed-response modes. An "immediate" mode means that the issuer will transmit a single RU and wait for a response before sending another RU. A "delayed"-control mode means that the user may send many requests before waiting for a response.

FIGURE 5.16.   IBM 3704 communications controller. (Photograph courtesy IBM Corp.)

Within the delayed-control mode there are two options: immediate request and delayed request. The immediate request indicates that the user may send a number of requests, but only the last such requests may indicate response. The delayed request allows the issuer multiple requests, without waiting for an intervening response. Each such request may require any particular form of response.

The immediate and response modes indicate the manner by which the receiver of a request returns a response. The immediate-response mode specifies that the responses must be returned in the same order in which requests are received. The delayed-response mode enables the receiver to accept a number of requests before responding, and the responses may be returned in an order different from that in which the requests were received.

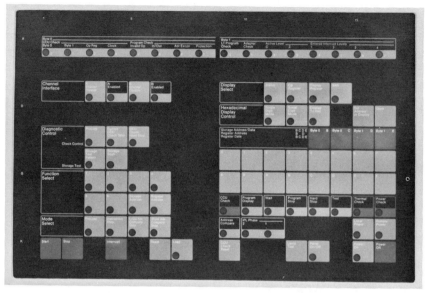

FIGURE 5.17.   IBM 3704 communications controller console. (Photograph courtesy IBM Corp.)

The function management protocol also enables the type of response to be specified. A definite response in which no more requests will be issued until an acknowledgment of the definite response has been received is one such specification. Another specification is that of an exception response which requests that the responses be acknowledged only on detection of an error condition. Such capabilities are implemented by means of control bits in the RH portion of a basic information unit.

Another type of control that may be implemented is that of chaining consecutive RUs. A chain consists of a predetermined number of RUs with a well-defined beginning and end, defined by specific control bits in each RH portion of the basic information units in the RU chain.

ADCCP

The advanced data communications control protocol (ADCCP) is the popular name for the protocol established by the American National Standards Institute, Inc. (ANSI), and initially defined in the X3.28–1976 standard entitled "Procedures for the Use of the Communica-

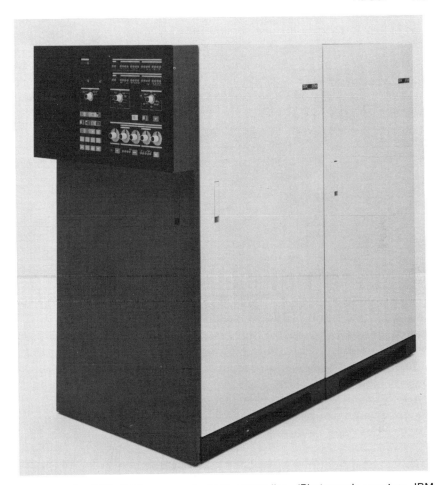

FIGURE 5.18. IBM 3705 communications controller. (Photograph courtesy IBM Corp.)

tion Control Characters of American National Standard Code for Information Interchange in Specified Data Communication Links.'' The ASCII control characters referred to in the title are

SOH: start-of-heading
STX: start-of-text
ETX: end-of-text
ETB: end-of-transmission block
ENQ: enquiry

FIGURE 5.19.   IBM 3705 communications controller console. (Photograph courtesy IBM Corp.)

ACK: acknowledgment
NAK: negative acknowledgment
SYN: synchronous idle
DLE: data link escape

The standard defines a number of generalized data communication control procedures based upon the combination of two subcategories: (1) establishment and termination (see Table 5.1) and (2) message transfer (see Table 5.2).

A particular category of data communication is specified by one type of establishment and termination procedure (selected from Table 5.1) with one type of message transfer procedure (selected from Table 5.2)—for example, category 2.2/B1 consists of the establishment and termination subcategory 2.2 together with message transfer subcategory B1.

Standards that prescribe the signalling speed and message format are being developed by Task Group X3S34.

The frame structure of the ADCCP data link control protocol is the same as that of SDLC. The command/response codes of the control field are summarized in Table 5.5 (p. 148) later in this chapter.

TABLE 5.1. Establishment and Termination Subcategories

Type of System	Salient Features	Subcategory Designation
One-Way-Only Systems		
Nonswitched multipoint	Master status permanently assigned Single or group selection without replies	1.1
Point-to-Point Two-Way Alternate Systems		
Switched	No identification Calling station has master status initially Terminate Mandatory disconnect	2.1
Switched	Station identification Calling station has master status initially Terminate Mandatory disconnect	2.2
Nonswitched	Contention Replies Terminate	2.3
Multipoint Two-Way Alternate Systems		
Centralized operation	Polling Selection (single slave) Control-tributary communication only Return to control on termination	2.4
Centralized operation	Polling Selection or fast selection (single slave) Control-tributary communication only Return to control on termination	2.5
Noncentralized operation	Polling Selection (single slave) Tributary-tributary communication permitted Return to control on termination	2.6
Centralized operation	Polling Selection (multiple slave) Control-tributary communication only Return to control on termination Delivery verification	2.7
Noncentralized operation	Polling Selection (multiple slave) Tributary-tributary communication permitted Return to control on termination Delivery verification	2.8
Point-to-Point Two-Way Simultaneous Systems		
Switched	Station identification Both stations have concurrent master and slave status Mandatory disconnect	3.1

Source: American National Standard X3.28-1976.

TABLE 5.2. Message Transfer Subcategories

Type of System	Salient Features	Subcategory Designation
Message-oriented	Without replies Without longitudinal checking	A1
Message-oriented	Without replies With longitudinal checking	A2
Message-oriented	With replies Without longitudinal checking	A3
Message-oriented	With replies With longitudinal checking	A4
Message-associated blocking	With longitudinal checking Retransmission of unacceptable blocks Single-character acknowledgment	B1
Message-associated blocking	With longitudinal checking Retransmission of unacceptable blocks Alternating acknowledgments	B2
Message-independent blocking	With longitudinal checking Retransmission of unacceptable blocks Alternating acknowledgments Noncontinuous operation Nontransparent heading and text	C1
Message-independent blocking	With longitudinal checking Retransmission of unacceptable blocks Modulo-8 numbering of blocks and acknowledgments Continuous operation Nontransparent heading and text	C2
Message-independent blocking	With cyclic redundancy checking Retransmission of unacceptable blocks Alternating acknowledgments Noncontinuous operation Transparent heading and text	D1
Conversational	Without blocking Without longitudinal checking	E1
Conversational	With blocking With longitudinal checking	E2
Conversational	With blocking With longitudinal checking With batch transmission capabilities	E3
Message-associated blocking for two-way simultaneous transmission	With longitudinal checking Retransmission of unacceptable blocks Alternating acknowledgments Embedded responses	F1
Message-independent blocking for two-way simultaneous transmission	With longitudinal checking Retransmission of unacceptable blocks Modulo-8 numbering of blocks and acknowledgments Continuous operation Nontransparent heading and text Embedded response	F2

Source: American National Standard X3.28-1976.

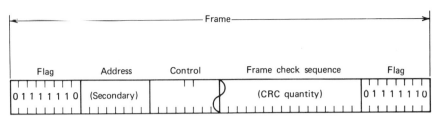

FIGURE 5.20.   X.25: frame format.

HDLC

High Level Data Link Control (HDLC) is the name of the protocol being formulated by the International Standards Organization. The frame structure standard, shown in Figure 5.20, has been approved and published as standard IS 3309. The procedure standard, which involves the definition and function of the bits in the control field of the frame, is being considered by member organizations and representatives at this writing. Details on some preliminary recommendations of the ISO are presented in Table 5.5 at the end of this chapter.

X.25

The X.25 protocol, proposed by the CCITT, and adopted by the International Standards Organization (ISO), is a recognized standard for international data communications. Both the European PTTs (Post, Telephone, and Telegraph authorities), and the ITU (Internation Telecommunications Union) have accepted X.25 as the data communications standard.

Because of the importance of X.25, it is worthwhile to describe some of its significant features in detail. All messages are assembled into frames which take one of two possible formats shown in Figure 5.20. There is an eight-bit opening flag, followed by an eight-bit address field, an eight-bit control field, an optional information field of *n*-bits, a 16-bit frame-checking sequence, followed by a final eight-bit flag.

The flags, address field, information field, and frame check sequence are standard in HDLC and other protocols, and need not be described further here. The control field does, however, merit our attention. There are three types of control field formats:

Information transfer (I frames)
Numbered supervisory functions (S frames)
Unnumbered control functions (U frames).

The contents of the specific bit locations of the control field for each of these frame types are shown in Table 5.3, similar to that for SDLC.

The similarity between the X.25 and SDLC control fields is readily apparent, but later in this chapter it will be noted that there are differences. Furthermore, the information field in SDLC is a multiple of eight bits long, while the information field in X.25 is an arbitrary *N* bits long.

Unlike SDLC, X.25 permits two different modes of operation to be implemented in the system: primary/primary and primary/secondary transmission. In primary/primary operation, each of two stations connected by the data link can act either as the primary station (i.e., initiating command and control functions), or the secondary station (i.e., executing the commands of another station). In primary/ secondary operation, one station is designated the "primary" station, and the other the "secondary" station. Primary/secondary operation is implemented by SDLC at the present time, but not primary/primary operation.

BDLC

Burroughs data link control (BDLC) protocol is a bit-oriented data link protocol designed for use with Burroughs equipment, including the TC 3500 intelligent terminal, the DC 140 intelligent communica-

TABLE 5.3.   Control Field Format

Control Field Bits	1*	2	3	4	5	6	7	8
I frame	0		N(S)		P/F		N(R)	
S frame	1	0	S		P/F		N(R)	
U frame	1	1	M		P/F		M	

N(S): transmitter send sequence count; N(R): transmitter receive sequence count; S: supervisory function bits; M: modifier function bits; P/F: poll bit when used by primary, final bit when used by secondary (one when poll or final).
*: The least significant bit, or first bit transmitted.

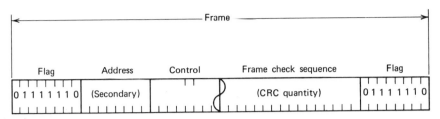

FIGURE 5.21. BDLC: frame format.

tions controllers, and the TC 1700 and TC 5100 terminals. A communications controller, the B 776, is also utilized in the data communications networks.

The basic structure of the unit of transmission in BDLC is shown in Figure 5.21. This transmission frame comprises the following fields:

Flag-bit sequence
Address field
Control field
Information field
Frame-check field
Flag-bit field.

The flag-bit field is placed at the beginning and end of each frame in order to provide frame synchronization. The address field designates the address of the secondary station to which the message is destined. The address field is normally eight bits long, but may be extended in eight-bit increments to accommodate additional secondary stations. This extended address field is the first distinction of BDLC from SDLC or X.25. (ADCCP and HDLC also allow an extended address field.)

The control field is an eight-bit field that is used to transmit commands from the primary station, responses from a secondary station and sequence numbers of transmissions. Three bits are normally used for the sequence numbers, permitting up to seven unacknowledged frames to be outstanding at any given time. The control field is, however, expandable to 16 bits, with the sequence number field being expanded to seven bits, so that the potential number of unacknowledged frames may be as high as 127.

The control field also includes a poll bit which serves to solicit a response from a secondary station.

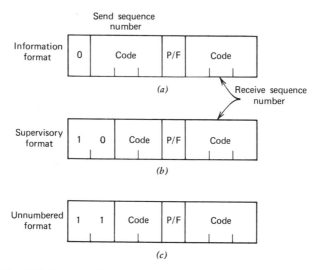

FIGURE 5.22.   BDLC: control field. (a) Information format; (b) supervisory format; (c) unnumbered format.

The particular format for the control field is shown in greater detail in Figure 5.22. There are three possible formats for the control field:

Information format
Supervisory format
Unnumbered format

The information format (Figure 5.22a) is basically used to keep track of the numbers of the last frames sent to and received by the secondary station. The information format includes the send sequence number of the frame being transmitted, and the received sequence number that is expected to be received in the next information frame coming from the addressed secondary station. The received sequence number thus informs the other station of the number of the last frame actually received. Thus, if the number is lower than the next send sequence number, then at the secondary station it is presumed that one or more frames were lost in transmission. The lost frames are then uniquely specified, and the transmitting station may retransmit the frames that have been lost.

The format identifier of the control field is specified by the left-most bit in the field. If the left-most bit is a zero, the control field has the information format. If the left most bits are one and zero, the control field is a supervisory format, and if the left most bits are one and one, the control field is in the unnumbered format.

Following the format identifier bit or bits are the specific control bits used in the type of control in question.

In the information format, the format identifier is followed by three bits of send sequence number, one bit designating a poll or final bit, and three bits specifying the received sequence number.

The supervisory format of the control field, as shown in Figure 5.22*b*, consists of the two-bit format identifier, followed by a two-bit command response field, a one-bit poll or final bit, and a three-bit sequence number. The supervisory format, as the name implies, is used to transmit numbered supervisory frames which indicate a particular link or device status: situations such as a readiness to receive information, a request for retransmission of information frames, and a temporary input of the receiving capability. Such supervisory commands permit the primary station to inform a particular secondary station of the type of transfer being performed.

The unnumbered format (Figure 5.22*c*) is utilized for transmitting supervisory commands or responses for different data link control functions. The particular format of the unnumbered control field format consists of the two-bit format identifier, followed by two modifier bits, the poll or final bit, and three modifier bits in the lower-most bit position.

Examples of the data link control functions specified by the format identifier are the disconnect command (DISC in Figure 5.15), which causes the address secondary to go off-hook; the setting of normal and asynchronous response nodes; and the acknowledgment of unnumbered frames. The normal response node command is used to set the addressed secondary to the "normal response," and thereby reset the send-and-receive sequence to zero to initiate operation in this mode. The asynchronous extended command is used for the same function while in asynchronous mode. An unnumbered acknowledgment message is used to notify the sending station of the receipt of an unnumbered frame.

Following the control field is the information field which may be of variable length. Following the variable length information field is a 16-bit frame-check sequence used for the cyclic redundancy check. The check sequence is then followed by the eight-bit final flag.

BOLD

BOLD is the bit-oriented data link control protocol announced by NCR Corporation. BOLD is a subset of ADCCP and need not be further described at this point. Details concerning the command and response codes defined in the control field are presented in Table 5.5 at the end of this section.

CDCCP

Control Data has announced a comprehensive network architecture in which multivendor host computers can be connected together in the network through Local Network Processors (LNP). The Control Data Communications Control Program (CDCCP) is expected to be implemented on the 2550-series network processors, which interface with the CDC Cyber 170, Cyber 70, 3000, and 6000 series. Communications software includes the CDC network operating system (NOS), together with a network access method (NAM) that permits large multihost networks to be implemented.

CDCCP is a bit-oriented protocol that is a subset of ADCCP. Since some of the key differences between CDCCP and the other bit-oriented protocols are the commands and responses defined by the control field bit encoding, Table 5.4 lists the CDCCP command/response repertoire.

Comparison of Bit-Oriented Data Link Protocols

One important formal means of comparison between the bit-oriented data link protocols is the definition of the bit encoding of the control field. Table 5.5 summarizes the command (CMD) and response (RES) repertoire of the key protocols. (The control field bit-encoding order and command/response definitions may be found in Table 5.4.)

DDCMP—DNA

Digital network architecture (DNA), the data communications architecture developed for Digital Equipment Corporation (DEC) products, utilizes three major protocols:

Digital data communications message protocol (DDCMP)
Network services protocol (NSP)
Data access protocol (DAP)

DDCMP is concerned with physical link control and error recovery practices within the digital communications network. DDCMP oper-

TABLE 5.4. CDCCP Command/Response Repertoire

Format	*Control Field Bit Encoding* 1	2	3	4	5	6	7	8	Commands	Responses
Information	0	—	N(S)	—	*	—	N(R)	—	I — Information	I — Information
Supervisory	1	0	0	0	*	—	N(R)	—	RR — Receive Ready	RR — Receive Ready
	1	0	0	1	*	—	N(R)	—	REJ — Reject	REJ — Reject
	1	0	1	0	*	—	N(R)	—	RNR — Receive Not Ready	RNR — Receive Not Ready
	1	0	1	1	*	—	N(R)	—	SREJ — Selective Reject	SREJ — Selective Reject
Unnumbered	1	1	0	0	*	0	0	0	UI — Unnumbered Information	UI — Unnumbered Information
	1	1	0	0	*	0	0	1	SNRM — Set Normal Response Mode	
	1	1	0	0	*	0	1	0	DISC — Disconnect	RD — Request Disconnect
	1	1	0	0	*	1	0	0	UP — Unnumbered Poll	UA — Unnumbered Acknowledge
	1	1	0	1	*	0	0	0	USER 0	USER 0
	1	1	0	1	*	0	0	1	USER 1	USER 1
	1	1	0	1	*	0	1	0	USER 2	USER 2
	1	1	0	1	*	0	1	1	USER 3	USER 3
	1	1	1	0	*	0	0	0	SIM — Set Initialization Mode	RIM — Request Initialization Mode
	1	1	1	0	*	0	0	1	RSPR — Response Reject	CMDR — Command Reject
	1	1	1	1	*	0	0	0	SARM — Set ASYNC Response Mode	DM — Disconnect Mode
	1	1	1	1	*	0	0	1	SARME — Set ARM Extended Mode	
	1	1	1	1	*	0	1	1	SNRME — Set NRM Extended Mode	
	1	1	1	1	*	1	0	0	SABM — Set ASYNC Balanced Mode	
	1	1	1	1	*	1	0	1	XID — Exchange Identification	XID — Exchange Identification
	1	1	1	1	*	1	1	0	SABME — Set ABM Extended Mode	

* = P/F

147

TABLE 5.5. Command/Response Repertoire of Selected Standards

ADCCP		HDLC		SDLC		CDCCP		BOLD		BDLC		SNAP/X25	
CMD	RES	CMD	RES	CMD	RES	CMD	RES	CMD	RES	CMD	RES	CMD	RES
	—		—	—	—		—		—	—	—	—	
RR	RR	RR	RR	RR	RR	RR	RR	RR	RR	RR	RR		RR
REJ	REJ	REJ	REJ	REJ	REJ	REJ	REJ	REJ	REJ	REJ	REJ		REJ
RNR	RNR	RNR	RNR	RNR	RNR	RNR	RNR	RNR	RNR	RNR	RNR		RNR
SREJ	SREJ	SREJ	SREJ*			SREJ	SREJ	SREJ	SREJ	SREJ	SREJ		
UI	UI	UI*		NSI	NSI	UI	UI	NSI	NSI				
SNRM		SNRM		SNRM	NSA	SNRM		SNRM	NSA	SNRM	UA		UA
DISC	RD	DISC		DISC		DISC	RD	DISC		DISC		DISC	
UP	UA		UA	ORP	ROL	UP	UA	ORP	ROL				
USR (4)	USR (4)					USR (4)	USR (4)						
SIM	RIM			SIM	RIM	SIM	RIM	SIM	RIM				
FRMR	FRMR	*	CMDR*		CMDR	RSPR	CMDR	RSPR	CMDR	RSPR	CMDR		
SARM	DM	SARM				SARM	DM	SARM		SARM		SARM	CMDR
SARME		SARME				SARME		SARME		SARME			
SNRME		SNRME				SNRME		SNRME		SNRME			
XID	XID	*				XID	XID						
SABM		*				SABM							
SABME		*				SABME							

* = Pending approval

148

ates utilizing existing hardware interfaces, full- or half-duplex transmissions facilities, and either synchronous-asynchronous or parallel lined circuits.

NSP is concerned with management of network functions, such as message routing between systems, and processor to processor communication within the network.

DAP is a specialized protocol for enabling programs or service routines on one particular node of the network to utilize I/O services available on different network nodes.

These DNA protocols are arranged in a hierarchic order so that various changes may be made in one or more of the protocols at each point or node a message is received. Such an arrangement is referred to as "layered" protocols. The particular layers are

Dialog layer
Logical link layer
Physical link layer
Hardware layer

These are illustrated in Figure 5.23.

The layering or envelopment of a message within two or three protocols is a key feature of DNA. By defining a hierarchic layer for each of the individual protocols, the message may be transferred from node to node, and each node will access the particular layer that the node itself is associated with within the network hierarchy. Thus, there is a one-to-one correspondence between software hierarchy in terms of protocols or layers, and a hardware hierarchy that distinguishes physical nodes or stations in the communications network.

As the message is sent from node to node, various parameters or other characteristics are added to or deleted from the message struc-

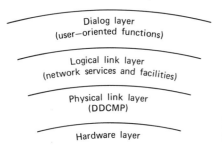

Dialog layer
(user—oriented functions)

Logical link layer
(network services and facilities)

Physical link layer
(DDCMP)

Hardware layer

FIGURE 5.23. Digital network architecture (DNA): layered structure.

ture. The highest hierarchic layer, or dialog layer, represents the user oriented functions, as shown in Figure 5.23. This layer includes user messages, programs, or data that are specifically coded by the user for his own use.

The next highest layer acts as a means for multiplexing various user messages into a single data stream for eventual transmission over a data link. This logical link layer therefore provides the network services and facilities required by the user in his interface with the communications network. This layer is defined by the network services protocol (NSP).

The next highest layer is concerned with physical link management—that is, the actual control of the data stream along the communications network. This physical link management layer, as typified by DDCMP, is concerned with message sequencing, synchronization, and error detection and recovery.

The last layer, referred to as the hardware interface layer, is concerned with physical hardware effects of transmission and reception of data bits over a physical link. This layer is concerned with the type of transmission mode (synchronous, asynchronous, or parallel), as well as physical device operation, including character synchronization and modem operation.

The advantage of the layered system implementation is to provide well-defined interfaces between network nodes, simple modification or replacement of layers by particular nodes, simplified error control and debugging, and consistent network integration procedures.

Figure 5.24 is a representation of how data flows through the layered network structure from a software or data structure viewpoint. The first block at the top of Figure 5.24 shows the user-created data labeled "user task data." The network services hardware and protocol then provides a routing header to the user task data log.

The physical link protocol hardware in turn provides a line protocol header and a block check trailer to the data block created by the network services hardware. It is this data block that is sent over the data communications link to another node, where a corresponding physical link protocol hardware unit is operative to strip the link protocol header and the block check trailer from the data block. Following the physical protocol interface hardware is the network services hardware, which is operative to strip the routing header from the data block.

Figure 5.25 is a simplified block diagram of the hardware used to implement these layered protocol functions in the data communications network.

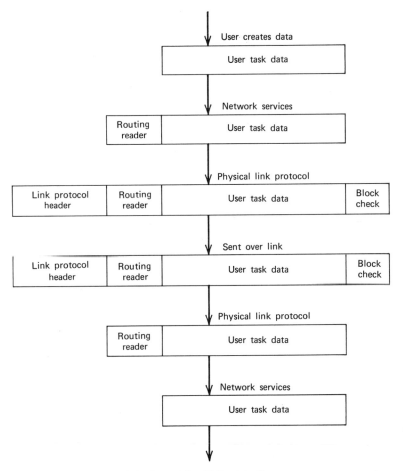

FIGURE 5.24.   DNA: data flow.

DDCMP

The basic format of the DDCMP unit of transmission is shown in Figure 5.26 (page 153). The unit of transmission consists of a header followed by a data field and a block check unit.

Figure 5.27 defines more explicitly the function of the particular bits in the header field. Table 5.6 more explicitly defines the functions of the various subfields within the header shown in Figure 5.27 (page 153).

There are basically two types of DDCMP messages: (1) data messages and (2) control messages. The data messages transmit user information over DDCMP links between a source and a sink station.

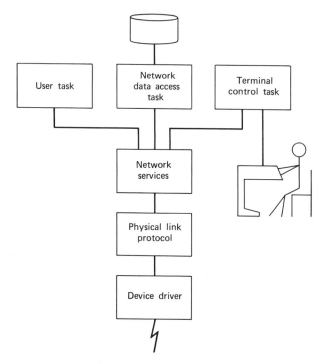

FIGURE 5.25.   DNA: hardware implementation.

Control information is sent by means of unnumbered control messages, or is incorporated within the headers of data messages going in the opposite direction. The particular format of the unnumbered control message block in DDCMP is shown in Figure 5.28. The interpretation of the various subfields in the header is in the unnumbered control message format of DDCMP as shown in Table 5.7.

DDCMP Operation

Transmission operation may be initiated by a start up (STRT) message by any one station. The message is transmitted to a receiving station, which responds to the start message by means of a start acknowledge (STACK) message. This technique of sending an inquiry and receiving an acknowledgment is known as a "handshaking" procedure. Once the sending station receives the STACK response and acknowledgment, it may begin transmitting data messages.

The data are transmitted in the form of numbered blocks or messages which are sequentially numbered. As the messages are received by the receiving station it uses the block check field to check for errors; if there are no errors detected, it accepts the message as correct. The station also checks for the correct numbering and sequence of message number. If both the data are received correctly sequenced, the receiving station acknowledges the receipt of the messages with an "acknowledgment" (ACK) statement. A single acknowledgment statement may imply the acknowledgment of up to 225 previous message numbers. In the case of error—for example, if the block check indicates a description error—the receiving station sends a "no acknowledgment" (NAK) statement with the number of

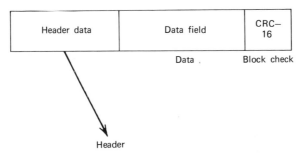

FIGURE 5.26. Digital data communications message protocol (DDCMP): frame format.

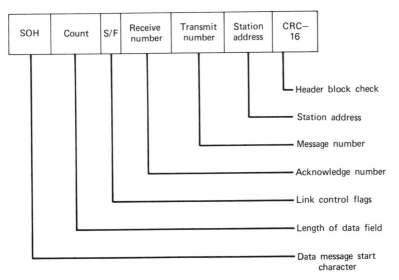

FIGURE 5.27. DDCMP: header field, data message.

TABLE 5.6.   Functions of the Subfields

SOH	The numbered data message identifier.
Count	The byte count field, specifies the number of 8-bit bytes in the DATA field.

S/F flags	The link control flags used to control link ownership and permission to send. These flags are
	
	    final flag: denotes end of current transmission stream;
	    select flag: requests receiving station to transmit.

Receive number	The response number used to acknowledge correctly received messages.
Transmit number	The transmit number, which denotes the number of this data message.
Station address	The station address field used to address the destination station on multipoint links. Control stations and stations on point-to-point links use the address value 1.
CRC-16 (first)	The block check on the numbered message header.
Data field	The numbered message data field consisting of COUNT eight-bit quantities. This field is totally transparent to the protocol and has no restrictions on any bit patterns. The only requirement is that it be a multiple of eight-bits.
CRC-16 (second)	The block check on the data field. Computed on DATA only.

the last good message received. A number of other conditions may also generate an NAK message, such as a failure to receive the correct header.

If the primary station receives an acknowledgment, it frees the message first up to the data message number that has been acknowledged, and continues to send data numbers in sequence.

If it receives a "no acknowledgment," it terminates the present transmission, freezes all messages from the message buffer through the message number not received, and retransmits the messages from the message buffer with the message following number r, preceded by a standard synchronization sequence.

If the sending station receives neither an acknowledgment or a no-acknowledgment message from the receiving station, the sending station may send a REP message. Upon receiving the REP message, the receiving station compares the number R with the number of the

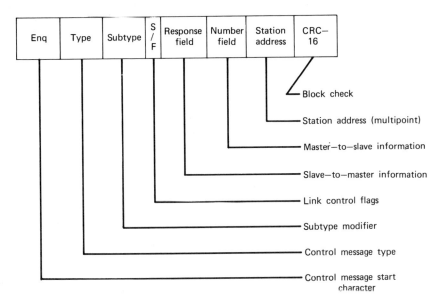

FIGURE 5.28. DDCMP: header field, control message.

TABLE 5.7. Unnumbered Control Message Format

ENQ	The unnumbered control message identifier.
Type	The control message type.
Subtype	The SUBTYPE or TYPE MODIFIER field provides additional information for some message types.
S/F	The link control flags described for numbered messages.
Response field	The control message response field used to pass information from the slave (numbered message receiver) to the master (numbered message sender).
Number field	The control message number field used to pass information from the master to the slave.
Station address	The station address field for multipoint use.
CRC-16	The block check on the control message.

last good message received. If the two numbers are equal, the receiving station sends back an ACKR message. If the numbers are not equal, it sends back a NAK message with the number of the last good message received, and indicates it is making a REP response.

DDCMP may be utilized both on duplex point-to-point communications and half-duplex point-to-point systems. In a half-duplex chan-

Flags	Route header	Message data

FIGURE 5.29.   Network services protocol (NSP): frame format.

nel, transmission from either station operates alternatively. The select and final bits are used to give up the channel, and indicate end of transmission.

NSP

NSP provides the following functions:

Maintenance of a logical link
Management of the logical link–physical link interface
Error detection and recovery
Error logging and administrative maintenance

The basic format of the NSP unit of transmission is shown in Figure 5.29. The unit of transmission consists of a NSP header followed by a user data field.

There are also two basic types of NSP messages: (1) data messages and (2) control messages. Data messages are used to transfer dialog-level information between processes, while control messages transfer information between NSP modules.

The particular format of the NSP data message is shown in Figure 5.30. The function of the various subfields in the header in the NSP data message is shown in Table 5.8.

The particular format for the NSP control message is shown in Figure 5.31. The function of the various subfields in the header is shown in Table 5.9.

NSP basically performs logical link functions which find the endpoints of a network connection.

The logical link operation consists of:

Creation of logical links
Message transfer over logical links
Interruption mechanism over logical links
Destruction of logical links

The creation of logical links consists of the specification of two

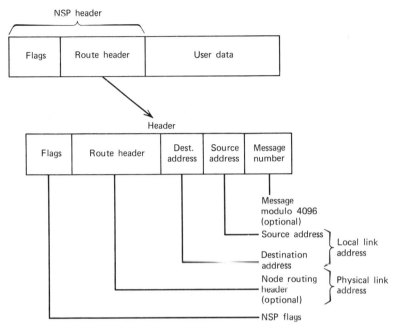

FIGURE 5.30. NSP: header field, data message.

TABLE 5.8. Definition of NSP Header Fields

DESTINATION ADDRESS. The logical link destination address for this message. This is the address for a conversation and is usually dynamically assigned via the connection procedure.

SOURCE ADDRESS. The logical link source address for this message.

MESSAGE NUMBER. The message number incremented modulo 4096 by one for each message. This field is optional.

USER DATA. The data the user process wishes to send or receive over a logical link. This field is totally transparent and may use all eight bits of each data byte.

---

particular processes between which a logical link is desired to be created. The logical link is created by a message which is sent to the destination NSP including the name of the origin process which the destination process is to be connected with.

The destination process interprets this information and makes a decision whether to complete the connection depending on traffic or

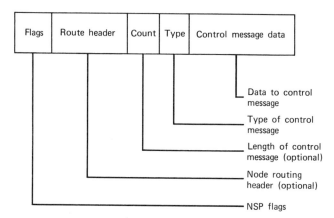

FIGURE 5.31.   NSP: header field, control message.

TABLE 5.9.   Definition of NSP Control Message Header Fields

COUNT.   The number of bytes in this Control Message—allows blocking of Control Messages. This field is optional.

TYPE.   The number representing the type of Control Message.

CONTROL MESSAGE DATA.   The data specific to each Control Message.

The following messages control logical link operation:

CONNECT.   The connect message is used to establish a logical link (communication path) between processes in the network.

DISCONNECT.   The disconnect message is used to destroy a logical link previously established and/or confirm that a connection rejection has been completed.

LINK STATUS.   The link status message is used for message requesting.

ERROR.   The error message is used to return error status to the sender of a message for a syntactical or semantic reason.

---

other conditions. If the message is desired to be completed, a connect command is sent back to the originating process and the logical link is created. If the destination process desires to reject the connection, it issues a connect reject command which causes the logical link to be broken. Other conditions include an error detection or a disconnect message.

Message transfer over logical link is the transfer of data or control message. The same type of counting is used for message verification, so that when the sending station receives a confirm request count message, it may release storage buffers allocated to storing the messages transmitted over the link.

NSP transmission is different from DDCMP transmission in that no acknowledgment occurs on unnumbered links. The transmission is completed by giving control over to the physical link level or DDCMP on unnumbered links.

An additional feature of the message transfer over logical links is the use of instrumental request counts. Furthermore, the detection of an error in the message causes the logical links to be disconnected.

NSP has a mechanism for permitting interruption to occur on a logical link. This feature permits interruption by means of a interrupt signal for initiating data transfer.

Logical links may also be terminated by means of three occurrences:

Request by the user
Failure of the user process
Failure of a communication link

If one of these occurred, the processors connected by the logical link are notified of the reason for disconnection. Messages received between the sending of a disconnect confirm are discarded.

DAP

The DAP provides the following functions in the data communications network:

File management operations
Input-output device operations
Format operations
Terminal control operations

The basic format of the DAP unit of transmission is shown in Figure 5.32. The unit of transmission consists of a DAP flag followed by a message operator, an optional channel number, an optional message length field, and finally the message data. Table 5.10 defines the functions of these various subfields more precisely.

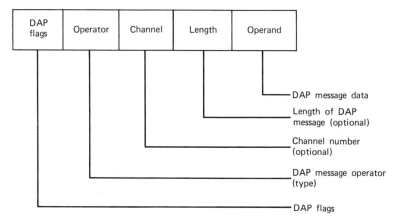

FIGURE 5.32.   Data access protocol (DAP): frame format.

TABLE 5.10.   Definition of DAP Fields

FLAGS—DAP Characteristic FLAGS.

CHANNEL.   The channel number field—optional. This is an address field used to allow up to 256 simultaneous transfers over a single NSP logical link (used primarily with terminal-type devices).

LENGTH.   Length of the OPERAND field in number of eight-bit bytes—optional.

OPERAND.   The information field for DAP messages. Dependent on the TYPE field. Described later.

The information field contained in the DAP message may contain various types of messages dependent upon the definition in the TYPE field. These defined fields are

Data without end of record
Data with end of record
Status
Continue transfer
Control device file
User identification
Access
Attributes
Error

The basic operation of the DAP depends on the I/O structure of the system in operation. There are two levels of commands or messages in DAP. The first level is a means for setting up the connection path and access verification and handshaking. The second level is device oriented, which provides means for controlling a particular feature of the specific I/O devices.

The specific process consists of the issuing of a command to a NSP for requesting specific logical link. Such a request is specified in actual process name, depending on the particular facilities supported at the destination node. The connection is completed by the return of a clarification command, thereby establishing a link.

Identification information is then sent to the node where the file or device is accessed. Various types of messages may then be interchanged between processes. These include a user identification message, an attributes message which indicates the desired mode and format of the data, an access message which indicates the desired operation, and control messages such as status messages or error messages.

OTHER NETWORK ARCHITECTURES AND PROTOCOLS

Other mainframe manufactures have also announced data link protocols. Control Data Corporation has developed the Control Data Communications Control Program (CDCCP), while Sperry Rand's Univac Division has its Univac Data Link Control (UDLC).

CDCCP is expected to be implemented on the 2550-series network processing unit (NPU), which interfaces with Control Data's Cyber 170, Cyber 70, 3000, and 6000 series models. The protocol operates with the CDC network operating system (NOS), or network operating system/batch environment (NOS/BE), together with a network access method (NAM) which enables large multihost networks with many communications nodes to be implemented.

UDLC is expected to be implemented on Univac computers and intelligent terminals. An end-to-end control scheme is also being developed which performs certain functions now performed by telecommunications access methods. Furthermore, the network operating system is expected to support SDLC protocol as well.

Comparison of Data Link Protocols

Some of the essential characteristics of the key data link protocols are summarized in Table 5.11. The table highlights basic characteris-

TABLE 5.11. Line Protocol Comparison

PARAMETER	Bi-Sync	SDLC,BDLC	ADCCP	HDLC	DDCMP
Character length (bits)	8	any	any	any	8-bit multiple
True full-duplex transmission capability	no	yes	yes	yes	yes
Control overhead	112 bits	24 bits	24 bits minimum	24 bits minimum	96 bits
Control sequence error checking	no	yes	yes	yes	yes
Allowed unacknowledged transmit frames (blocks)	2	8	8 minimum	8 minimum	256
Bit parallel capability	yes	no	no	no	yes

tics such as character length, control overhead, and the number of allowed unacknowledged transmission frames.

A more detailed comparison of data link protocols is a determination of throughput based on typical communication parameters. One measure of throughput or data communication efficiency is called the transfer rate of information bits (TRIB). TRIB is defined as:

$$TRIB = \frac{K\,(M - C)\,(1 - P)}{(M/R) + T}$$

where K is the number of information bits per character, M is the total number of information characters in a message block or packet, C is the number of noninformation characters in a block or packet, P is the probability of one or more bit errors in a block or packet, R is the raw line speed in characters per second, and T is the time between blocks in seconds.

Using this formula, or similar formulas, one can then compare the relative efficiency or throughput of data link protocols and make certain conclusions.

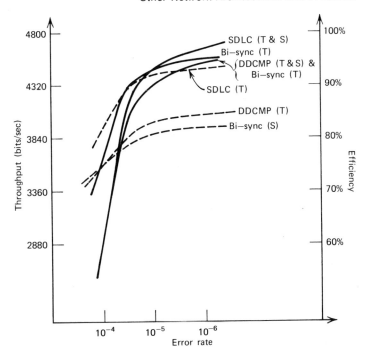

FIGURE 5.33.   Data communications protocol throughput comparison.

Notes: 1. Solid curves are for 2000-bit frames (more suitable for satellite circuits).
           Dashed curves are for 500-bit frames (less suitable for satellite circuits).
        2. Terms in parenthesis:
           (T) terrestrial circuits; assumed 50-msec one-way delay. (S) satellite cir-
           cuits; assumed 400-msec one-way delay.
        3. Curves are for 4800-baud full-duplex communication channel.

Figure 5.33 is a graph of the relative throughput of bi-sync, SDLC, and DDCMP for terrestrial and satellite circuits, using both 2000-bit and 500-bit frames. The calculated data are based upon the assumption of 4800-baud full-duplex communication channels, and is plotted as a function of the error rate.

Of course, the formula and graph are not meant to demonstrate that any one data link protocol is "better" than any other, but to present a method for quantitative comparing the features and throughput of such protocols as a function of the characteristic communication parameters of a given system.

REFERENCES

2740/2741

"IBM 2740/2741 Communication Terminal, Original Equipment Manufacturers Information," IBM Systems Reference Library (SRL) GA27-3002-0.

BSC

"General Information—Binary Synchronous Communications," IBM SRL GA27-3004.

SDLC—SNA

"IBM Synchronous Data Link Control, General Information," IBM SRL GA27-3093-1.

"Systems Network Architecture, General Information," IBM SRL GA27-3102-0.

R. A. Donnan and J. R. Kersey, "Synchronous Data Link Control: A Perspective," *IBM Systems Journal*, May 1974, pp. 140–162.

"System Network Architecture Format and Protocol Reference Manual: Architecture Logic," IBM SC30-3112-0.

ADCCP

ANSI Doc. X3.28—1976

Carlson, D. E., "ADCCP—A Computer-Oriented Data Link Control," *IEEE Compcon*, 1975, pp. 110–113.

HDLC

International Organization for Standardization: ISO/TC 97/SC 6N, "HDLC Proposed Balanced Class of Procedures" and "Proposed Enhancement to DIS 4335."

X.25 / SNAP

CCITT Doc. AP VI-No. 55-E, May 1976.

BDLC

Bedford, M. J., *Data Communications* 4(6), November/December 1975, pp. 41–47.

CDCCP

J. W. Conrad, "Control Data's CDCCP," Control Data Corporation, Santa Ana, Calif.

DDCMP

Digital Equipment Corporation, "Decnet," Maynard, Mass.

six
TRANSMISSION SYSTEMS AND TECHNOLOGIES

There are a variety of different transmission systems using different technologies that might be used for transmitting information through a data communication network. These are

- Common-carrier microwave networks
- Value-added common carriers
- Satellite networks

After considering these basic transmission systems, we turn our attention to the various transmission technologies:

- Voice-grade telephone lines
- Private lines
- Terrestrial microwave radio
- Satellite technology
- Millimetric waveguides
- Optical fiber technology

Each of these distinct transmission systems and transmission technologies will be considered in the sections below.

TABLE 6.1. Authorized Interstate Terrestrial Telecommunications Common Carriers

American Satellite Corporation (ASC)
American Telephone and Telegraph Company (AT&T)
CPI Telecommunications Inc. (CPI)
Data Transmission Company (DATRAN) [discontinued]
MCI Telecommunications Corporation (MCI)
Nebraska Consolidated Communications Corporation (N-Triple-C)
Packet Communications, Inc. [discontinued]
Southern Pacific Communications Company (SPCC)
Telenet Communications Corporation
United States Transmission Systems Inc. (USTS)
United Video, Inc. (UVI)
Western Tele-Communications Inc. (WTCI)
Western Union Telegraph Company

TRANSMISSION SYSTEMS

Common-Carrier Microwave Networks

The common-carrier networks are perhaps the most common means of implementing a data communications network. There are today a number of "common-carrier" services for interstate or international telecommunications. Such services are regulated by the Federal Communications Commission (FCC) pursuant to the Communications Act of 1934. The FCC grants and regulates the franchise for specific telecommunications services to private companies.

Table 6.1 lists the currently authorized interstate terrestrial telecommunications common carriers.

AT&T LONGLINES. AT&T Longlines holds the franchise for telephone, private line, radiotelephone, and picturephone services on an interstate basis throughout the United States. Digital data transmission over voice-grade telephone lines has existed since the 1950s, but the quality of the transmission link has significantly limited the use of such lines for high-speed data transmission. In view of this, the Bell System developed the Digital Data System (DDS), which is described in greater detail in the next section.

The other common carriers shown in Table 6.1 are known as "specialized common carriers" that offer private-line services to users. Such specialized common carriers were originally formed in the late 1960s to provide more reliable data communications than were then available over other facilities. In 1971 the FCC finally authorized such services, and opened up a new market to competition. Although such services were originally intended for the data communications market, more recently telephone services, such as Foreign Exchange direct dial services, have been offered by some carriers. The nature and impact of such telephone services will be discussed below.

Digital Data System.   The Dataphone Digital Service (DDS) is a new digital communications network service offered by the Bell System. By 1979 the network is projected to connect the 96 metropolitan areas shown in Figure 6.1.

Certain criteria were used in selecting the primary cities in the network:

• Data circuit demand of region
• Geographic location
• Access to transmission facilities

The DDS cities are organized in a three-level hierarchy, shown in Figure 6.1 as class I, II, and III digital serving (DSAs). The purpose of the hierarchic design is to maximize the digital transmission efficiency and use of existing digital facilities, and minimize the cost of multiplexers by clustering facilities so that each multiplexer is able to meet its projected load.

DDS provides private-line, point-to-point, and multipoint digital channels operating at 2.4, 4.8, 9.6, and 56 kb/sec. Such digital links mean that the customer is able to utilize Bell System digital transmission facilities directly, without being connected in analog form. The result is that transmission efficiency is greater and the error rate is lower.

The implementation of the DDS is relatively straightforward. The customer's data processing system is connected to a local telephone central office over a four-wire loop, thus permitting duplex operation. At the central office the data signals are multiplexed with other data signals and transmitted to a centrally located hub office. At the hub office the signal is demultiplexed and transferred to the intercity digital channel.

It would be worthwhile to describe the digital transmission hierarchy in the Bell System. Figure 6.2 illustrates the hierarchy beginning with the T1 Line. As shown, the T1 carrier handles the DS-1 digital signal rate (1.544 Mb/sec) through a DSX-1 cross-connect frame.

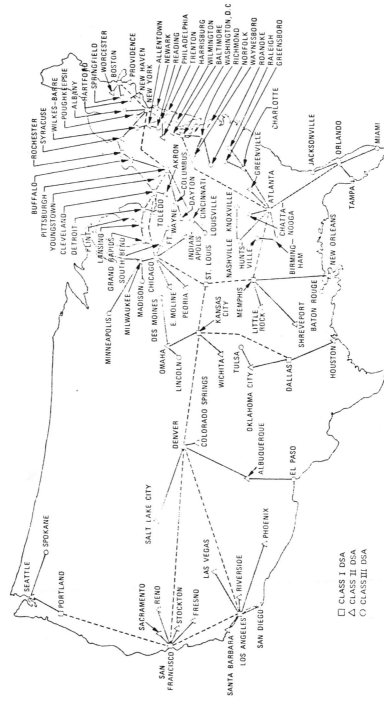

FIGURE 6.1. Bell System digital data system network.

□ CLASS I DSA
△ CLASS II DSA
○ CLASS III DSA

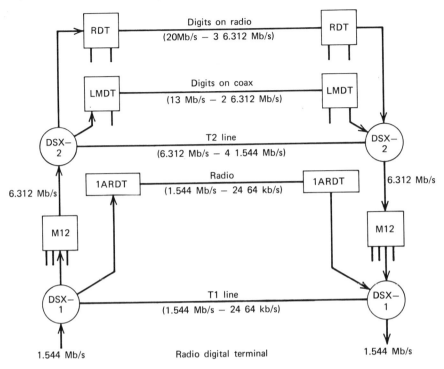

FIGURE 6.2. Bell System digital transmission hierarchy.

The T1 system is a short-haul cable-carrier system based on PCM modulation. The PCM frame used in T1 voice transmission is shown in Figure 6.3. The voice signal is sampled 8000 times/second and quantized according to a seven-bit code—that is, to one of 128 possible levels. Each voice signal is therefore represented by a data stream of 56 kb/sec.

Twenty-four such 56-kb/sec voice channels are time-division multiplexed into a single frame with a duration of 125 msec. An eighth or signaling bit is added at the end of each voice channel, and a framing bit is added at the end of each 125-msec frame for synchronizing purposes.

The T1 carrier requires amplifiers and repeaters about 1 mile apart, and therefore is generally used for short-haul applications, such as interconnecting local end offices to the hub office.

The next level in the digital hierarchy are the long-haul carriers. DDS is expected to use the 1A radio digital system (1A RDS) which operates at the same signal rate as the T1 carrier.

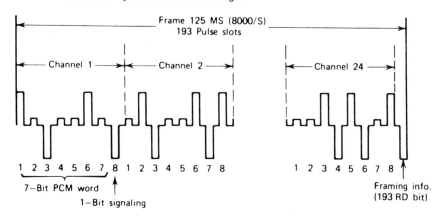

FIGURE 6.3.   PCM frame.

The 1A RDS compresses the signal to a bandwidth that occupies the lower 500 kHz of the radio signal through multilevel encoding and shaping techniques. Since the 1A RDS transmits voice channels over its higher frequencies, the system is sometimes called the Data Under Voice (DUV) system.

As data transmission requirements increase as the DDS expands, other levels of the hierarchy shown in Figure 6.2 may be utilized. Up to four DS-1 signals may be combined with the M12 multiplexer to form a DS-2 signal (6.312 Mb/sec). This signal may be transmitted directly over a T2 digital line, or applied to the L-mastergroup digital terminal (LMDT) for transmission over the L4 or L5 coaxial cable-carrier system. Figure 6.2 indicates still another transmission alternative, by being applied to the radio digital terminal (RDT) for transmission over a 20.2 Mb/sec radio link. The latter system is sometimes called the 2A radio digital system (2A RDS).

Two types of multiplexers are particularly adapted for DDS: the T1DM, which has a capacity of 23 synchronous 64-kb/sec channels and is used exclusively for data; and the T1WB4, which combines PCM voice signals with synchronous 64-kb/sec data for transmission over T1 channels.

The DDS is synchronized by means of a master-slave tree timing network. A master timing supply sets the frequency for the entire network, and is passed on through the transmitted DS-1 signals as discussed above in conjunction with Figure 6.2. The master timing supply synchronizes the local timing supply which is of sufficient

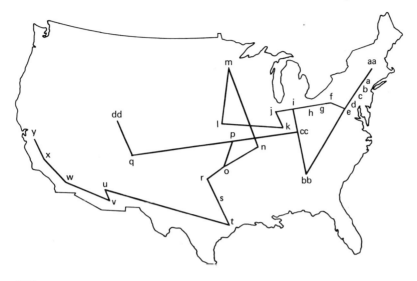

MCI
Operational

a	New York	l	Omaha	w	Los Angeles
b	Newark	m	Minneapolis	x	San Diego
c	Baltimore	n	St. Louis	y	San Francisco
d	Philadelphia	o	Tulsa		
e	Washington	p	Kansas City		
f	Pittsburgh	q	Denver		Future
g	Cleveland	r	Oklahoma City	aa	Boston
h	Toledo	s	Dallas	bb	Atlanta
i	Detroit	t	Houston	cc	Cincinnati
j	Chicago	u	Phoenix	dd	Salt Lake City
k	South Bend	v	Tucson		

FIGURE 6.4. MCI network.

accuracy to run several days even if all input synchronization signals fail. The local timing supply then supplies common clock signals to all DDS equipment in the local office. Eventually, a new highly accurate Bell System frequency standard located near St. Louis will become the master timing supply.

MCI TELECOMMUNICATIONS CORP. MCI provides leased-line communications services currently between the cities shown in Figure 6.4, and serves over 750 customers.

MCI provides a variety of different services for the business or government user, not just limited to "data" communications. Since voice-transmission services are often intermixed with data-transmission services by the customer, it would be worthwhile to review such services here:

Tie-Line Service.   The tie-line service enables the user to tie a switchboard in one city to a switchboard in another city. Each individual telephone in either location can be used to communicate directly with any other telephone connected to either of the two boards. The service also permits a user in one city to dial an "outside line" to call any number in the other city at local rates.

Off-Premise Extension Service.   A service similar to a tie-line service is known as an off-premise extension. This is a private-line connection of a remote telephone to a switchboard. Even though the remote phone may be in a distant city, the user can operate it exactly as if it were in the same location as the other telephones connected to the board.

Metropolitan Area Telecommunications Service (MATS).   For businesses that have an office in one city but need to make frequent calls to outside numbers in another city, or to receive calls, MCI offers a Metropolitan Area Telecommunications Service (MATS). The effect of this is, through a private-line channel, to provide an "office-by-telephone" so that the business can operate in a distant city at local telephone rates, as if it actually had an office there. With MATS, the user also gets a local phone number in the distant city which is listed in both the "white pages" and the "yellow pages." Prospects can call this number at local rates and the user answers the phone in his own city.

Quickline Service.   MCI's Quickline Service is a direct phone-to-phone automatic-ring line that gives the user instant contact with a phone in another city. No dialing or operator intervention are needed.

Alternate Voice/Data Service.   For users who need to transmit both voice and data communications, MCI Alternate Voice/Data Service enables a user to switch instantly from direct voice communication by telephone to a direct data communication between two data terminals. Data communication is at various speeds with a maximum error rate of 10^{-6} and transmission reliability of not less than 99.994%.

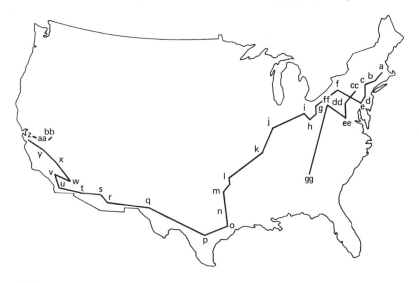

SPC
Operational

a	Boston	m	Oklahoma City	y	Fresno
b	Providence	n	Dallas/Ft. Worth	z	San Francisco/Oakland
c	Hartford	o	Houston	aa	San Jose
d	New York	p	San Antonio	bb	Sacramento
e	Philadelphia	q	El Paso		
f	Buffalo	r	Tucson		Future
g	Cleveland	s	Phoenix	cc	Jersey City
h	Toledo	t	Yuma	dd	Baltimore
i	Detroit	u	San Diego	ee	Washington
j	Chicago	v	Los Angeles/Anaheim	ff	Pittsburgh
k	St. Louis	w	San Bernadino	gg	Atlanta
l	Tulsa	x	Bakersfield		

FIGURE 6.5.   SPC network.

Facsimile Service.   For transmission of graphic material such as pictures, letters, and technical drawings, users can hook up a facsimile terminal at either end of any MCI line and use the line for this function when it is not being utilized for voice communication.

SOUTHERN PACIFIC COMMUNICATIONS.   SPC currently provides leased-line services between the cities shown in Figure 6.5. Among the specialized services offered are:

Voice tie lines
Foreign exchange service (similar to MCI's MATS)
Data channels
Measured-time and part-time lines
Voice plus data

CPI MICROWAVE.   CPI presently provides leased-line services between eight cities in Texas (Figure 6.6). Although most traffic is voice communications and video for television networks, data services are also provided.

UNITED STATES TRANSMISSION SYSTEMS.   USTS provides a network between several cities shown in Figure 6.7. The network is particularly designed for small- to medium-scale users.

CPI Microwave, Inc.
Operational

a	Dallas	e	Corpus Christi
b	Waco	f	Houston
c	Austin	g	Beaumont
d	San Antonio	h	Harlingen

FIGURE 6.6.   CPI network.

USTS (ITT)
Operational

a	Houston	g	Norfolk
b	New Orleans	h	Washington
c	Birmingham	i	Philadelphia
d	Atlanta	j	New York
e	Columbia	k	Hartford
f	Charlotte		

FIGURE 6.7. USTS network.

DATRAN. DATRAN (Data Transmission Co.) is no longer operational, and is only mentioned for historical interest. DATRAN offered a digital switched data communications service between 20 cities from 1974 until 1976, when the network terminated operations in view of continued financial difficulties.

WESTERN TELE-COMMUNICATIONS INC. (WTCI). WTCI provides voice/data service from San Diego to Yuma, and from Los Angeles to San Diego, Phoenix, and Tucson. Figure 6.8 illustrates these services, along with some planned facilities.

Value-Added Networks

The concept of a value-added network originated in 1973, when the FCC approved the application of a new type of common carrier that would provide service by leasing communication channels from other

Western Tele-Communications, Inc.

FIGURE 6.8.   WTCI network.

carriers and "adding value" thereto in the form of additional services such as switching, error control, code conversion, and so on.

At the present time, four value-added networks (VANs) have been approved by the FCC: Packet Communications, Inc.; Telenet Communications Corporation; Graphnet Systems, Inc., and Tymshare, Inc. In the present section, we will consider the Telenet system in greater detail as an example of a VAN.

TELENET.   Telenet is a packet switching network that provides high-speed digital transmission services between the cities shown on the map in Figure 6.9. The packet switching technique organizes data messages into packets of up to 1024 bits or 128 characters each. The number of characters transmitted in each packet depends on the application and is under user control. Packets are given an identification and sequence number, and are transmitted to the next node in the network. The routing is selected dynamically by computers in the switching center as each packet passes through the node.

The particular advantages of a VAN over regular carrier service are:

• Lower cost for certain applications
• Lower error rate
• Flexibility and adaptive routing
• Single-source network management

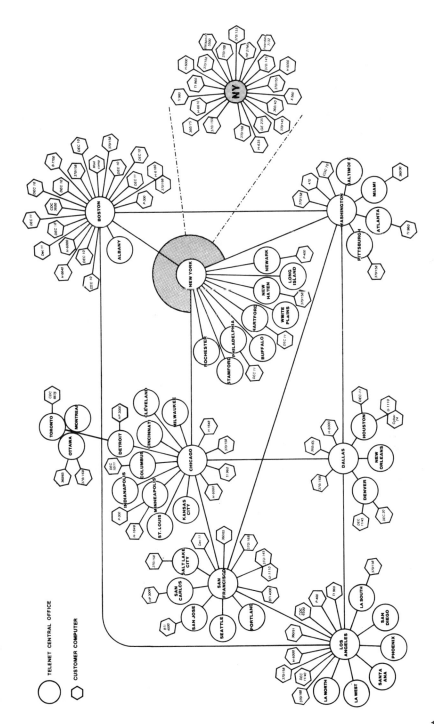

FIGURE 6.9. Telenet logical map, November 1976.

The first point, lower cost, is an important commercial factor in selecting a VAN. The reason for lower cost is that VANs do not charge as a function of the transmission distance, and therefore are able to offer lower rates for medium- to long-haul transmission for low- to medium-volume communications users. Common-carrier offerings, such as direct distance dialing (DDD), or WATS, charge on a per-mile or per-sector basis at higher rates. Of course, very high volume users between two or three fixed locations may consider a leased-line or specialized common-carrier circuit an economic alternative to a VAN.

The second point, lower error rate, is achieved by means of internal error detection and correction techniques built into the network structure. By error detection and retransmission, the error rate is able to be kept down to one in 10^{11} bits between nodes.

The third point, flexibility and adaptive routing, is an important feature for making the Telenet VAN appeal to a wide variety of users. The network is able to accommodate any terminal or computer, at any standard data rate from 50 bps to 56 kbps. The user is able to change his configuration or location at any time without degrading performance. Routing in the network is adaptive, so that transmission will occur to bypass congested or failed links, and thereby adapt to traffic conditions without the user being aware of the different routing.

Finally, a VAN offers the user a single-source network management, thereby relieving him of the problem of network design and selection of communications processors, modems, software, communications circuits, and so on. A VAN installs, operates, and maintains all facilities, optimizing the access lines, and tailoring the software parameters to meet the user's traffic and application requirements.

Because of the importance of economics to the selection of a transmission carrier, it would be worthwhile to analyze the cost factors of a VAN. There are essentially five types of charges:

1. Network port charges per hour: these charges are based on whether the user is in a low-, medium-, or high-density zone (as designated by the particular carrier), and the type of port
2. Host-to-network interface cost: a fixed monthly charge
3. Traffic charges: based on the number of characters transmitted per hour, or kilopackets
4. Equipment charge for the local terminal
5. Local communications cost—that is, the local telephone charge for connecting the user's terminal to the closest node of the VAN

At the time of writing, for a 110–300-bps adaptive speed port, Telenet charges $1.40/hour in a high-density zone (Boston, New York, Washington D.C., etc.), $2.40/hour in a medium-density zone (Denver, St. Louis, Pittsburgh, etc.), and $4.80 in a low-density zone (Kansas City, Portland, Salt Lake City, etc.).

The host-to-network interface cost, the Telenet Access Controller, is a $600 one-time installation charge, and a $400/month charge.

Traffic charges are $0.60/kilopacket (each containing up to 128 characters of user data).

In analyzing and comparing data transmission services, one can draw a curve such as that shown in Figure 6.10, which shows the average cost as a function of usage for Telenet.

Satellite Networks

AMERICAN SATELLITE CORPORATION (ASC). ASC provides a nationwide network for voice and data communications utilizing leased transponders on the Western Union WESTAR I satellite, with backup service on the WESTAR II satellite. A diagrammatic illustration of the service provided is shown in Figure 6.11, indicating some of the designated earth station locations.

SATELLITE BUSINESS SYSTEMS (SBS). SBS is a partnership formed by subsidiaries of COMSAT General Corporation, IBM, and Aetna Casualty and Surety Company for the purpose of developing a domestic satellite communications system. Applications were filed with the FCC in December 1975 for authority to implement a domestic

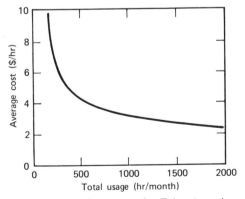

FIGURE 6.10. Cost curve for Telenet service.

American Satellite Corporation (ASC)

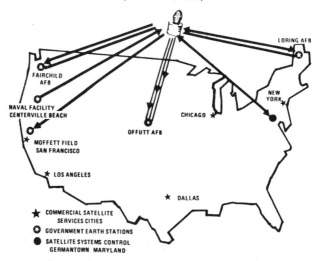

FIGURE 6.11. ASC network.

satellite system for the 12/14 Ghz band for providing end-to-end, all digital, switched private communications services using small earth stations located on a customer's premises.

The Satellite Business Systems (SBS) satellite communications earth station shown in Figure 6.15, installed on IBM premises at Los Gatos, California, began traffic tests in April 1977 with a similar SBS antenna on IBM premises at Poughkeepsie, New York. SBS plans to install a third such antenna on IBM premises at Research Triangle Park, North Carolina, in late 1977. In Phase Two of its pre-operational program, SBS plans to provide a common carrier service to IBM for intracompany communications among IBM facilities at Raleigh, Los Gatos, Poughkeepsie, and Kingston, New York, which will be interconnected with Poughkeepsie via a terrestrial microwave link. The stations operate in the 4 and 6 Gigahertz bands via capacity leased by SBS in an existing U.S. domestic satellite.

WESTERN UNION TELEGRAPH CO.   Western Union launched its WESTAR I domestic communications satellite in April 1974, and began service later that year. The satellite network uses five earth stations, shown in Figure 6.12, along with Western Union's regular terrestrial transmission facilities.

The Western Union Telegraph Company

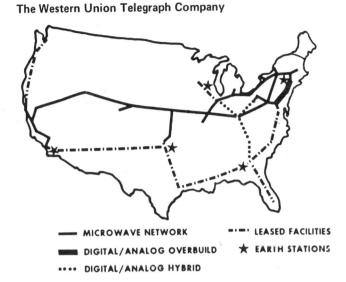

> — MICROWAVE NETWORK ▪—▪ LEASED FACILITIES
> ▬ DIGITAL/ANALOG OVERBUILD ★ EARTH STATIONS
> •••• DIGITAL/ANALOG HYBRID

FIGURE 6.12. Western Union network.

The WESTAR service offers a wide range of options, including:

- Full transponder service
- Voice band services—single channel (group or supergroup)
- Alternate data/voice channel service
- Wideband channel service

SATELLITE BROADCASTING. Another important role for satellites is broadcast communications, that is, the use of a satellite for "broadcasting" to several geographically remote receiving stations. By using a narrow beam and relatively high transmitter power at the satellite, small-diameter antennas can be used at the ground receiving station, making possible individual home or community group reception.

According to discussions of a European Planning Conference on broadcast satellite communications, planned experiments are expected to use frequency modulation at 12 GHz. For a service area the size of the United Kingdom, for example, a satellite with about 300 watts of r.f. signal power would be necessary. The CTS satellite, which has a 200 watt transmitter, is expected to participate in such experiments.

TRANSMISSION TECHNOLOGIES

Voice-Grade Telephone Lines

As pointed out above, digital data transmission over voice-grade telephone lines existed since the 1950s. Such systems utilize data modems to encode the digital data signals, such as through band-limiting techniques, so that data can be transmitted through the randomly selected unconditioned voice-grade telephone lines.

Private Lines

For higher data rates, leased or "private" lines are available from the common carriers. There are four basic categories of leased-lines:

> Teletype
> Subvoice
> Voice
> Wide-band

Teletype-grade lines, as the name implies, are suitable for use with ordinary teletype equipment operating at speeds of up to 75 baud.

Subvoice-grade lines are suitable for use with 15 character-per-second terminals, and operate at speeds up to 180 baud.

Voice-grade lines, used normally for ordinary voice communications, can transmit data at rates up to 9600 baud. Generally, these high-speed data transmissions require custom individually adjusted line conditioning known as line equalization to control the amplitude and delay characteristics for the frequencies used. Such devices are known as variable-line equalizers. The device has many parameters to adjust so that the amplitude and envelope delay characteristics of the composite line and the equalizer become constant for the wide range of frequencies. With the aid of these variable equalizers, the telephone channel bandwidth can be equalized for a range as wide as 2500 Hz bandwidth. With this bandwidth, 2400 bits per second, 3600 bits per second, or more can be transmitted.

Such "conditioned" voice-grade lines are designated C1, C2, C3, and C4, and are made available under special tariffs by the common carrier for the data communications user. C1 conditioned lines are suggested for 2400 baud usage, C2 lines for 4800 baud usage, and C4 lines for usage at data rates higher than 4800 baud.

Wide-band lines, or broad-band cable networks (BCN), provide transmission means with a bandwidth of several megahertz, and are primarily used for reception of cablecast video signals.

Microwave Radio

Microwave radio is a form of transmission technology for point-to-point communications that accounts for some 70% of all interstate voice channel mileage. In 1959 the FCC authorized other carriers to operate and use microwave communications systems, which has led to the development and growth of the specialized common carrier industry described earlier in this chapter.

Satellite Technology

Satellite technology is one of the most important and rapidly growing transmission technologies. Moreover, there are many important social and economic implications of satellite networks that go far beyond their utility for commercial data communications.

Satellites make possible many of the services that are normally available only in metropolitan centers (such as education, health, social, and entertainment services) in sparsely settled areas where alternative communications would be prohibitive. The extensive transmission distances, coupled with the low population density of such areas are technologic and economic constraints which make satellite communications the most economically feasible alternative.

A communications satellite is typically orbited over the earth in a geosynchronous orbit, which means that the satellite appears fixed in position relative to any point on the surface of the earth. Such an orbit enables continuous coverage of a given area on the surface of the earth, thus eliminating the requirement of expensive tracking systems on the earth station.

The satellite design itself is relatively simple, consisting of a repeater that amplifies the received signals and retransmits them back to earth. The various types of communications satellites that are presently in operation are shown in Table 6.2. The INTELSAT IVA is shown in Figure 6.13; INTELSAT and SBS earth stations are shown in Figures 6.14 and 6.15, respectively.

Some of the typical specifications of the WESTAR satellite are shown in Table 6.3.

Millimetric Waveguides

Increased telecommunications traffic over high-density routes has led to the consideration of alternative potential transmission systems. The use of very high frequency microwave signals (50 GHz and above) through waveguides is one such technique. Such "millimetric waveguide" systems represent complex technology, and only re-

TABLE 6.2. Present Communications Satellites

Name	Organization	Builder[a]	Freq. Band	XPNDRS	Capacity TV or Voice	L/V[b]	E/S dia[c] (M)	Oper. Date
INTELSAT IV	INTELSAT	HAC	C	12	12 or 16,000	Atlas/Centaur	30	1971
ANIK	TELESAT	HAC	C	12	12 or 6,000	Delta	98,30, 8, 4	1972
WESTAR	Western Union	HAC	C	12	12 or 6,000	Delta	10	1974
SYMPHONIE	France/ Germany		C	2	2 or 1,200	Delta	16,8,4	1975
INTELSAT IVA	INTELSAT	HAC	C	20	20 or 10,000	Atlas/Centaur	30	1975
SATCOM	RCA	RCA	C	24	24 or 12,000	Delta 3914	13,10	1975

[a]HAC—Hughes Aircraft Company
RCA—RCA Corporation
[b]L/V—launch vehicle
[c]E/S dia—earth station diameter (meters)

FIGURE 6.13.   INTELSAT IVA.

cently may be considered to be commercially feasible. A number of millimetric waveguide experiments are underway, both in the United States and Europe, to justify the feasibility of such transmission systems.

Such experiments are concerned with several issues:

1. Performance and reliability of the technology under field conditions
2. Cost of installation, maintenance, and repair of the system
3. Propagation characteristics

FIGURE 6.14.   INTELSAT earth station at Etam, West Virginia.

The experiment directed by the British Post Office utilized a 50-mm internal diameter lightweight helix waveguide over a 14-km route in Suffolk. The waveguide itself was constructed from glass-reinforced plastic, which offered good transmission performance and economy compared to a dielectric-lined waveguide.

One important parameter that is measured in such experiments is the attenuation along the route due to bends in the path of the waveguide. In the BPO experiment, the attenuation averaged 0.15 dB/km at 80 GHz, and 0.45 dB/km at 110 GHz.

TABLE 6.3.   WESTAR
Characteristics

Height:	11 ft., 3 in.
Weight:	658 lbs.
Solar power:	300 watts

FIGURE 6.15.   SBS Earth Station at Los Gatos, California.

Optical Fiber Transmission

Optical fiber transmission is expected to be an important communication transmission technology. Although technical problems still exist concerning the most suitable and economic light source and detectors, sufficient progress has been made so that optical data transmission systems are practical for systems when their technical advantages are more significant than cost. Avionics applications, where the transmission distance is not great, is an example of such a system which is feasible because of the lower weight of optical fiber paths than the equivalent wire paths.

The thrust of research in the optical fiber area is concerned with the following issues:

Suitable system applications
Fiber type and composition
Source and detector type

SYSTEM APPLICATIONS. As a transmission technology that provides a physical interconnection between the signal source and the signal receiver, an optical fiber link can most suitably be compared with copper. The most important advantages of optical fiber over copper are:

Greater information bandwidth
Not sensitive to electrical interference
Smaller physical size and weight
Transmission security
No crosstalk
No spark or fire hazard
Wide operating temperature range

Some of the present disadvantages are:

Cost
Incompatibility with existing systems
Signal loss and distortion

FIBER TYPE AND COMPOSITION. Optical fiber transmission is implemented by transmitting a signal-encoded beam of light through an optical cable, consisting of a group of discrete optical fibers each transmitting a light signal from one end of the cable to the other.

A single optical fiber is constructed as shown in Figure 6.16. The fiber has a center core of some material (a glass or plastic) with a high index of refraction, surrounded by a cladding layer of some material having a slightly lower index of refraction. With such a basic construction, three distinct fiber types are possible, shown in transaxial cross-sectional view in Figure 6.17.

The first type, shown in Figure 6.17a, has a small core and is typically used from monomode transmission (i.e., transmitting a

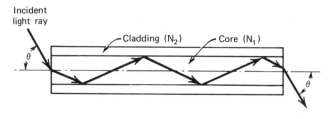

FIGURE 6.16. Optical fiber.

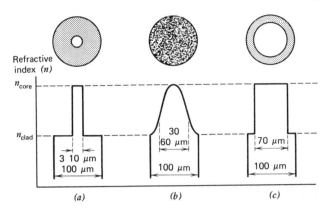

FIGURE 6.17.   Optical fiber: transaxial view. (a) Small core; (b) large core, graded index; (c) large core, step index.

single mode of linearly polarized electromagnetic radiation). The second type (Figure 6.17b) is a large-core multimode graded index; the third type (Figure 6.17c) is a large-core multimode step index fiber. In all cases, the relative difference in the index of refraction between the core and the cladding is only about 1%.

The transmission of light is based on total internal reflection of the light as it travels along the core of the fiber. The cladding layer thus isolates the fibers and prevents crosstalk between adjacent fibers.

The composition of the fiber itself determines the transmission attenuation, caused either by scattering or absorption by trace elements present in the core. The manufacturing process of such fibers, using ultrafine and ultrapure compounds, is therefore critical in producing the fiber with the most desirable characteristics, or optimum tradeoff between cost and attenuation.

Attenuation of optical fibers cables is usually measured in decibels per kilometer at a given frequency. The cables presently available range from high loss plastic-composition cables for illumination purposes, to extremely low loss, ultrapure-glass cables (typical attenuation losses in the range of 2–10 dB/km).

BELL LABS EXPERIMENTAL SYSTEM.   The technical feasibility of lightwave communications has been demonstrated in a Bell Labs/Western Electric experimental system in Atlanta. The experimental system transmits digitized voice and data at a rate of 44.7 megabits/second along a cable containing 144 glass fibers, a data rate equivalent to 672 digitized voice channels over a single glass fiber.

In the Atlanta system 12 glass fibers are encapsulated into a flat ribbon. In the transmission cable 12 such ribbons are stacked together and twisted along the length of the cable. Reliable communication is possible at distances of up to 7 km (4 miles) before regeneration of the light signals is necessary, with an average loss in the cable of 6 dB/km.

seven
COMPUTER
NETWORKS

I n order to illustrate many of the concepts presented in the preceding chapters, it would be worthwhile to consider in detail some specific computer networks and data communications systems. These include:

ARPANET
Commercial time-sharing networks
Industry data networks
European data networks
Satellite networks

ARPANET

ARPANET is a fully distributed message-switching network that interconnects a wide variety of computers at different contract research centers of the Advanced Research Projects Agency (ARPA) of the U.S. Department of Defense. Although ARPANET is an experimental computer network, a significant amount of financial resources and development effort have been expended with the project. Technologically significant results with ARPANET have been achieved, however, and therefore we will consider ARPANET in considerably greater detail than other data networks. We will consider three important aspects of ARPANET: network organization, packet switching, and network performance measurements.

Network Organization

ARPANET was initiated as an experimental network in 1968 to study the interconnection of geographically dispersed computer systems of different manufacture, model, and characteristics. The basic goal of ARPANET was the development and testing of such a large-scale computer communications network in which resources were shared among network participants.

ARPANET today consists of a network of some 50 computers extending from Hawaii across the U.S. to Europe, as shown in the geographic map of Figure 7.1. The actual logical configuration of the computers attached to each of the ARPANET nodes is shown in Figure 7.2.

Each of the principal ARPANET computers is known as a host. The hosts are connected to smaller computers known as interface message processors (IMPs), as illustrated in Figure 7.3. The IMPs handle all network communications for their hosts, as well as packet switching functions.

The various users of the system interface with ARPANET through a terminal interface processor (TIP). Access to the TIP is either through a hardwired connection or through remote access, such as a dial-up telephone connection. Up to 63 terminals or other devices may be connected to a given TIP. As suggested in Figure 7.3, the path of communication from sending terminal to receiving terminal is through a series of IMPs until the desired destination host computer is reached.

Packet Switching

As pointed out previously, ARPANET is a packet-switched network. The characterizing feature of packet transmission is that the messages are broken down into "packets" of a finite length that are burst-transmitted over the communications link. Such packets share the communications link with other packets in transit which have originated from other sending stations. In ARPANET the maximum message length is 8063 bits long, which is divided into packets that are at most 1008 bits long.

There are a number of variations on the protocols of packet transmission. "Pure ALOHA" refers to the system in which each user is free to transmit anytime. The pure ALOHA system is named after the ALOHA system of the University of Hawaii, a packet broadcasting system utilizing ground-based and satellite-based channels.

The second protocol is known as "slotted ALOHA" in which the transmission channel is divided into time slots equal to the transmission time of one packet. Transmissions must be synchronized with the time slots.

A third protocol utilizes TDMA or FDMA to assign specific time slots to specified users. Such techniques are particularly suited for high-density traffic, and they result in maximal channel utilization.

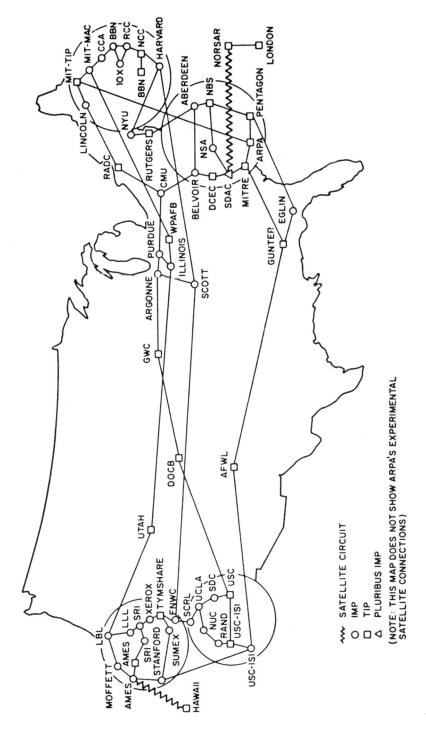

SATELLITE CIRCUIT
○ IMP
□ TIP
△ PLURIBUS IMP

(NOTE: THIS MAP DOES NOT SHOW ARPA'S EXPERIMENTAL SATELLITE CONNECTIONS)

FIGURE 7.1. ARPANET: geographic map, April 1976.

193

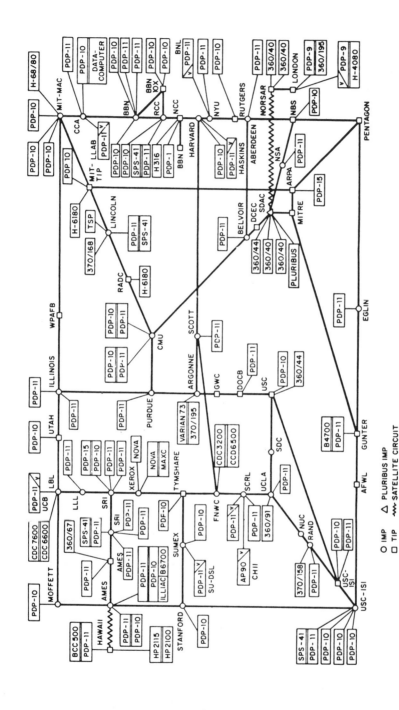

FIGURE 7.2. ARPANET: logical map, April 1976.

○ IMP △ PLURIBUS IMP
□ TIP ∿ SATELLITE CIRCUIT

(PLEASE NOTE THAT WHILE THIS MAP SHOWS THE HOST POPULATION OF THE NETWORK ACCORDING TO THE BEST INFORMATION OBTAINABLE, NO CLAIM CAN BE MADE FOR ITS ACCURACY)

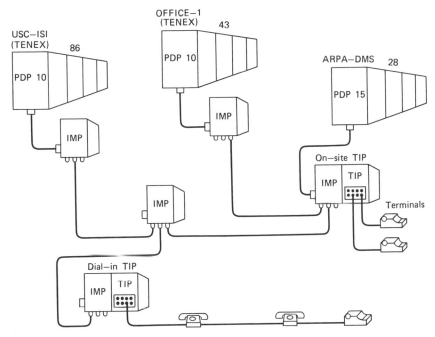

FIGURE 7.3. ARPANET interface message processors (IMPs).

Yet a fourth protocol is carrier sense multiple access (CSMA). In CSMA the station "senses" the channel to determine whether it is clear or busy; if busy, it postpones transmission until clear is detected. A variation of CSMA is known as busy tone multiple access (BTMA). In BTMA, the communication channel is divided into two separate channels: one the message channel and the other the "busy tone" channel. By sensing a carrier on the busy tone channel, the station knows that the message channel is not clear.

Network Performance Measurements

Since the basic design of ARPANET was experimental, a considerable amount of information has been developed concerning network performance under a wide variety of conditions. Although such data are directly applicable only to ARPANET and similar packet-switching networks, it would be worthwhile to review some of the basic concepts of network performance in that context.

The basic network performance measurements made on ARPANET include:

- Network throughput for different protocols
- Network congestion and delays
- Network deadlocks and degradations
- Network performance as a function of message and packet size
- Channel utilization
- Network behavior

Many of these measurements were made at the UCLA Network Measurement Center (NMC) and reported in NMC publications.

NETWORK THROUGHPUT FOR DIFFERENT PROTOCOLS. Throughput is the measurement of the transmission rate of useful data through the channel, excluding any control information or retransmissions that the protocol requires. The throughput for various radio access protocols is summarized in Table 7.1 below.

TABLE 7.1. Throughput for radio access protocols.

Protocol	Capacity
Pure ALOHA	0.184
Slotted ALOHA	0.368
1-persistent CSMA	0.529
Slotted 1-persistent CSMA	0.531
Nonpersistent BTMA	
100 kHz bandwidth	0.680
1000 kHz bandwidth	0.720
0.1-persistent CSMA	0.791
Nonpersistent CSMA	0.815
0.03-persistent CSMA	0.827
Slotted nonpersistent CSMA	0.857
Perfect scheduling	1.000

Source: Kleinrock, L., *IEEE Transactions of Computers,* **C-25** (1976) 1326–1335.

NETWORK DEADLOCKS AND DEGRADATIONS. There are a number of different types of network deadlocks and degradations that can affect network performance which have been observed in ARPANET. Among the deadlocks are:

Reassembly deadlock
Store-and-forward lockup

Buffer lockup
Piggyback lockup

Reassembly deadlock refers to the situation in which buffer space is not provided at the destination for the reassembly of the message. The messages and packets back up around the destination, and no reassembly can take place.

Store-and-forward lockup refers to the situation in which the buffers of two adjacent IMPs are fully occupied and such IMPs attempt to transfer packets to each other. The result is a stand-off, with neither of the IMPs able to transfer messages in its buffers.

Buffer lockup refers to the unavailability of sufficient buffers either because of a lack of sufficient pointers to the buffers, or because buffer assignments can not easily be disengaged.

Piggyback lockup refers to the situation where network messages are handled in a piggyback fashion, which in turn leads to buffer lockup.

Among the degradations that have been observed in ARPANET are routing loops and deadlocks, message transmission gaps, single packet turbulence, and system phasing.

COMMERCIAL TIME-SHARING NETWORKS

The commercial time-sharing networks are good examples of computer networks. The time-sharing service vendors offer the computer user convenient batch or interactive use of a centralized computer, together with access to proprietary applications programs in a wide variety of commercial areas. Although the nature of the network is transparent to the user, it is significant from the point of view of the vendor. In the present section we briefly consider a variety of time-sharing services:

CYBERNET
MARK III
TYMNET
INFONET
Scientific Time-Sharing

CYBERNET

CYBERNET is the commercial time-sharing service network of Control Data Corporation. Computer centers are located in the United

States, Canada, Australia, Brazil, France, Germany, Greece, Israel, Mexico, Netherlands, South Africa, Sweden, and the United Kingdom. Some of the CYBERNET applications program capabilities include structural analysis, electrical engineering, data base management, financial planning, management analysis, and graphics.

MARK III

MARK III is the interactive computer network of GE Information Services, based on two large computer centers in the United States and one near Amsterdam in Europe.

Although MARK III provides remote batch service, some of its most important applications concern its centralized data base services. For example, MARK III provides customers with access to its Currency Exchange Database, which features daily open-and-close exchange rates for 46 currencies. Financial analysts can make use of such data, together with other economic databases, in the preparation of reports analyzing the impact of currency exchange fluctuations on a company's specific financial situation.

TYMNET

TYMNET (Figure 7.4) is an example of a commercial computer network in the United States. Although TYMNET was initially developed as part of the time-sharing system offered by Tymshare, Inc., the network recently became a value-added common carrier.

INFONET

INFONET is the commercial time-sharing service network of Computer Sciences Corporation. The INFONET network is shown in Figure 7.5.

Scientific Time-Sharing Corporation

Scientific Time-Sharing Corporation offers interactive computer time-sharing services using the APL language, a very high level language. The Scientific Time-Sharing Corporation network is shown in Figure 7.6.

INDUSTRY DATA NETWORKS

Various industries have their own computer/communications networks which are managed by industry organizations and subscribed to by individual enterprises in the industry. These include NASDAQ in

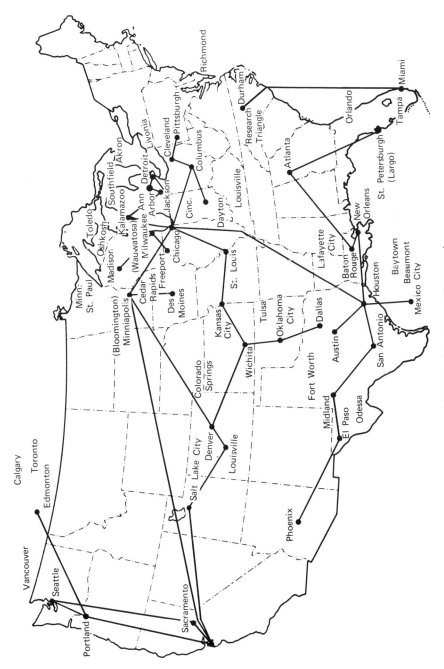

FIGURE 7.4.   TYMNET network.

199

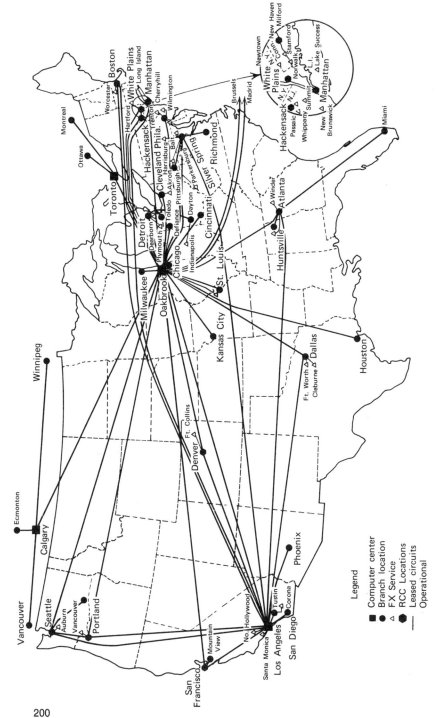

FIGURE 7.5. INFONET network.

Legend

■ Computer center
● Branch location
△ FX Service
⬟ RCC Locations
— Leased circuits
  Operational

200

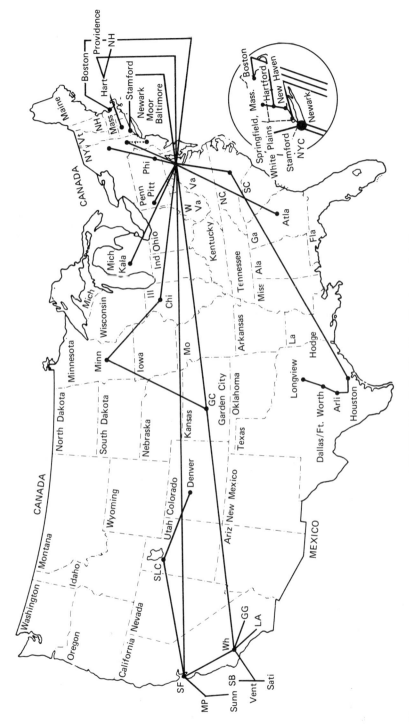

FIGURE 7.6.   Scientific Time-Sharing network.

201

the over-the-counter securities industry, and SWIFT in the banking industry. Mention should also be made of the Canadian shared-user data network Datapac, as well as defense networks.

NASDAQ

The National Association of Securities Dealers Automated Quotation (NASDAQ) system, shown in Figure 7.7, interconnects member firms of the NASD for providing quotations on over-the-counter securities in the United States.

SITA

The SITA (Société Internationale de Télécommunications Aeronautiques) network is the message switched data communications network of the air carrier industry. Computer centers, located in London, Amsterdam, Frankfurt, Paris, Rome, Madrid, Beirut, Hong Kong, and New York, switch the inquiry/response messages between reservation computers geographically dispersed and terminals located in airline offices. Telegraphic message traffic service is also provided for administrative communication.

FIGURE 7.7.   NASDAQ system.

SWIFT

The Society for Worldwide Interbank Financial Telecommunications (SWIFT) is expected to interconnect some 400 of the largest banks in 15 countries in North America and Europe. The system presently uses two dual-processor Burroughs B3700 systems at switching centers in Belgium and the Netherlands.

ZENGIN

ZENGIN is the data communications network of the banking industry in Japan. Some 88 banks with a total of 7500 branches are connected, which is in addition to the internal networks of individual banks. An automatic cash dispenser system, operated by Nippon Cash Service Company, is expected to be coupled to the ZENGIN network by 1979. Furthermore, the SWIFT network is also expected to be connected to ZENGIN in the future.

Datapac

Datapac is a shared data network for data communications using packet technology over the Dataroute digital transmission network, the private line digital data service in Canada. Service is presently provided between 15 Canadian cities.

Datapac provides two types of service: Datapac 1000, which utilizes the BSC protocol and is suitable for short message transmission, and Datapac 1500, for general data communications, which uses the SNAP protocol based on the CCITT X.25 protocol.

INFOSWITCH

INFOSWITCH is another Canadian packet-switching network under development by Canadian National/Canadian Pacific Telecommunications (CN/CPT).

DDX

DDX is a Japanese packet-switching network presently in the prototype stage under development by Nippon Telephone and Telegraph (NTT).

Defense Networks

The SATIN IV communications network (Figure 7.8) is designed as a component of the U.S. Department of Defense Worldwide Military Command Control System (WWMCCS) for providing a highly reliable, direct channel of communications from the National Command Au-

SATIN IV

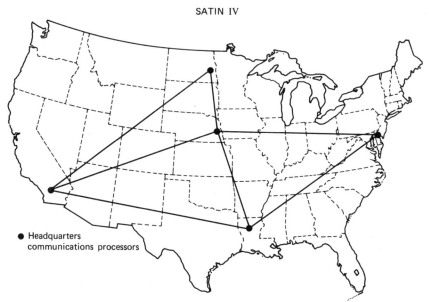

FIGURE 7.8.   SATIN IV network.

thorities (NCA) to Strategic Air Command (SAC) executing command-
ers. The SATIN IV network is similar to the AUTODIN II network for
worldwide computer communications.

The SATIN IV network consists of a family of communications
processors which automatically perform message switching, distribution, and logging functions. The network has two important features:
internetting and communications security.

Internetting refers to the ability to reconfigure the network when a
predetermined error threshold is exceeded. The affected communications processors automatically seek out a better quality transmission
path to the desired switching node.

Communications security is also of high priority in a defense communications network. The basic design goal of SATIN IV is end-to-end
encryption, in which the message remains encrypted from the sender
to the destination.

EUROPEAN DATA NETWORKS

In Europe, data networks have been developed in cooperation with
the various national PTT (Post, Telephone, and Telegraph) agencies.
We consider a few of them in this section:

NPL (U.K.)
EPSS (U.K.)
RCP (France)
CYCLADES (France)
EIN (London-Zurich-Milan-Ispra)
CTNE (Spain)
NORDIC
TRANSPAC
Other Data Networks

NPL

The NPL network is a small, experimental packet-switched data communications network developed by the National Physical Laboratory (NPL) in the United Kingdom.

The network interconnects about 100 terminals through a single packet-switched node. Network hardware includes a pair of DDP 516 computers used for message switching of the packets. The network is eventually expected to be interconnected with the EPSS and EIN networks.

EPSS

The Experimental Packet Switched Service (EPSS) network is a packet-switched commercial data communications network connecting London, Glasgow, and Manchester, and operated by the G.P.O. (Post Office) of the United Kingdom (Figure 7.9).

The network provides duplicate 48 Kbit/second lines over the route, together with a Ferranti packet-switching exchange in London. The network can service up to 150 character terminals and 50 packet terminals.

RCP

The Reseau à Communication par Pacquets (RCP) network is a packet-switched commercial data network connecting Rennes, Paris, and Lyons, with multiplexers in Lille, Bordeaux, and Marseilles, and operated by the French P.T.T. (Figure 7.11).

The network utilizes PDP-11 as packet-switching computers, interconnected by 4800-baud lines.

CYCLADES

The CYCLADES network is an experimental packet-switched data communications network connecting Paris, Grenoble, Toulouse, and

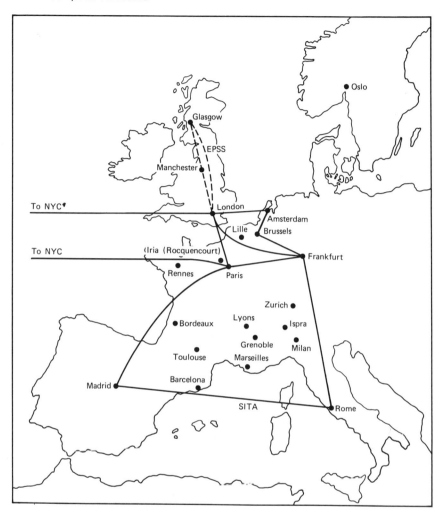

FIGURE 7.9.   EPSS and SITA networks.

Rennes, and operated by the Institut de Recherche d'Informatique et d'Automatique (IRIA) of the French government (Figure 7.10).

Actual packet communications take place over a communications subsystem known as CIGALE. CIGALE utilizes a CII Mitra 15 computer for transporting packets, and maintaining sequence and error control.

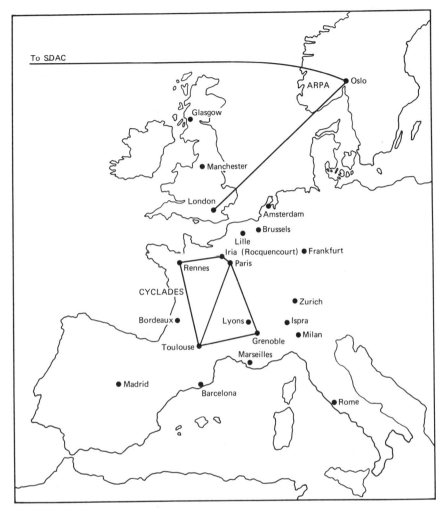

FIGURE 7.10.   CYCLADES and European ARPA networks.

EIN

The European Information Network (EIN) is a joint effort by France, Italy, Norway, Portugal, Spain, Switzerland, the U.K., and Yugoslavia to develop a European packet-switching network. The initial nodes are London, Zurich, Milan, and Ispra, which utilize the same format and hardware (the Mitra 15) as the CYCLADES network (Figure 7.11).

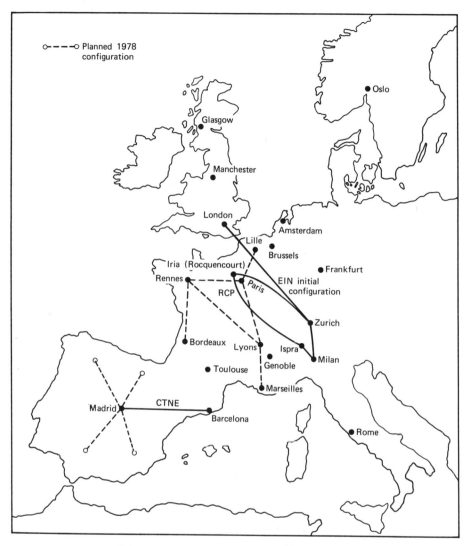

FIGURE 7.11.   EIN, RCP, and CTNE networks.

CTNE

The Compagnia Telefonica National de España (CTNE), the communications agency in Spain, operates a packet-switched network connecting Madrid and Barcelona along 4800-baud duplicate lines (Figure 7.11).

NORDIC

NORDIC is a proposed data network that is expected to connect over 10,000 subscribers in Stockholm, Oslo, Copenhagen, and Helsinki by 1980. The network is expected to be operational in Denmark in 1978 and in the other countries in the following year. The network is being developed by Oy Nokia (Finland) and Electrisk Bureau (Norway), and will utilize the LM Ericsson AXB 30 switching system. The network will handle both synchronous and asynchronous transmission.

TRANSPAC

TRANSPAC is a proposed public packet-switching network in France expected to be operational in 1978. Switching centers are expected to be located in Lille, Strasbourg, Dijon, Lyon, Marseille, Toulouse, Bordeaux, Nannes, Rennes, Rouen, Orleans, and Paris. The network is a service of the French PTT, and will handle both synchronous and asynchronous transmission.

EURONET

EURONET is a European data communications network under development by a consortium of six companies—Cardata, Christian Rousing, Italsiel, Logica, Sait, and Sesa—and expected to be operational in 1978.

OTHER DATA NETWORKS

In addition to the packet-switched data networks considered above, the government telecommunications agencies have begun development of digital transmission and switching networks for normal communications transmission. The advantages of digital transmission is that all information, whether digitized speech, television pictures, or digital data, would be transmitted in the same format. Of course, digital transmission throughout a network is most expeditiously implemented by digital switching. Present switching technology is mostly analog, and the digitally encoded signals must be converted into analog form, sent through the switching system, then reconverted back into digital form for transmission along the digital link. The conversion process introduces noise into the system, so an eventual change-over to an all-digital integrated network is seen as the eventual objective.

SATELLITE NETWORKS

Satellite networks are becoming increasingly important not only for data communications but also for other forms of telecommunications. A list of satellite systems, in one stage of development or another, is as follows:

1. National and Regional Systems
   Canada
   Indonesia
   INTELSAT National and Regional Systems
   United States
   USSR
2. Organizations and Companies
   American Satellite Corporation
   Comsat General
   EUROSAT
   RCA
   Satellite Business Systems
   Western Union
3. Maritime/Aeronautical Systems
   MARISAT
   INMARSAT
   MAROTS
   AEROSAT
4. Experimental Systems
   ATS-6
   CTS
   SYMPHONIE
   Japanese Experimental Systems
   SIRIO
   LES
5. Defense Systems
   FLTSATCOM (AFSATCOM, TACSATCOM)
   NATO III

National and Regional Systems

CANADA. The Canadian domestic satellite system, operated by Telesat Canada, utilizes three geostationary earth satellites, called "ANIK" ("anik" is the Eskimo word for brother). The first ANIK satellite was launched in 1972 and began providing communication services the following year. The second and third-satellites are used for in-orbit back-up and future system expansion.

The Telesat satellites feature 12 transponders, each with a usable bandwidth of 36 MHz. The principal usage of the bandwidth is for national television distribution, followed by east-west telephone message traffic. Modulation techniques include video-FM, FDM-FM, and FDM-PCM-PSK-TDMA.

INDONESIA. The Indonesian domestic satellite Palapa I was launched in July 1976 and covers the regions shown in Figure 7.12. The satellite is the same type as the Canadian Telesat; however, the single-channel-per-carrier (SCPC) demand assignment access technique is used.

INTELSAT NATIONAL AND REGIONAL SYSTEMS. A number of nations are using or planning to use the available capacity of the INTELSAT networks for domestic national or regional systems. These countries include Algeria, Norway, and (potentially) the Andean Group, Argentina, Denmark, and Malaysia. Such usage is referred to as the INTELSAT SPADE system, for "single-channel-*per*-carrier PCM multiple-*a*ccess *d*emand-assigned *e*quipment."

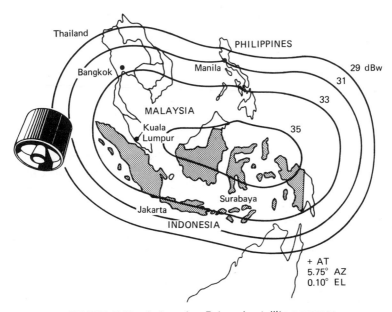

FIGURE 7.12. Indonesian Palapa I satellite coverage.

UNITED STATES.   Domestic satellite services are now provided in the United States by American Satellite Corp., Comsat General, RCA, and Western Union, and eventually by Satellite Business Systems. These companies and their programs are reviewed in the second section of this chapter.

USSR.   Domestic satellite services are provided in the Soviet Union by the MOLNIYA II satellite, which was first launched in 1971 ("molniya" is the Russian word for lightning). The MOLNIYA satellites are large (1000 kg.), high-powered (over 700 watts rf output) systems designed to serve a large number of small, geographically dispersed ORBITA earth stations. There are over 50 ORBITA earth stations, which provide television distribution services to over 75% of the population of the USSR, as well as telephone message traffic.

PROPOSED NATIONAL AND REGIONAL SYSTEM.   There are several nations and regional groups that have proposed or are planning satellite systems, including the Arab Group, with its ARCOMSAT; the Asean nations; Australia; Brazil; the Federal Republic of Germany; India; Iran; and the United Kingdom.

Organizations and Companies

AMERICAN SATELLITE CORPORATION.   American Satellite Corporation (ASC) provides a full range of communications services through eight satellite earth stations and three leased transponders on Western Union's WESTAR satellites. Five of the earth stations are dedicated for Air Force use.

COMSAT GENERAL.   Comsat General Corporation, a subsidiary of Communications Satellite Corporation, has responsibilities with four satellite network programs: AEROSAT, MARISAT, Satellite Business Systems (SBS), and COMSTAR. The first three programs are considered in sections below; the COMSTAR program is discussed here.

The COMSTAR program exclusively provides domestic satellite communications capability for AT&T. The program includes two orbiting satellites with a third expected to be launched in 1978, and tracking, telemetry, and command earth stations located at Southbury, Connecticut and Santa Paula, California. Communications earth stations operated by AT&T are located near major switching centers in Pennsylvania, Georgia, Illinois, and California. The COMSTAR satellite, first launched in 1976, has 24 transponders on board, each transponder having a capacity of 600 telephone circuits, equivalent to a 48 megabit-per-second digital data stream.

EUROPEAN REGIONAL SATELLITE ORGANIZATION (EUROSAT).
EUROSAT is an international organization founded in 1972 to promote the establishment of operational satellite systems for European regional subscribers by providing the administrative, technical, and financial services required by the ultimate users. The shareholders of EUROSAT consist primarily of industrial organizations, banks, and financial institutions.

EUROSAT is concerned with several distinct areas of space technology, much like Comsat General: AEROSAT, MARISAT, meteorological satellites, and communications satellites. Although government agencies have the principal responsibility for the regulation and development of space technology through the European Space Agency (ESA), the operational aspects and commercial use of such satellite systems have been delegated to EUROSAT.

AEROSAT and MARISAT are considered in sections below. EUROSAT's participation in meteorological satellite programs is centered on the METEOSAT, launched in 1976 as part of the Global Atmosphere Research Project of the World Meteorological Organization.

RCA GLOBAL COMMUNICATIONS–RCA ALASKA COMMUNICATIONS. RCA Globcom and RCA Alaska provide a full range of communications services through satellite earth stations in California, Pennsylvania, and Alaska, and two leased transponders on Western Union's WESTAR satellite. Meanwhile, RCA has an FCC application pending to launch two satellites of its own.

SATELLITE BUSINESS SYSTEMS (SBS). SBS is a joint venture of Comsat General, IBM, and Aetna Life and Casualty to establish a domestic satellite communications system for business and other users. SBS plans to operate with hundreds of small earth stations located at the customer's plant or office, using 5- to 7-meter antennas and the 12/14 GHz band. SBS will thus enable direct computer-to-computer communications to take place, bypassing other common-carrier facilities. Initial evaluation will take place at IBM facilities in Poughkeepsie, New York and Los Gatos, California. Five additional preoperational stations will be chosen from the following locations: Gaithersburg, Maryland; Manassas, Virginia; Boca Raton, Florida; Atlanta, Georgia; Lexington, Kentucky; Greencastle, Indiana; Rochester, Minnesota; Austin, Texas; and Boulder, Colorado.

WESTERN UNION.   Western Union provides a full range of satellite communications services with two satellites, each having 12 transponders. In addition, Western Union owns and operates earth stations located in New Jersey, California, Alabama, Texas, and Wisconsin.

Western Union's satellite, the WESTAR, is similar to the ANIK satellites built for Telesat Canada by Hughes Aircraft Company. Further details and specifications of the WESTAR satellite are presented in the satellite technology section of Chapter 6.

Maritime Systems

MARISAT (COMSAT).   The Marisat satellite was launched in February 1976 and was the world's first maritime satellite. There are presently two Marisat satellites, one over the Atlantic Ocean and the other over the Pacific Ocean, with coverage shown in Figure 7.13.

The Marisat system was designed and developed by COMSAT General, a subsidiary of COMSAT. The system is owned under a joint venture of COMSAT General, RCA Global Communications, Western Union International, and ITT World Communications.

Shore stations for the Marisat system are located at Southbury, Connecticut and Santa Paula, California. Each of the shore stations is a network control point for commercial traffic in its ocean area. The shore stations also interconnect with existing domestic and international terrestrial telecommunications networks for transferring telex, data, and telephone communications.

INMARSAT.   The development of an international maritime satellite has been under consideration by the Inter-Governmental Maritime Consultative Organization (IMCO) for the past few years. IMCO plans to create an international organization responsible for such an international maritime satellite system (INMARSAT), and much of the discussion has centered on the institutional and legal nature of the organization, and the respective responsibilities of the governments and private entities participating in the system. It has been generally agreed that the participating states could designate an entity, public or private, to assume the financial, technical, and operational responsibilities associated with participation in INMARSAT. The five largest participants are expected to be the United States, the United Kingdom, the U.S.S.R., Norway, and Japan.

MAROTS—ESA.   The MAROTS system (Maritime Orbiting Technology Satellite) is a project of the European Space Agency (ESA), the

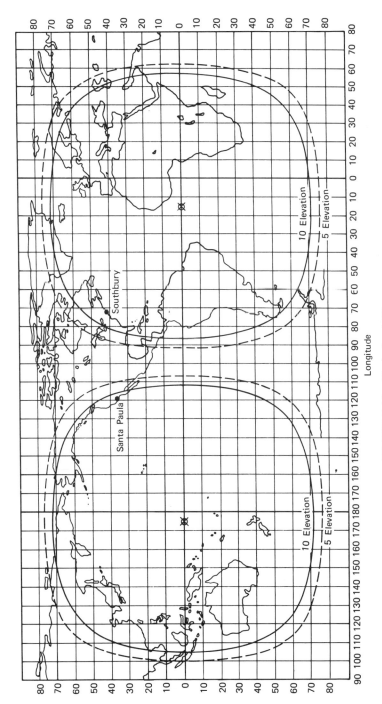

FIGURE 7.13. Marisat satellite coverage.

single coordinated space agency with 10 European member countries (Belgium, Denmark, France, Federal Republic of Germany, Italy, Netherlands, Spain, Sweden, Switzerland, and the United Kingdom) formed in 1975.

AEROSAT (COMSAT/ESA).   The AEROSAT system (Aeronautical Satellite) was a project of the ESA and the governments of the United States and Canada to establish an aeronautical satellite experimentation and evaluation program. The program would have been concerned with such experiments as air traffic control communications, aircraft navigation and surveillance, and aircraft/airline company communications such as maintenance and service requirements, passenger and cargo customs data, and estimated arrival and scheduling information.

In the United States, COMSAT General Corporation was the designated organization concerned with system operations. Since funding for the project has not been appropriated, the program's future is uncertain.

Experimental Systems

ATS.   The ATS-6 (Applications Technology Satellite) was launched by NASA in 1974 for providing communications support to various independent research groups in North America. Prior ATS systems 1 through 5 were concerned with such projects as super high-frequency (SHF) voice and television experiments, propagation measurements, and aeronautical and maritime applications.

Some of the key ATS-6 experiments include:

1. Demonstration of television distribution by satellite for public service Information (satellite instructional television experiment, or SITE)
2. Use of the satellite for television relay (television relay using small terminals, or TRUST)
3. Position location and aircraft communication experiments (PLACE)
4. 18/13 GHz millimeter wave-propagation measurements
5. Measurements of radio-frequency interference between satellites and terrestrial systems
6. Evaluation of technology for an operational tracking and data relay satellite system

CTS. The CTS (Communication Technology Satellite) system is a joint effort of the United States and Canada for experiments in communications. The satellite was launched in 1975 and was designed for performing the following experiments:

1. Communication experiments with low-cost transportable ground terminals, such as for:
   television broadcast to remote communities
   radio broadcast to small ground terminals
   telephony service between small transportable ground stations
   digital data transmission, and investigation of time-division multiple-access techniques
   television transmission origination for transportable terminals for retransmission and network distribution
2. Development and flight testing of new satellite components, including:
   a highly efficient power amplifier tube
   a lightweight extendable solar array
   a new satellite stabilization system

SYMPHONIE. The SYMPHONIE program is a joint effort of France and West Germany for telecommunications research using a geostationary satellite stationed over the Atlantic Ocean and earth stations in France, West Germany, and on the island of Reunion in the Indian Ocean. The first SYMPHONIE satellite was launched in December 1974.

JAPANESE EXPERIMENTAL SYSTEMS. The Japanese have several experimental satellite systems either in operation or under development. The ETS-II (Engineering Test Satellite) was built by Aeroneutronic Ford Corporation and launched in February 1977. The CS (Communication Satellite), also built by Aeroneutronic Ford, will be launched in November 1977. The BSE (Experimental Broadcast Satellite), built by General Electric, is expected to be launched in February 1978. Finally, the ECS (Experimental Communications Satellite), built by Aeroneutronic Ford, is expected to be launched in February 1979.

SIRIO. SIRIO (for Satellite Italiano Ricerca Industriale Orientata) is the Italian experimental communications satellite launched by NASA for the Italian government in August 1977. The satellite is particularly designed for studying transmission in the SHF (superhigh-frequency) bands from 12 to 18 GHz. Experiments concerned with transmissions during extreme weather conditions (rain, snow, fog) have been planned.

LES.   LES refers to the Lincoln Laboratory series of satellites which were first launched in 1965. The LES satellites are concerned with a wide variety of experiments at UHF and K bands, including aircraft and ship communications and intersatellite relay communications. Intersatellite tests are expected to take place in the 36 to 38 GHz bands.

Defense Systems

AFSATCOM.   The Air Force Satellite Communications System (AFSATCOM) is designed to provide a highly reliable UHF (225–400 MHz) communication capability to various high-priority Air Force and Defense Department users, including the Strategic Air Command (SAC), National Command Authorities (NCA), CINCEUR, CINCPAC, and others.

The AFSATCOM is primarily intended for providing teletype communications between command facilities and mobile forces, particularly the airborne forces, at a data rate of about 75 baud. No voice facilities are planned. The AFSATCOM space segment will include two operational satellites. Overall control is the responsibility of the Air Force Communications Service (AFCS), which schedules the various users on the various channels according to predetermined plans and priorities.

FLTSATCOM.   The Navy Fleet Satellite Communications System (FLTSATCOM) is similar in objectives to that of AFSATCOM.

NATO.   The NATO III satellite, designed and developed by Aeroneutronic Ford Corporation, was launched in April 1976 and is positioned in a stationary orbit midway between Africa and South America. NATO III is designed to provide real-time communications for nations of the NATO military alliance; the NATO SATCOM system control center in Belgium schedules and controls communications via the satellite. Earlier NATO II satellites were launched in 1971 and 1972.

eight
DATA COMMUNICATIONS APPLICATIONS

We review the range of applications of data communications networks by considering some typical examples in greater detail. The following industries will be considered in the present chapter:

Banking and finance
Insurance
Retailing
Government
Health care
Manufacturing
Telephony

BANKING AND FINANCE

Banking applications of data processing are more intensively concerned with data than many other industries, and illustrate the gradual evolution from batch processing to on-line processing and distributed processing through data communications. Moreover, the increased interest in the implementation of electronic funds transfer (EFT) through telecommunications networks is an even more significant area.

On-Line Processing

A typical on-line processing system is the IBM 3600 Finance Communication System. The IBM 3600 interfaces with a System/370 in an integrated network that permits tellers in remote locations to enter, update, and retrieve customer data and financial information. The IBM 3600 consists of several components:

IBM 3601 finance communication controller
IBM 3604 keyboard display terminal
IBM 3610 document printer
IBM 3612 passbook and document printer
IBM 3618 administrative line printer
IBM 3614 consumer transaction facility, or self-service teller terminal

In operation, the teller enters the transaction information on the 3604 keyboard display. The information entered is sent to the 3601 controller, which automatically performs any required computations. The customer's passbook is then inserted into the 3612 passbook and document printer, as shown in Figure 8.1, and the controller supervises the printing of the updated information in the passbook. The 3601 also relays the transaction to the host computer so as to immediately revise the centralized files, thereby enabling any teller at any remote station to obtain the updated customer data.

FIGURE 8.1.   IBM 3600 finance communications system. (Photograph courtesy IBM Corp.)

The 3618 administrative line printer is used to obtain running totals or balances for all transactions for management report or auditing purposes.

Distributed Processing

The next stage in the evolution of data processing in the banking and financial industries is the transition from on-line processing to distributed processing and decentralized processing. Such a transition is only possible if the organizational environment makes such processing advantageous over traditional centralized processing.

The banking and financial industry is one example where the operational environment of branch offices makes distributed processing feasible. Data entry, verification, processing, and hard-copy output for the customer, internal records, and auditing purposes may all be economically performed at the branch office level, rather than through a centralized location. The branch offices may be "loosely coupled" in a data communications network so that a customer may make use of a branch office that is not identified as his own branch office for certain transactions. The branch offices may also be interconnected to a supervisory office which periodically collects pertinent summary data from the branch offices for management purposes.

Since the transition from a on-line centralized data processing system to a fully decentralized system requires significant organizational and operational coordination and planning, we review the experience of one such financial institution making such a transition—Citibank N.A., in New York.

CITIBANK DECENTRALIZED DATA PROCESSING NETWORK. The Citibank decentralized data processing network is a reflection of the bank's decentralized management policy rather than any single network architecture philosophy. Each operational unit is responsible for its own activities, including all data processing operations associated with its operations. Since the management within that operational unit is most familiar with the data characteristics and processing requirements for its own activities, it therefore selects its own computer configuration most suited to its needs. Although such processing is done independently of central corporate management, financial control and management auditing and review is achieved by interacting with the computer system of the operational unit over a communications network.

The most important consequence of the decentralized management concept is the complete decentralization of the bank's data base, and the gradual downgrading of the centralized data base and computer processing facilities. The comparative efficiency of a single large-scale, multiprogrammed, multiprocessing computer system compared to a heterogeneous mix of smaller computers at remote locations was carefully considered before the bank committed itself to decentralized processing. Some of the key considerations in evaluating the comparative efficiency of centralized and decentralized should be noted.

First, the bank observed that, to be effective, large-scale, centralized data processing systems require a high level of operational knowledge of the business. The management of a large-scale data processing operation is practically a business in itself, and the experienced professionals in management of data processing operations generally do not have the business understanding to effectively design the computer configuration to satisfy the user's requirements.

Stated in other terms, the data processing managers of large data processing systems may be able to produce highly efficient computation, measured in terms of throughput, virtual memory, optimized compilers, and performance monitoring, but may not always be able to supply the specific information that is valuable to the bank's operation managers in an efficient fashion.

Of course, the experience of Citibank in evaluating the efficiency and effectiveness of its centralized data processing facility is not necessarily applicable to other organizations, or even other banks. Indeed, for many organizations the economics of scale and centralized management of a single large-scale data processing operation could possibly be more efficient than a distributed or decentralized data processing network. However, very large organizations (i.e., those using several large-scale computer systems) may well consider whether several smaller data processing operations may be managed more effectively, and provide more useful information to the end user, than a single large-scale, centralized data processing operation.

The second consideration of importance to Citibank concerns the logistics of system planning, development, and implementation. The planning and development of large-scale computer installations, or the upgrading of existing installations, required much longer lead times than was desirable. The bank was unable to rapidly respond to changing customer requirements, and found that when system designs were finally implemented, they were no longer suited to user requirements.

In short, large-scale computer systems require much longer planning, proposal, and delivery schedules than the rapidly changing banking business justified. Once such systems were installed, they were not flexible enough to adapt to changing market conditions and consumer preferences.

The third consideration in evaluating the comparative efficiency of centralized and decentralized data processing operations concerned the installation and facilities management of large-scale computer systems. The environmental requirements of back-up power, air conditioning, raised floors, and security devices all contribute to the complexity and decreased effective efficiency of centralized data processing operations.

The final consideration was the increased technical complexity of large-scale computer facilities. Business problems and user requirements were not simply translatable into the hardware/software capabilities of complex computer systems. The business managers did not speak the jargon of priority queues and partitions, and the systems analysts could not always relate such technical issues to the basic user needs.

The Citibank decentralized data processing network is implemented primarily with minicomputers of various manufacturers, including Digital Equipment Corporation (DEC), Interdata, Data General, and Hewlett-Packard. Over 50 such minicomputers were installed in 1975, and over 100 were installed in 1976.

Citibank's minicomputers operate in different corporate divisions, performing different applications, and are not intended to routinely communicate with each other. The heterogenous makeup of the network is a consequence of the decentralized management decision to implement a particular computer system which is most efficient and effective for its particular operation, regardless of the types of computers used by other divisions or operations. Compatibility is not necessary since the computers do not share a common data base, and information between divisions or operations is exchanged on a special request basis, rather than through an automatic procedure. Financial control and management review is achieved at present by magnetic tape output or a simple data communications transfer to another processing facility.

One example of such a system is the letter-of-credit channel. Four CRT terminals are used as input devices, while the processor supervises the issuance, amendment, and payment of commercial letters of credit. The processor maintains its own database of letters of credit outstanding, and hands off on magnetic tape the pertinent information for the customer accounting system, and the loan liability system for account and loan liability updating.

Another example is the Lockbox Automation System, which utilizes an Intel 8080 microprocessor controlling a display and a Burroughs Check Encoder. The Lockbox system captures the customer check information and amount at the same time that the check is being encoded, and updates the customer files by a magnetic tape handoff to the customer accounting system.

Both of these systems are implemented on a DEC PDP 11/70 configured with two tape drives, three 88 megabyte disk drives, and two 300-line/minute printers. Operators interface with the system through some 64 communications ports and 60 terminals.

Other on-line applications at Citibank include:

Foreign bank accounts
Foreign exchange processing
Commercial loan data entry
Domestic money transfer
International money transfer
Federal Reserve Bank interface automation
Automated loan processing
Clearing House interface automation
Corporate accounting and information

The decentralized data processing applications described above will eventually be tied together through a data communications network, thereby automating the financial control and management review functions now performed by the physical transport of magnetic tape financial summary listings. Such a network would use a general line control procedure so that machines from different manufacturers in the network would be able to communicate with each other.

Another application of such a data communications network would be for direct customer communications with the bank. Large corporate customers would have a terminal for entering transactional information into the network. The network will connect to a Transaction Processing Computer which will handle the transaction and perform the routine accounting and general advice function. Finally, account and MIS data will be sent to the head office for generating internal reports.

Electronic Funds Transfer

Electronic Funds Transfer (EFT) refers to the concept of a checkless, cashless transaction mechanism by which funds are transferred automatically by electronic means. EFT is an extremely controversial and complex issue in data communications, and it would be worthwhile to consider some of the issues in greater detail. The following basic issues are considered in the sections below:

EFT background
Economic issues
User concerns
Regulatory and consumer interests

EFT BACKGROUND. There are many different types of EFT systems, depending on the application and environment. These include:

1. Preauthorized banking services, which provide for the automatic deposit of a payroll or Social Security funds in a designated account, or the automatic debiting of mortgage or loan payments from a designated account.
2. Customer-directed payment systems, which enable a bank customer to utilize a telephone or EFT terminal to direct the bank to pay funds to a designated account.
3. Point-of-sale systems, which use a terminal on the premises of a merchant that enables the customer to authorize payment from his account to the merchant's.

One could also include as EFT systems the following:

4. Credit verification/authorization systems, which enable a merchant to check the credit of a customer by automatic query of a centralized bank or credit card company computer.
5. Automated banking facilities, such as automatic cash or travelers'-check dispensers, providing 24-hour service to the customer.

EFT must be considered as an evolutionary step in society's payment media. As technology changes, and as the nature and cost of transaction processing change, there has been an increased interest among large-scale transaction-processing organizations, such as the government and financial institutions, to use the new technology to improve the transaction processing mechanism. Some of the early experiments in EFT were also carried out by smaller financial institutions such as the Hempstead Bank on Long Island, New York and the First Federal Savings and Loan Association of Lincoln, Nebraska in the early 1970s.

ECONOMIC ISSUES.   The basic impetus to EFT is an economic one. Present-day transaction media consist of cash, checks, and credit cards. The costs associated with such media are very high:

Currency ($71 billion in circulation)—an annual cost of over $4 billion for printing, security, and so forth
Checks (32 billion clearing annually)—an annual cost of over $7 billion in processing
Credit cards (over 6.5 billion transactions, involving $85 billion)—an annual cost of $3.9 billion

The total cost of all funds transfer is over $22 billion for handling some 325 billion transactions annually (i.e., a cost of over 6 cents per transaction). Such costs are expended for personnel, document processing equipment, losses from forgery or fraud, security and protection, and so on.

It is difficult to compare the cost of electronic funds transaction systems with present-day systems: there are simply too many variables that affect the cost an order of magnitude or more. However, with standardization, widespread market acceptance, and high volume use, EFT costs measured over suitable periods (e.g., 10 years) can be very attractive.

In the short term, however, EFT offers a number of distinct features:

1. Simplicity of establishing new EFT outlets or terminals
2. Increases merchant competitiveness by offering consumers a new, more convenient payment technique
3. Minimizes merchant handling costs and credit losses
4. The increasingly lower cost of processing technology (microprocessors and related components).

USER CONCERNS.   One of the major problems in EFT is the competitive implications of such systems and the attendant user concerns. We can identify two major competitive areas:

1. Competition between financial institutions
2. Competition between financial institutions and merchants

EFT systems are a high-risk, high-capital-investment item. Large financial institutions are in a much better position to enter the field and experiment with EFT systems than small ones. Furthermore, EFT systems are highly visible to the customer, and the intense competition for the retail depositers makes the availability of EFT systems an important competitive factor. EFT complicates the competitive balance between different financial institutions: large versus small institutions, urban versus rural and suburban institutions, and commercial banks versus savings banks and other depository institutions.

EFT systems open up a new prospect of competition between financial institutions and merchants. As in many other interdisciplinary and interindustry activities, the basic question is: Where does the "banking" function end, and the "retailing" function begin? Associated with one industry or the other are unique regulatory, labor, and legal interests and customs which cannot be assumed by the other.

In addition to competitive issues, EFT raises significant technical and administrative issues which must be answered:

Equipment compatibility
Code and protocol standardization
Security and system integrity
Compatibility with related systems (e.g., UPC)
Ownership of systems
Supervision and control of systems

REGULATORY ISSUES. The regulatory and legal issues may not be the most significant, but they are clearly issues that must be settled before EFT systems can be implemented.

There are many forms of regulation that relate to EFT, ranging from state and Federal regulation of banks and the legal infrastructure of commerce such as the Uniform Commercial Code (UCC), to consumer law. Fundamental changes must take place in all these areas before total implementation of EFT can be possible.

The National Conference of Commissioners on Uniform State Laws is moving forward in one area—automated stock transfers—by amending the relevant statutes to allow corporations to establish and maintain stock ownership data by computerized records rather than the issuance of engraved certificates.

Already, new mutual funds—for example, cash management and municipal bond funds—do not routinely issue certificates, but instead send their shareholders a monthly or quarterly statement of their shareholdings. Such recordkeeping particularly simplifies automatic dividend reinvestment procedures.

There are of course some who oppose such automated reform. The cost of manual stock transfer is high—several dollars per transfer—and such costs mean significant revenues for banks or stock transfer companies. New regulations may also impose periodic shareholder notification requirements that may be burdensome on companies with many small shareholders or infrequently traded securities.

Discussion of consumer law aspects of EFT is also important. Some of these issues are:

1. Recordkeeping and account information: when is written documentation to be supplied to the user concerning an EFT transaction, and what minimum information should be contained therein?

2. Error control: what means should be established to correct for errors, or provide recourse similar to a stop payment order? What effect does EFT have on well-established legal doctrines such as the "holder in due course" (UCC 3-305), which provides that the holder in due course of an instrument (such as a check or its EFT equivalent) takes the instrument free from all claims to it on the part of any person?

3. Standardization: does EFT require standardization of technology, coding, use, and disclosure, and what degree of regulation is appropriate or sufficient?

INSURANCE

Insurance applications of data communications networks are quite different from banking and financial applications. Such applications are concerned with the preparation and processing of individual insurance policies at agency locations throughout the country. It must be emphasized that, unlike banking transactions, the preparation of insurance policies are tailored to the individual background and requirements of the customer. The data communications network could be used to implement an on-site preparation of insurance policies at remote agency locations by interacting with the centralized files at the host computer location.

In the implementation so described, the independent or company agent enters the required customer information on a terminal in his local office. The centralized host computer processes the application by examining claims history and other characteristics, and calculates the premium. The actual policy itself may be printed out on an on-line printer associated with the terminal, so that copies of the policy are supplied to both the agent and the customer for signature on the spot. Meanwhile, the host computer establishes a billing cycle for the customer, and credits the local agent with the sale. Renewal notices are also generated automatically.

RETAILING

Retailing is one of the most significant applications for data communications networks and specialized terminals. The data generated by department stores and mass merchandisers in the ordering, handling, inventorying, and selling of goods is extremely important for the efficient management of transactions involving vast quantities of assorted merchandise. More importantly, the analysis and interpretation of such data enables managers to react even more quickly to consumers' demand patterns.

One typical retailing data processing system is the IBM 3650. The individual components of 3650 system include:

IBM 3651 store controller, which controls all other devices in a store network and communicates directly with an IBM System/370 host computer

IBM 3653 point-of-sale terminal, which includes a sales-slip printer, customer and operator guidance displays, a data entry keyboard, and an optional "wand" for reading magnetically encoded data

IBM 3657 ticket unit, which prints, encodes, and reads information from price tags

IBM 3275 display station and 3284 printer which attaches to the 3651 store controller, for administrative message handling or special customer services

By integrating both purchasing and selling activities into a single communications loop, a distributed processing network for a retailing operation makes possible a more coordinated, efficient flow of merchandise through the firm. A narrative review of how such a system would be implemented in a retailing environment is worthwhile discussing here. A more detailed discussion of a "management information system" will be postponed to the section on manufacturing applications, although it must be realized that a management information system could also be implemented in the retailing industry.

The first step of the retailing cycle processed by the system is the buyer's original purchase order, which may be entered at a distribution center, store, or administrative headquarters through the 3275 terminal, for example. The record of the purchase order is entered into the host computer storage, and the original copy is printed out at the 3284 printer for mailing to the vendor.

When the shipment arrives at the receiving dock, the foreman utilizes the 3275 terminal to access the host computer storage. The purchase order is then displayed on his screen, enabling him to check it against the shipper's bill of lading. If the merchandise is in order, he accepts it by making appropriate entries on the 3275 terminal. The use of a remote terminal or distributed processor for such functions is often called a "point-of-purchase" system.

The host computer updates the outstanding purchase order file, updates the appropriate inventory file, records the amount due the vendor on the accounts payable record, and alerts the ticketing file that price tickets should be prepared for the received merchandise.

When the merchandise is received at the ticketing station, the 3657 ticket unit prints out the appropriate price tag, which also indicates merchandise class, size, color, or model for inventory control purposes.

The final step of the retailing cycle is the "point-of-sale," at which the customer brings the merchandise to the cashier. Data from the price tag is either entered manually on the keyboard of the 3653, or read by the optional wand. The inventory control file is updated, and the printer produces a receipt and journal tape for auditing purposes. Special services, such as credit sales, back-ordering of a particular size or color, and similar requests may also be implemented through the system.

Another important application of a distributed processing network is the airline reservation and ticketing system. Although such networks may be built around a large host computer, it should also be noted that they can be built around minicomputer networks. The AEROFLOT network is such an example.

The AEROFLOT network, installed by the Compagnie Generale de Construction Telephonique (C.G.C.T.) is based on 23 DS6-400 hardware/software modules built around the SPC-16/85 General Automation minicomputer. The network includes five major switching centers in Moscow, Rostov, Novosibersk, Alma-Ata, and Sverdlovsk. In addition to message switching, the centers also handle real-time file interrogation and data base management. The centers are expected to handle some 4 million messages, or about 1 billion characters, every day. Each of the processing modules is designed to handle at least eight messages per second.

GOVERNMENT

Government applications of data communications networks has been briefly discussed in Chapter 1 in terms of the general administrative and operational functions of government that may be assisted by information-handling facilities. In this section a specific operational function will be discussed in greater detail: the function of patent searching as part of the statutory responsibility of the government in granting an inventor a patent.

Patent Searching

Patent searching is the process of examining a patent application for novelty and unobviousness in view of previously published "prior art," such as previously issued patents. The patent searcher or examiner analyzes the application to determine the particular classifications of technology the application is related to, and physically "searches" the Patent Office files in those classifications for similar or related patents and other publications.

The process of patent searching is a good example of the potential application of distributed processing computer technology to an important government function. The U.S. Patent Office processes more than 100,000 patent applications per year, and the searching process is a time-consuming, manual task which limits the effectiveness and efficiency of patent examination.

The first step to a distributed processing patent searching system was taken in 1975 with the introduction of a high-speed computer controlled microform search system (CCMSS).

The CCMSS is not a true on-line system, but demonstrates the capabilities of such a system in the user environment. Every issued patent and many important publications are classified into one or more technological classes or subclasses. In performing a search, the searcher considers the various classes that the application is related to, and searches both classes. If the invention is concerned with both classes of technology, the searcher must still search both individual classes.

The distributed processing capability of the CCMSS enables at least some portion of the searching process to be performed more efficiently through the use of logical operators which may be specified during the search. By "logical operator" we mean a function such as AND or OR applied to two or more classes. If the searcher only wishes to examine those references in classes 250 and 283, for example, which are classified in both class 250 *and* class 283, he may enter the search command "250 AND 283" on the terminal console. The system then performs the logical AND operation on all elements of classes 250 and 283, and stores the reference numbers of those which are common to both classes. The searcher may then enter a DISPLAY function on the console, and sequentially examine each of the references.

U.S. PATENT OFFICE CLASSIFICATION SYSTEM: DIGITAL DATA PROCESSING SYSTEMS

I. APPLICATIONS
  1. Control systems
    adaptive
    models/simulations
    learning/training
    sampled data or signal
     processing
    multiplexing/Time-Sharing
    multiple mode
    testing/monitoring
    signal function generator
  2. Process control
  3. Machine control
  4. Environment
  5. Communications/data
    transmission
    telephone
  6. Traffic/vehicular
  7. Security
  8. Material/article handling
    systems
    conveyor systems
    dispensing systems
  9. File maintenance
    inquiry/deletion/updating
    sort/merge
 10. Scientific
    aerospace
    astronomy
    biology
    chemistry
     spectroscopy
    civil engineering

 10. Scientific *(continued)*
    electrical engineering
    earth sciences
     seismology
    mathematics
     statistics
     data analysis
     other
    mechanical engineering
    medical
     patient monitoring
    physics
     optics
     nuclear
     other
 11. Business
    accounting
    banking
    document analysis
    document retrieval
     film
    document or display
     preparation
     justification/hyphenation
     editing
     typesetting
     photocomposing
     other
    education
    inventory control
    language translation
    law enforcement
    libraries

11. Business (*continued*)
    manufacturing/industry
    public utilities
       Electric power companies
    reservation
    sports/amusement
    stock market
    other
12. Other

II. MULTIPROCESSOR SYSTEMS
  1. Different internal structure
    (heterogeneous)
  2. Shared memory
  3. Virtual processors
  4. Plural CPs (redundant)
  5. CPU + terminal processor
  6. CP + interface processor
  7. Processor interconnection
    direct
    parallel (common bus)
    loop
    reconfigurable
    other
  8. Multiprocessor Control
    priority assignment
    interrupt handling
    task assignment
    supervisory (master/slave)
    other
  9. Other

III. COMPUTER/DATA PROCESSOR
  1. Mini
    desk
    hand-held
    other
  2. Timeshared
    peripheral devices
    plural programs
    other
  3. Pipelined
  4. Parallel array
  5. Orthogonal
  6. Virtual
  7. Adaptive
  8. Simulator/emulator
  9. Hybrid (A-D)
  10. Electro-optical
  11. Magnetic bubble
  12. Modular
  13. Integrated circuit
  14. Multiple-mode

15. Parallel (common. bus.)
16. Other

IV. INPUT/OUTPUT DEVICES
  1. Keyboard/switch
    data
    function
    program select
    other
  2. Printer
    bar
    chain/belt
    disc/drum
    matrix/dot
    single character
    multiple character
    other
  3. Typewriter
  4. Drum storage
  5. Disc storage
  6. Tape
    magnetic
    paper
    cartridge/cassette
    other
  7. Card reader/punch
  8. Pen/pointer
  9. Display
    Cathode ray tube
    lights
    other
  10. Character recognizer
  11. Plotter
  12. Analog
  13. Other

V. INTERFACING OF PROCESSOR-
PERIPHERALS
  1. Multiplexed
  2. Central switch
  3. I/O interface switch
  4. I/O controller
  5. Memory controller
  6. Line adaptor/modem
  7. Buffer structure
    shift register
    recirculating
    other
  8. Buffer functions
    rate control
    serial/parallel conversion
    formatting
    program data control

8. Buffer functions (*continued*)
   alternating load/unload
   status checks
   I/O device
   other
9. Other

VI. PROCESSOR-PERIPHERAL
    COMMUNICATION TECHNOLOGY
    1. Direct polling
    2. Loop polling
    3. Priority interrupt
       fixed
       variable
       multilevel
       other
    4. Time continuous interface
    5. Conditional/mode interface
    6. Queued/tabled interface
    7. Direct access
    8. Real time
    9. Other

VII. STORAGE MANAGEMENT
    1. Plural memory configurations
       plural main memories
       main memory and external
        bulk memory
       data and program
       fast and slow
       main memory and I/O local
       multiplex access
       other
    2. Single memory configurations
       compound types
       logic-in-memory
       Queue/Stack
       recirculating
       shifting
       ROM/microprogram
       other
    3. Storage reconfiguration
       variable length
       relocatable
       defective storage substitution
       other
    4. Storage dedication
       I/O devices
       processors
       users
       other

5. Storage assignment
   resolution between mems.
   resolution within single mem.
   mapped/part.
   interleaved
   other
6. Storage protection
   boundary address
   locked/unlocked
   other
7. Other

VIII. STORAGE ELEMENTS (SPECIFIC)
    1. Drum
    2. Disc
    3. Tape
    4. Core
    5. Thin film
    6. Bubble
    7. Delay line
    8. CRT storage tube
    9. Cryogenic
    10. Semiconductor
        Charge coupled
        Integrated circuit
        Other
    11. Optical
        hologram
        other
    12. Capacitive
    13. Other

IX. STORAGE ACCESSING
    1. Sequential
       unit increase/decrease
       nonunit increase/decrease
       counter control
       timer control
       chained
       tree structure
       other
    2. Random
       shortest distance
       other
    3. Key/partial
       key
       masking
       Word Byte/Field
       Other

4. Associative
    matching data
    user
    other
5. Group
    multiple instructions/words
    multiple locations/access
    block/page
    chip/module
    queue/stack
    linked
    other
6. Multiple mode
7. Variable length
8. Substituted
9. Address modification
    indexing
    prefixing
    bit insertion
    base + seg./tag + set
    table lookup
    other
10. Complementary
    digit
    other
11. Virtual
    table lookup
    converted
    other
12. Other
X. OPERATIONAL CONTROL
    1. Arithmetical
        add/subtract
        multiply
        divide
        other
    2. Logical
        and/or/other
        compare
        sense
        special character detect
        shift
        masking
        other
    3. Data transfer
        external
        internal
        other
    4. Transform
        invert

4. Transform (*continued*)
    compress/expand
    pack/unpack
    set/reset
    other
5. Modify
    command
    other part
6. Branching
    unconditional
    conditional
    trap
    look ahead
    timed
    other
7. Repeating
    interated function
    error detection
    other
8. Instruction sequences
    chaining/linking
    fixed (hardwired)
    macro instructions
    micro instructions
    other
9. Execution overlap
10. Lookahead (prefetch)
11. Interrupt (internal)
12. Other
XI. PERFORMANCE MONITORING
    1. Anticipated
        internal
        external
        simulated
        statistical
        with control response
        busy/idle/on-off-line
        other
    2. Error detection
        data transmission
        data encode/decode
        storage/addressing
        arithmetic/logic
        input/output
        executive sequence control
        monitor/error circulation of
            synch error
        intermittent/transient errors
        parity/validity

2. Error detection (*continued*)
   comparison with expected
     result
   with automatic recovery
   other
3. Diagnosis/tracking routine
   schedule/performance
   real time
   with repeated operation
   program control
   operator control
   hardware control
   with fault isolation
   other
4. Alternate/backup
   concurrent
   periodic
   redundant elements
     arithmetic/logic
     memory/sectors
     input/output
     channels
     other
   synchronous system/elements
     with majority vote
     with element substitution
     other
5. Other

XII. TIMING (PROCESSOR)
   1. Interval generator
      fixed
      variable
      multiple
      other
   2. Asynchronous time control
      between processor & I/O
      between processors
      within processor
      other
   3. Synchronous control
      external device
      plural processors
      plural programs
      other
   4. Time delay
   5. Cycle control
      cycle stealing
      other
   6. Other
XIII. POWER
   1. Sequenced
   2. Reduction
   3. On demand
   4. Partial
   5. Failure
   6. Other

HEALTH CARE

The application of distributed processing and data communications networks to health care delivery systems is expected to be a much more significant use of data processing technology than the suggested "remote medical literature searching," "remote medical diagnosis," and "electrocardiogram analysis" projected for 1990 considered in Chapter 1. Although ideally the world of 1990 should be able to allocate more of its resources to medical research than the present, it is very doubtful that such resources be extensively applied to medical literature searching as opposed to basic or clinical research.

The application of distributed processing to hospital and medical services is similar to other "delivery systems," in which billing for a wide variety of services is generated, with specific items being prorated for third-party billing. Furthermore, extensive documentation and reporting to federal and local agencies must be supported.

Remote Medical Diagnosis

The prospect of remote medical diagnosis through the use of data communications facilities is significant where diagnosis can be performed at a location remote from the patient. One actual example of remote medical diagnosis and data processing is the use of computed tomography x-ray equipment at different locations connected by a data link.

A computed tomography (CT) scanner is an x-ray device that records several projected views through a patient's cross-section, and then mathematically "reconstructs" the cross-sectional image on a television screen using a computer. Typical cross-sectional images which are obtained of the head and torso are shown in Figure 8.2.

CT scanners are particularly suited for implementing remote diagnosis because of the high cost of the equipment, the distinct types of operations needed to be performed by the equipment, and the digital nature of the processing itself. As a high-cost item (costing upwards of $500,000), not all hospitals would be justified in acquiring such equipment based on their potential patient load. However, because of the modular nature of the equipment, several hospitals over a given region may have sufficient patient load to justify a "distributed" arrangement of CT scanning gantries, connected by data links to a centralized processing facility. The processing facility does the mathematical reconstruction of the image, copies are made for the referring physician or hospital, and more detailed analysis and diagnosis can be made at the remote location.

MANUFACTURING

The application of distributed processing and data communications in the manufacturing environment is similar to that in the retailing industry; however, the different data inputs and processing variables presents a more sophisticated processing task.

One simple application has been to link sales offices with manufacturing plants through the use of intelligent terminals and a data communications network. The salesmen can immediately inquire about the production schedule of the particular unit ordered, so that the customer knows exactly when he can expect to receive the goods.

The salesmen can also use the terminal and network to his advantage to provide special customer services. If, for example, another model of the desired product is available from a different manufactur-

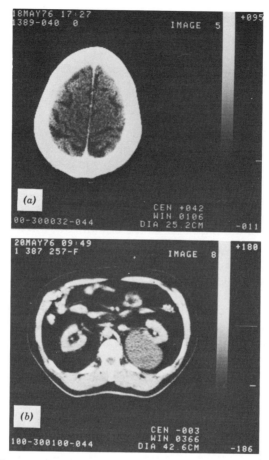

FIGURE 8.2.   Cross-sectional images obtained by CT scanner of (a) the head and (b) the torso.

ing plant, or is available from stock at a different location, the salesman would be able to so advise his customer.

When the goods are ordered, the transaction is entered through the terminal, thereby generating a customer invoice within 24 hours. The system deletes the goods ordered from the master inventory file and credits the salesman with the order.

There are a wide variety of intelligent terminals that can be used in a data communications network in the manufacturing environment. The IBM 3770 Data Communication System is just one example of a family of operator-oriented remote terminals which connect with a

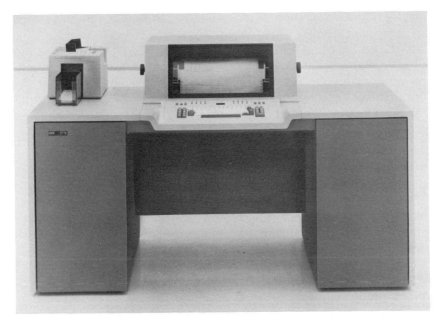

FIGURE 8.3. IBM 3776 communication terminal. (Photograph courtesy IBM Corp.)

host computer. The IBM 3770 family includes various types of terminals with different keyboard, printer, and on-line storage combinations. Figure 8.3 illustrates one such terminal, the IBM 3776 Communication Terminal.

These intelligent terminals are connected to the host computer through a communications processor, such as the 3704 or 3705 in the case of the IBM 3770 system. The host computer maintains the master inventory file, as well as records of the individual salemen orders.

Another more sophisticated application of distributed processing is in a management information system (MIS). The MIS is the most detailed and comprehensive data processing system that could be implemented in a manufacturing industry. As the name implies, an MIS is concerned with *information* that can be presented to management on demand.

MIS should not be confused with a management decision system. A management decision system is one that takes given information and performs specific decision-making algorithms on that information to derive characteristics or parameters concerning such information that is useful for management decision-making. A simple example of management decision-making algorithms in the area of financial analysis is the calculation of discounted cash flow (DCF) and return on investment (ROI).

A MIS, on the other hand, is directed at the initial task of providing the user—a designated manager—with certain up-to-date information on demand. Once that information is displayed to the user, he may then call decision-making subroutines which will operate on that data. The essential point is the obtaining of information, not the processing of it.

TELEPHONY

Telephony may not seem at first to be a particularly significant application of data communications until two specific applications are considered:

• The use of the public telephone network for the transmission of digital information
• The gradual conversion of certain analog facilities of the public telephone network to digital facilities

Data communication presently accounts for about 15% of the public telephone network. The public telephone network, being an analog system, was never really designed for digital communications, and the demand for such services has not been fully met to complete satisfaction. However, the growth of specialized common carriers catering to data communications users has been a difficult one, and there is still no clear indication that such alternative carriers will be viable over the long run. Some estimates project the data communication usage of the public telephone network at about 30% by 1980. It must be pointed out, however, that projections of usage for specialized communication services have always been overly optimistic, both inside and outside of the Bell System and other carriers. In any event, the public telephone network is and will continue to be the most important transmission medium for data communications.

The second aspect of digital communications is the conversion of the analog facilities of the telephone network into digital facilities. The use of digital facilities for voice transmission is economic for long-haul transmission; and as the volume of such intertoll communication increases, more and more digital facilities will be implemented.

The significance of the conversion to digital facilities is that data performance is greatly enhanced through digital facilities compared with analog facilities. Analog facilities are susceptible to a variety of impairments such as amplitude and delay distortion and phase jitter that significantly affect the error rate.

The introduction of the ESS No. 4 (Electronic Switching System) in 1976 was a major step forward in the implementation of digital facilities in the common carrier telephone network in the United States. ESS No. 4, shown in Figure 8.4, is a *digital* switching system as opposed to previous analog systems. ESS No. 4 is able to handle

FIGURE 8.4. ESS No. 4. (Photograph courtesy American Telephone and Telegraph Co.)

550,000 calls per hour, also significantly more than the previous analog systems. The switching element is only one part of the telephone network, and the implementation of digital carriers is equally as important.

The Bell System in the United States already utilizes a digital short-haul carrier known as T1. The T1 system utilizes pulse code modulation (PCM). Each voice frequency channel is sampled 8000 times per second, and converted into a seven-bit PCM word (7-bit quantization). An eighth bit is added for signaling information. Twenty-four of such voice frequency channels are combined into a single time-division multiplexed frame of 193 pulse slots or bits. The 193rd bit, as shown in the representation of a single frame in Figure 8.5, is used for framing information. With a frame rate of 8000/second, the total bit rate of the carrier is 1.544 Mb/second (megabits per second).

The T1 carrier is only the first of a hierarchy of digital transmission systems shown in Figure 8.6. As shown, four T1 carriers are multiplexed through the M12 multiplier to form one T2 carrier, which operates at 6.312 Mb/second, and carries 96 voice frequency channels. Similar multiplexing is performed to form the T3 and T4 levels.

PABX

The PABX (private automated branch exchange) equipment industry gained importance in the United States after 1968, when the FCC ruled that private companies may connect their own terminal equipment to the exchange network. Although PABX systems are principally used for telephony, many PABX utilize digital encoding and

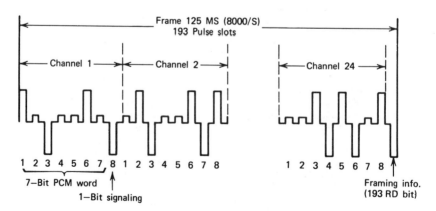

FIGURE 8.5. T1 PCM frame.

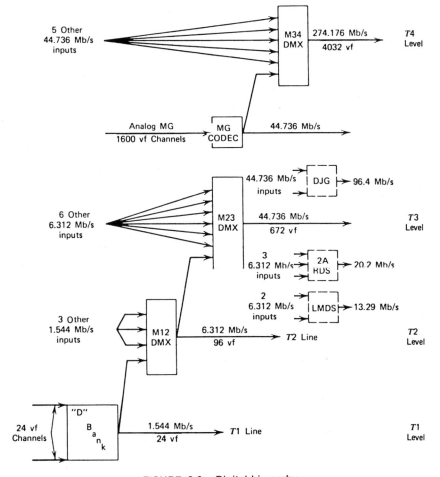

FIGURE 8.6. Digital hierarchy.

switching, and could be used for data switching as well. In the next section we will consider one very important PABX system which is intended not only for telephony but for data communications switching.

PABX systems may be analyzed and classified according to a number of distinct characteristics:

- Type of service
- Type of control

- Technology
- Type of switching cross-point
- Number of station lines
- Number of trunk lines

The type of service refers to the operational characteristics and features of the PABX system, such as direct inward dialing, identified outward dialing, conference calling features, and other specialized services.

The type of control refers to the use of relay logic, solid-state wired logic, or solid-state stored program control for performing the common control function of the PABX system. The type of technology refers to the type or level of technology used in the common control unit: electromechanical, or electronic (discrete circuits, integrated circuits, large-scale integrated circuits/microprocessors). The common control system may also be designed as either a time- or space-division multiplex system.

The type of switching cross-point refers to the use of crossbar, reed, or solid-state switches for making the switched connection between lines.

The number of station lines refers to the number of extensions, while the number of trunk lines refers to the number of external lines or "trunks." Some of the features that are important in analyzing such characteristics of PABX systems include trunk-trunk connection capabilities and TDM-trunk connections.

IBM 3750

The IBM 3750 is an integrated network for voice and data communication switching presently being marketed in several European countries. The 3750, successor to the earlier 2750, was developed and manufactured in France, and announced in 1972.

The 3750 was primarily designed to offer a range of data communications capabilities operating either as a stand-alone unit or linked to a computer system for performing more advanced functions. Push-button telephone can be used for data collection and inquiry purpose, as well as standard telephone voice communication facilities of a conventional PABX. The IBM 3750 is configured with up to 2264 station lines and 192 trunk lines.

The voice communication features of the 3750 include facilities for three-party conference calls, access at each extension to a paging

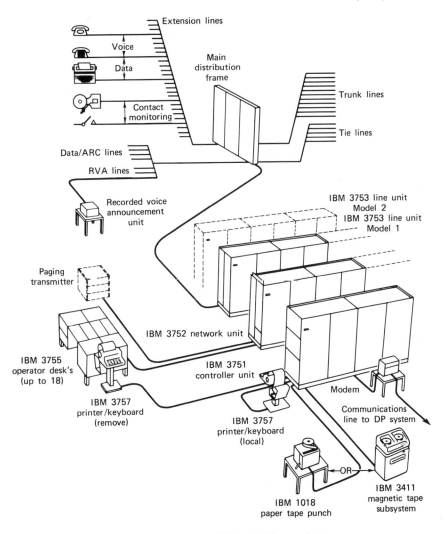

FIGURE 8.7. IBM 3750 switching system.

system, and direct inward dialing to extensions from the public network without operator intervention. Additionally, users can dial three-digit codes for frequently used outside telephone numbers rather than the number in full.

The system can automatically record the particulars of outgoing calls made from each extension, including the number called, caller's extension, call duration, and cost information. The system can also provide an analysis of traffic density on both trunk and internal extension lines to assist in efficient administration of the network.

For data collection, the 3750 can assemble, check, and identify each input message and store this information on its disk. This information can be transferred directly to a computer via a telephone line, or via punched paper tape. When the IBM 3750 is connected to the computer via communications lines, push-button telephones can be used, for example, as inquiry terminals with audio response.

Via contact sensing and operating lines, the system can monitor the condition of devices such as alarms, or the open-or-closed status of doors or valves.

The basic IBM 3750 configuration consists of an IBM 3751 control unit, IBM 3752 network and IBM 3753 line units, from 2 to 18 IBM 3755 operator desks, and an IBM 3557 keyboard-printer unit for system control. The control and switching hardware is all-electronic and incorporates solid-state monolithic technology.

The switching function and other related operations such as scanning, path marking, and signal distribution are handled by the duplexed controller. It operates under stored program control. In addition to controlling the basic switching operations, these programs control supervisory, traffic analysis, and diagnostic functions. Diagnostic routines monitor the system's own logic, automatically signaling any malfunction that might occur.

FIGURE 8.8. IBM 3750 switching system. (Photograph courtesy IBM World Trade Corp.)

The switching system stored program for the 3750 is generated by IBM from a master program to meet the specific requirements of each individual user. Routine changes in program-controlled functions are handled by the customer. For example, the reassignment of telephone extensions can be made rapidly by updating tables in the machine memory rather than through hardware or program modifica-

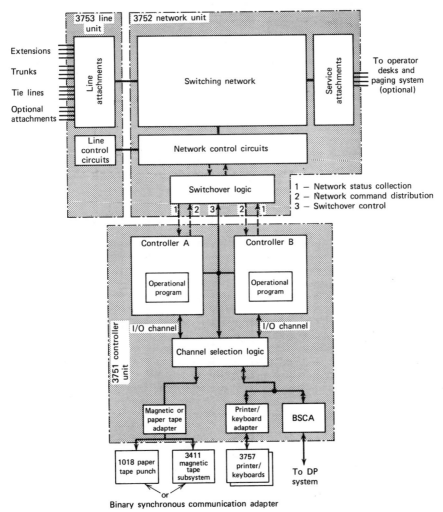

FIGURE 8.9.   IBM 3750: functional organization. (Reprinted courtesy IBM World Trade Corp.)

Codes for Voice Functions

Code Name	Code Type[a]	Function	Used for
Call to 3750 Operator	P	Connects extension to any free 3750 telephone operator	Calls to operator
DOD	P	Connects extension to public switched network	Direct outward dialing (DOD)
Personal DOD	P	Connects extension to public switched network, and instructs the 3750 to record call duration for charging as personal call	Direct outward dialing (DOD)
Selective DOD	P	Connects extension to a specified exchange on the public switched network	Direct outward dialing (DOD)
Public exchange operator recall	S	Connects extension to public switched network operator	External calls
Tie-line access	P	Connects extension to a remote 3750 or other switching system via a tie line	Tie-line calls
Inquiry to extension	S	Holds a call while inquiry is made to another extension and, if required, transfers the call to the other extension	Hold, shuttle, transfer
Inquiry to 3750 operator	S	Holds the call while inquiry is made to a 3750 telephone operator and, if required, transfers the call to the operator	Hold and transfer to operator
Return	S	Enables an extension user to return to held party after making an inquiry to an extension or to the telephone operator. Also enables an extension to shuttle between two parties after making an inquiry or accepting a camp-on request	Hold and shuttle calls

248

			Camp-on
Accept	S	Enables extension to accept a camp-on request	
	S	Enables extension to accept a stacked call	Stacking
	S	Enables extension to accept an external call transferred from another extension	Transfer
Camp-on request	S	Signals a busy extension that another extension is waiting on the line, and connects both extensions when the busy extension either dials the accept code or hangs up	Camp-on, shuttle call
Protection	S	Prevents intrusion into a confidential conversation. Same code as used for data protection	Protection
Intrusion	S	Enables extension to break into established call	Intrusion
Short-code dialing	P	Enables associated extensions to call each other	
	S	Initiates inquiry and transfer with one digit	
Bar extension	P	Causes all incoming calls to be diverted to an associated extension (for example, the secretary's)	Manager/secretary call assistance
Free extension	P	Terminates diversion mode established by the bar extension code	
Reclaim	P	Reclaims a rerouted call	Call assistance

FIGURE 8.10. IBM 3750: dialing codes. (Reprinted courtesy IBM World Trade Corp.)

Codes for Voice Functions *(contd.)*

Code Name	Code Type[a]	Function	Used for
Store external number	S	Stores in the 3750 an external number that is busy, answers, or does not answer, allowing later recall by the repeat external number code	External number repetition
Repeat external number	P	Causes the 3750 to pulse out an external number that has been stored by the store external number code	
Add-on third party	S	Introduces a third party into a call established between two other parties	Add-on third party
Paging request	S	Enables extension to set paging device into action	Dialed paging
Paging answer	P	Connects paged party to caller	
Abbreviated dialing	P	Enables an extension to call selected external numbers by dialing only three digits	External abbreviated dialing
Night service answer	P	Enables extensions to accept incoming calls when the 3750 is in Special-Night-Service Type-2 status	Special night service type 2

Codes for Data Functions

Protection	S	Prevents intrusion while data is being transmitted from an extension equipped with talk/data switch	Data transmission

	Code	Description	
Data collection	P	Enables data to be sent from an MF terminal through an extension line for storage on the disk file. The code can have up to 30 different values, each corresponding to a different message format (four values only in basic data collection)	Data collection
Autoconnection request	P	Connects local serial terminal to the DP system via data line	Auto-connection
Autoconnection end	P	Terminates link between local serial data terminal and the DP system	
Teleconnection request	P	Establishes transmission link between two internal data terminals associated with extensions	Tele-connection
Teleconnection end	P	Disconnects data transmission link	

Codes for Contact Monitoring Functions

	Code	Description	
Contact sensing	P	Checks whether a contact is open or closed	Contact sensing
Contact operating	S	Changes the status (open or closed) of a contact	Contact operating

FIGURE 8.10. (*contd.*)

ᵃP: prefix; S: suffix.

tions. Only major changes—such as the addition of new features —require the preparation of new switching system stored programs or the installation of additional hardware. This is archived with little or no system interruption.

Figure 8.7 is a schematic of the basic IBM 3750 configuration, shown in the photograph in Figure 8.8.

The functional organization of the system is shown in Figure 8.9. Some of the services performed by the 3750 are represented by specific dialing codes which are tabulated in Figure 8.10.

The operators of the 3750, shown at a cluster of 3755 operator desks in Figure 8.11, handle all connection and call supervision procedures that are not carried out automatically on the 3750. These functions include:

- Connecting incoming calls from the public switched network to extensions
- Making connections between extensions and tie-lines
- Performing supervisory functions

FIGURE 8.11. IBM 3750: operator desks. (Photograph courtesy IBM World Trade Corp.)

FIGURE 8.12.   IBM 3221: numeric multifunction device. (Photograph courtesy IBM World Trade Corp.)

Another important terminal for use with the 3750 is the 3221 Numeric multifunction device, shown in Figure 8.12. The 3221 has been designed as a low-activity data collection and inquiry device, and contains a voice data switch which enables alternate use of the extension line for either data or voice communications. The 3221 contains a keyboard of 16 punch buttons, a reader, a speaker, and an amplifier for audio response.

appendix one
TECHNOLOGY FORECASTING AND ASSESSMENT

A data communications system is a long-term undertaking that requires significant capital investment and operational expense. The rapid pace of technologic change in the computer and communications industries has therefore created an increased interest in the long-range forecasting, planning, and assessment of such systems. Appendix One develops the basic concepts of technology forecasting and assessment that are applicable to the planning of data communications systems. To this end, the following subjects are discussed:

Decision-making process
Objectives of technology forecasting
Sources of technology forecasting
Applications of technology forecasting
Methodologies of technology forecasting
Technology assessment

DECISION-MAKING PROCESS

In the last few years there has been an increased interest in technology policy making and the decision-making process both in government and in industry. With technology making an important impact on personal life styles, and having long-range social and environmental consequences, much of this interest and attention is being focused on technology forecasting and assessment.

Ideally, technology forecasting and assessment should be an important step in the corporate or government decision-making process. In reality, the decision makers are often more responsive to the political and legal clout of the proponents of a particular technology forecast and assessment than the substance of the forecasts or assessments themselves. With this more realistic perspective in mind, we can go on to define technology forecasting and place it within an admittedly idealized decision-making process.

A technology forecast is a presentation of possible new and useful machines, processes, or materials, or improvements of the same, for assessment by decision makers.

Technology assessment is the evaluation of such forecasts in terms of predetermined technologic, economic, social, and political goals.

Thus, in our definition, a forecast aims to present alternatives, constrained only by physical laws or technologic development, rather than concentrating on the prediction of the statistically most likely event. In order to clearly understand the role of technologic forecasting in the decision-making process, we must situate forecasting in a seven-step planning development methodology:

1. Prescribing goals.
2. Presenting alternative futures
3. Presenting specific forecasts
4. Defining policies
5. Formulating plans
6. Implementing programs
7. Budgeting and allocating resources

Each of these seven steps is an independent discipline in its own right, with its own methodology, jargon, practitioners, and research journals, each with little overlap or relation to the others. The prescription of goals—social, economic, political, or technologic—is often a matter of prerogative or politics. The consideration of alternative futures, through intuitive techniques, associative methods, or interactive models, is the subject of the new discipline of futuristics.

It is in this context of possible alternative futures, possible alternative social or political systems or life styles, that specific technologic forecasts are made. Then considering the goals, futures, and forecasts in a broad socio-economic-political framework, executives define and describe policy, a process quite properly called policy analysis. In planning, policies are delineated and scaled according to time dimensions and objectives, and programs created. Then, finally, the programs are implemented at the staff level for individual projects, for which budgeting and allocating of resources takes place.

The latter steps, planning, programming, and budgeting systems (PPBS) have been used in the U.S. Department of Defense throughout the 1960s. The process of defining policies is part of the discipline of policy sciences initiated over 20 years ago by Harold D. Lasswell. The earlier steps, goal prescription, alternative futures, and forecasting, are disciplines still in their initial stages of development. This work concerns forecasting, and must be clearly distinguished from other steps in the methodology.

In order to define the subject matter more clearly, we must outline the objectives, the sources, the applications, and the methodology of forecasting—and technological forecasting in particular.

OBJECTIVES OF TECHNOLOGY FORECASTING

The objectives of technology forecasting fundamentally depend on the organization doing the forecasting: private industry, a public research institute, or a government agency.

Government agencies, particularly those concerned with defense and national security, have been long engaged in technology forecasting. The principal objectives of such research is to assess potential developments which might threaten national security, and to develop countermeasures to them. In the legislative area, the objective of forecasting is to evaluate the effect of technologic change on the interpretation and execution of laws, and to indicate the necessity of future legislation. One particular area of interest is the problem of computer software and copyright and patent laws. Technologic change has strained the interpretation of these laws, and further legislation is called for by many industry groups. Another area is the assessment of the effects of technology arising from new legislative programs on society.

Public research institutes are most effective in undertaking broad research programs in the area of social, political, economic, and technologic forecasting and interactions. Examples include jointly sponsored programs in the area of alternative political futures, studies of resources, and other interdisciplinary topics.

Forecasting in private industry is probably the least developed area, and accordingly commands most of our attention in this appendix. Forecasting is done in the securities industry as a technique in evaluating venture capital situations, merger and acquisition opportunities, and in securities analysis. In other industries, technology forecasting is often a part of a research and development program. As such, we can cite some specific objectives of a forecasting activity:

1. Identify projects for research and development
2. Evaluate and assess ongoing research projects
3. Prepare alternative strategies should conditions change
4. Provide input for organizational changes to meet future needs
5. Evaluate options for technology transfer

SOURCES OF TECHNOLOGY FORECASTING

Technology forecasting utilizes a number of well-developed disciplines as sources of information: operations research, cybernetics, information theory, decision theory, the theory of games, systems analysis, and general systems theory. Perhaps too much attention has been placed on attempting solutions of the problem, rather than understanding the problem itself. Only through a clear analysis of the nature of the problem itself can a solution be formulated according to the methodologies treated in the next section.

The first question we ask concerning the problem of technology forecasting is: Is the problem well posed?, or more popularly: Is technologic forecasting possible at all?

The standard solution to this problem is to do something that sounds sophisticated, call it "technology forecasting," and thus dismiss the question out-of-hand.

However, the question is a nontrivial one. By a "well-posed" problem is meant that the solution exists, is unique, and depends on the data in a continuous manner. The actual proof of the existence and uniqueness of a solution to a system is often a difficult matter, but is a fundamental step in the development of the theory. This is in fact the case in nonlinear analysis, optimization theory, and even the theory of games. A rigorously formulated utility theory of technological forecasting will have to do the same.

Such a theory of technological forecasting can be formulated along the same lines as mathematical theories of economics. One must select the appropriate variables, describe the interaction, and apply the given initial and boundary conditions. One may not be able to find an explicit solution, but one can make some statements concerning the nature of the solution.

The second question we ask: Is the input data valid and consistent? The input data must be carefully evaluated, and two standard criteria applied: validity (i.e., how closely the actual data reflects reality), and consistency (i.e., how different sources agree on the data). Numeric indices reflecting these criteria should be presented as part of the forecast.

The final question we ask: What is the nature of the interaction between the variables (i.e., what is the nature of the uncertainty)? Forecasting may be considered as a problem of decision making under uncertainty. We can characterize such uncertainty under four general frameworks:

1. Epistemic uncertainty: system behavior is uncertain due to ignorance or lack of full knowledge concerning the variables
2. Stochastic uncertainty
   a. Markovian: the change in the variables depends conditionally on the previous changes in the variables
   b. semi-Markovian: a more general Markov process in which the possibility of no change in variables could be allowed over a certain time period
   c. non-Markovian: the change in variables depends on events not described by one of the above processes
3. Game theoretic uncertainty: the system behavior is determined by "moves" of independent players following specific strategies. The behavior may be:
   a. stable: a small change in strategy produces a small change in system behavior
   b. unstable: a small change in strategy produces a large change in the system behavior
4. Canonical uncertainty: although the outcome may be uncertain, a standard or canonical procedure exists for determining the solution, which is fully determined by the variables and initial data

Another way to look at this framework is to call the characterizations decision making under (1) ignorance, (2) risk, (3) conflict, and (4) ambiguity.

The problem of doing a technologic forecast must be posed in this general framework in order to ask a meaningful question, and hope to arrive at a meaningful answer. Of course, it depends on the forecast whether the problem is well posed, whether the data is valid and consistent, and the nature of the uncertainty.

What should be clear from posing these questions is that technologic forecasting is not just a matter of technology—there are marketing, economic, and social variables as well. These variables, combined with the source disciplines of operations research, decision theory, game theory, and others are the foundations of the technologic forecast.

APPLICATIONS OF TECHNOLOGY FORECASTING

The application of technologic forecasting broadly fits into two categories:

1. Input to a strategic planning system
2. Source of feedback for ongoing research projects

In both cases, the forecast should not be expressed simply in terms of technologic devices or machines, quantified by some numerical parameter which indicates an advance in technology or utilization. A forecast, solely parameterized in terms of performance indices, may miss some important points of technologic development.

A comparison between the computer industry and the early automobile industry has often been made. Similarities are numerous:

1. The product requires extensive design and development
2. The product is standard and functional, different only in size, speed, or other characteristics
3. The product is sold "unbundled," with accessories or peripherals available at extra charge
4. Marketing and service plays an important part in the selection of the product
5. The industry has been characterized by mergers and consolidations, with the result that a few large firms dominate the industry
6. The industry has spawned a competitive industry in the area of replacement parts, accessories, and peripherals
7. Changes in the product models are made at periodic intervals
8. The emphasis is placed on the technology and engineering of the product, rather than human factors; thus developments in automobile safety and data security were rather late developments

One particular application of this comparison would be to compare the growth of processing speed of computers with the average cruising speed of automobiles. In the early days of both industries the curves are similar, almost exponentially increasing functions of time. Writers described future automobiles traveling between cities at 150 miles/hour; indeed, there is no technologic reason why they could not. And so today, writers are describing the development of superfast computers much in the same manner.

It is important to avoid a narrow-minded view of technologic forecasting simply as a blind projection of characteristics or parameters, ratios, or other indices, which signify improvements in size, speed, efficiency, or cost/performance. We should not even stop with improvements in design or architecture, application or use.

It is important to avoid seeing new devices and technologies, and even industries, as extensions of old ones. When we look back at photographs of early-century automobiles, we remark how funny they look. Indeed, the early automobile industry was not manufacturing cars, but horseless carriages. Similarly, the early computer industry thought it was producing fast data-processing equipment, rather than information systems.

It is even more important to avoid restricting oneself to what one considers as developments in "the industry." Again, a narrow-minded view should be avoided. The early railroad industry was confident of its market and its growth plans. However, it did not view itself as a part of a "transportation" industry; and while changes were taking place outside the "railroad" industry, it failed to capitalize on them.

With these remarks in mind, we can apply technologic forecasting to planning situations. The forecast, if it contains purely information on the technology or device in question, is of little value to the decision maker to which it is presented. The technologic forecast must go through two distinct and detailed evaluation processes: feasibility and assessment.

The technologic forecast only demonstrates technologic feasibility. Feasibility must be indicated at other levels, including:

1. Technical resources: Does the corporation have the staff and facilities to undertake the proposed venture?
2. Financial resources: Does the corporation have the funds available to support the project through development, production, and marketing?
3. Marketing resources: Does the corporation have the outlets, customer contacts, and sales personnel to handle the product? Are service facilities and personnel available?
4. Legal considerations: What are the patent, tax, antitrust, unfair competition, and product liability aspects of the development?
5. Strategic considerations: What is the relationship of the development with present or other planned product lines in the corporation, in the industry, or in other industries?

These questions, among others, are posed in the feasibility study to separate departments, namely:

1. Research and development
2. Financial
3. Marketing
4. Legal
5. Corporate planning, and product planning departments, respectively.

Each department should rate the proposed development with a feasibility index between zero and five, specifically:

0: the project is not feasible
1: the project is probably not feasible
2: the project may probably be not feasible
3: the project may probably be feasible, although there may be difficulty in obtaining the required resources
4: the project is probably feasible, and the required resources may be obtained with little difficulty
5: the project is feasible, the required resources are on hand

These feasibility indices should also be expressed over a definite time period—that is, feasibility index 4 to 1980, index 3 thereafter. In this manner the decision makers have a clear basis for establishing the most optimum time to initiate and execute the project.

Following the feasibility evaluation, if the project meets minimal requirements for feasibility, a technologic assessment is made. The question is not "can it be done," but "what are the consequences if we do it?" The specific questions that the separate departments consider include:

1. Research and development: What effect will the development have on the organization, staff, and facilities of the department?

2. Financial: What are the potential sales, profits, returns on investment associated with the project? What does a discounted cash flow analysis indicate? What are the opportunity costs of embarking on the project?

3. Marketing: What market share can the product achieve? What are the costs of marketing, servicing the product? What is the long-term nature of the market for the product, including questions of replacements, substitutions, and by-products?

4. Legal: What are the governmental, international, and social aspects of introduction of the products?

5. Strategic: What effect will the product have on the company, the industry, and other industries? What are the effects on the long-range planning goals of the company, including

   a. merger and acquisition plans
   b. plans for joint ventures
   c. plans for acquisitions of new facilities and staff
   d. plans for licensing agreements

One must be very careful not to reject a promising technology based on the limitations the assessment may present.

Once the assessment is complete, the forecast, feasibility, and assessment studies are presented to the management review committee for evaluation and decision. Under the framework of the general corporate goals, and separate studies of alternative futures, a final decision can be made.

METHODOLOGIES OF TECHNOLOGY FORECASTING

There are a wide variety of different methodologies for technologic forecasting, often overlapping, contradictory, or conflicting. In order to differentiate between them, we can classify the methods into three general categories, each increasing in the level of sophistication or complexity (but not necessarily correctness):

1. Intuitive methods
2. Associative methods
3. Interactive methods

Intuitive Methods

Intuitive methods rely on the opinions of knowledgeable persons, often "experts," in the field or technology in question. The opinions are developed in a spontaneous, random fashion, usually over a short period of time. Examples include the Delphi technique, brainstorming, science fiction, and scenario writing.

Perhaps the most fashionable intuitive method is the Delphi technique. The technique utilizes interviews, or more likely questionnaires, sent to selected participants to elicit their comments on possible future developments. Typical questions are posed in terms of parameters, such as a time scale as to when a particular technology will be readily available. After the results are compiled, followup questionnaires incorporating the results are sent to the participants to determine whether further refinement or modification of the responses is justified.

Of course there are significant limitations to the Delphi technique:

1. The participants may have no particular competence, background, or expertise in the technologies, or in the questions posed.
2. The questions asked reflect the background and interests of the group writing the questionnaire.
3. There is little opportunity to incorporate data concerning feasibility or assessment, effectiveness or efficiency, of the technologies considered.
4. The resulting "statistical" data often confuses rather than clarifies the essential relevant questions concerning the technology.

Associative Methods

Associative techniques are highly developed and frequently used in practice. By "associative" we mean that the predictions of a forecast are associated with the behavior of another system, whether a historical trend, a model, or an analogy. Some specific examples of associative methods are:

TREND ANALYSIS. The analysis of historical trends is probably the best known method of technologic forecasting. Refinements of pure-curve extrapolation include envelope fitting, regression analysis, time series, and spectral analysis. Some examples of trend analysis as applied to the computer industry are illustrated in Figure A1.1.

MORPHOLOGIC AND ANALOGIC TECHNIQUES. The morphologic method enumerates all possible "forms" or configurations of the problem or device under study; the forms are broken up into functional units, with characteristic parameters being varied. Thus, for example, one will generalize a wheel to "a rotating element," or a light to an "illuminating device."

The technique is an interesting application of language and semantics to technologic problems, but is probably of more use in claiming broad patent rights to a product then achieving an initial insight into the product or technology itself.

Other techniques in the same area include historical analogy and relevance tree methods.

MODEL TECHNIQUES. The model approach associates the problem with a set of variables, and a system of structural relationships and constraints between the variables. In economics, various sophisticated models have been developed to analyze the economic behavior of national economies, firm's inventory and resource allocation problems, interindustry dynamics, and international trade. These models may be either static—referring to behavior at a specific time—or dynamic—referring to expected behavior over a period of time.

The application of models to technologic forecasting is an extension of such dynamic economic decision models. The question usually posed is: What are the most efficient, or optimum, solutions of the problem? In a forecasting model, additional questions are posed to determine the values of various unknown variables at a later time.

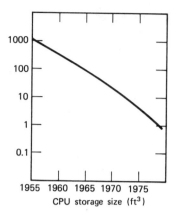

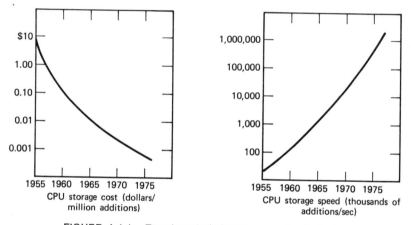

FIGURE A.1.1. Trend analysis in the computer industry.

The efficiency of a model is usually measured in terms of an extremal value of an objective function measuring "utility." The finding of an extremal value of a function subject to constraints is a standard problem in mathematics.

It must be pointed out, however, that although the mathematical problem is often straightforward, the application of the solution to specific problems in economics is not immediate. In any real life situation, variables are not easily quantized, and relationships between variables are not expressible in simple functional form. A specification of what constitutes "utility"—that is, what functions should be optimized—is a one-time value judgement that again may not reflect reality.

A model may also be described in terms of a "game." In game theory the constraints are reflected as "rules" of the game; the decision makers are the "players," and the utility or objective function is the "payoff." The dynamic characteristics of the model, reflected as sequences of decisions over time, are the "moves." The uncertainty of variables is equivalent to knowledge of previous moves by other players. The relationship between the variables is equivalent to the game "strategy" by the respective players.

The advantages (mathematical precision), and shortcomings (difficulty to relate to actual reality) of games are the same as for models. However, games are somewhat more general than models in their ability to incorporate a large number of decision makers as part of the descriptive specification of the game. These cases generally fall into the interactive methods of forecasting, and will be described more fully there.

CROSS-IMPACT, CLUSTERING, AND INPUT/OUTPUT ANALYSIS. We are often interested in focusing our attention on a discrete set of events and the relationship between them. These events, for example, may lie in the social, political, or economic spheres and may be positively or negatively correlated with one another—that is, one event may directly imply the other, have no relationship to the other, or may imply that the other event is inconsistent.

The forecasting methodology of cross-impact analysis consists of selecting the significant events, determining the relationship among one another quantitatively in terms of correlation coefficients, and displaying the results in tabular form permitting easy visual identification.

If the events can be described by a continuously varying parameter rather than as a series of discrete events, or if there is a great quantity of data that must be simplified, the techniques of clustering and aggregation are indicated. In that situation, two parameters are represented on x and y axes, and various regions of the x-y plane are designated to indicate a correlation relationship. By varying the partitions, scale, and weights assigned to the various parameters, and critical cutoff values for the correlation coefficients, various conclusions and predictions can be drawn.

Input/output analysis is a particular example of aggregation analysis where the parameters are the inputs and outputs of various elements of the system. Usually certain end outputs are known, and the problem is to determine the internal input/output mixes that would determine the known output. The solution of this problem is the same as with clustering and aggregation analysis.

Interactive Methods

Interactive methods are higher-order associative methods in which the decision makers "interact" not only with the data but with one another. Thus, whereas associative methods include linear or nonlinear programming in the static case and game theory in the dynamic case, interactive methods entail dynamic programming in the static case and differential games in the dynamic case.

MODEL TECHNIQUES. The model techniques involve two or more independent, interacting decision makers. In the static case, the problem is approached through generalizing the calculus of variations to dynamic programming. Optimal control theory, applied in a multistage fashion, is the general technique of solution.

In the dynamic case, the problem is that the different "players" change their strategy over time. These "differential games" may either be "discrete" or "continuous," depending on whether time is measured in discrete intervals or continuously. Furthermore, since the strategies change over time, the nature of the uncertainty is no longer simple "game theoretic," but is either stochastic or deterministic. Games are also classified as to the number of players—that is, as a "two-person" or "n-person" game—as well as the relationship of the objective or payoff function to all of the players—that is, as a "zero-sum game," in which what one player gains, another loses—or a "nonzero-sum game." The technique of solution is a nontrivial mathematical problem, often involving nonlinear partial differential equations.

SEVERAL-VARIABLE IMPACT ANALYSIS AND CLUSTER ANALYSIS.   Multiple-impact analysis, correlation analysis, clustering, and aggregation analysis in the interactive case are a straightforward generalization of the two-variable-at-a-time approach of the associative methods, and will not be detailed here.

CONCLUSIONS

We have surveyed the objectives and methodologies of technologic forecasting in this appendix for the purpose of introducing the reader to the wide range of possibilities the subject offers. We have not attempted to describe in detail any particular method, nor shall we apply any of these techniques to any aspect of the computer industry, such as planning a distributed computer network.

Our feeling is that a true technologic forecast is a major undertaking, done within a specific area of technology to meet some predetermined objectives. The objectives of the forecast should determine the techniques and resources to be used. The objectives of a small market research house, a major computer company, or a government technologic planning group are quite different, as are their financial and scientific resources.

The forecasting techniques we cite can only be more appropriately amplified in terms of the specific context of the forecast: the uncertainties, the parameters, the decision makers. Out of context, it is pointless or even meaningless to give more concrete examples. Indeed, such details are probably proprietary information anyway—or if not, usually just good guesses.

The actual use of econometric model forecasting techniques is, moreover, useful in the case of a corporate planning model, which is analogous to a technologic forecasting model with similar parameters and decision making structure.

The previous chapters have treated the computer-communications facilities industries in detail—systems, hardware, software, communications, and applications. The purpose of these surveys is to make an initial step toward a comprehensive technologic forecast in any specific area of the computer and telecommunications industries.

We again emphasize that the purpose of a technologic forecast is to present alternatives for decision makers, and not to make any vacuous "predictions" for popular consumption. There is no point in making innocuous statements about any of the technologies surveyed—such as suggesting when certain technologies may be commercially available—and no such forecasts will be found in this work. As we have noted in the Applications chapter, such decisions are as much financial and marketing decisions as they are technologic ones.

Thus, the chapters in this book present the state-of-the-art of available technology, present directions of research and development, and possible future research explorations. It is hoped that the analyses presented in this manner will deepen the consideration of future alternative computer systems and technologies, and motivate comprehensive technologic forecasts in those areas.

appendix two
DATA ENCRYPTION ALGORITHM*

T he algorithm is designed to encipher and decipher blocks of data consisting of 64 bits under control of a 64-bit key. Deciphering must be accomplished by using the same key as for enciphering, but with the schedule of addressing the key bits altered so that the deciphering process is the reverse of the enciphering process. A block to be enciphered is subjected to an initial permutation IP, then to a complex key-dependent computation, and finally to a permutation which is the inverse of the initial permutation IP^{-1}. The key-dependent computation can be simply defined in terms of a function f, called the cipher function, and a function KS, called the key schedule. A description of the computation is given first, along with details as to how the algorithm is used for encipherment. Next, the use of the algorithm for decipherment is described. Finally, a definition of the cipher function f is given in terms of primitive functions which are called the selection functions S_i and the permutation function P. S_i, P, and KS of the algorithm are contained in Appendix Three.

The following notation is convenient: Given two blocks L and R of bits, LR denotes the block consisting of the bits of L followed by the bits of R. Since concatenation is associative, $B_1B_2...B_8$, for example, denotes the block consisting of the bits of B_1 followed by the bits of B_2 ... , followed by the bits of B_8.

ENCIPHERING

A sketch of the enciphering computation is given in Figure A2.1. The 64 bits of the input block to be enciphered are first subjected to the following permutation, called the initial permutation IP:

*Reprinted from the Federal Information Processing Standard Publication *Specifications for the Data Encryption Standard*.

$$IP$$

58	50	42	34	26	18	10	2
60	52	44	36	28	20	12	4
62	54	46	38	30	22	14	6
64	56	48	40	32	24	16	8
57	49	41	33	25	17	9	1
59	51	43	35	27	19	11	3
61	53	45	37	29	21	13	5
63	55	47	39	31	23	15	7

That is, the permuted input has bit 58 of the input as its first bit, bit 50 as its second bit, and so on with bit 7 as its last bit. The permuted input block is then the input to a complex key-dependent computation described below. The output of that computation, called the preoutput, is then subjected to the following permutation, which is the inverse of the initial permutation:

$$IP^{-1}$$

40	8	48	16	56	24	64	32
39	7	47	15	55	23	63	31
38	6	46	14	54	22	62	30
37	5	45	13	53	21	61	29
36	4	44	12	52	20	60	28
35	3	43	11	51	19	59	27
34	2	42	10	50	18	58	26
33	1	41	9	49	17	57	25

That is, the output of the algorithm has bit 40 of the preoutput block as its first bit, bit 8 as its second bit, and so on, until bit 25 of the preoutput block is the last bit of the output.

The computation that uses the permuted input block as its input to produce the preoutput block consists, but for a final interchange of blocks, of 16 iterations of a calculation that is described below in terms of the cipher function f, which operates on two blocks—one of 32 bits and one of 48 bits—and produces a block of 32 bits.

Let the 64 bits of the input block to an iteration consist of a 32-bit block L followed by a 32-bit block R. Using the notation defined above, the input block is then LR.

Let K be a block of 48 bits chosen from the 64-bit key. Then the output $L'R'$ of an iteration with input LR is defined by:

(1)
$$L' = R$$
$$R' = L \oplus f(R,K)$$

where $\oplus$ denotes bit-by-bit addition modulo 2.

As remarked previously, the input of the first iteration of the calculation is the permuted input block. If $L'R'$ is the output of the 16th iteration, then $R'L'$ is the preoutput block. At each iteration a different block K of key bits is chosen from the 64-bit key designated by KEY.

With more notation we can describe the iterations of the computation in more detail. Let KS be a function that takes an integer n in the range from 1 to 16 and a 64-bit block KEY as input and yields as output a 48-bit block K_n which is a permuted selection of bits from KEY. That is

(2)
$$K_n = KS(n,\text{KEY})$$

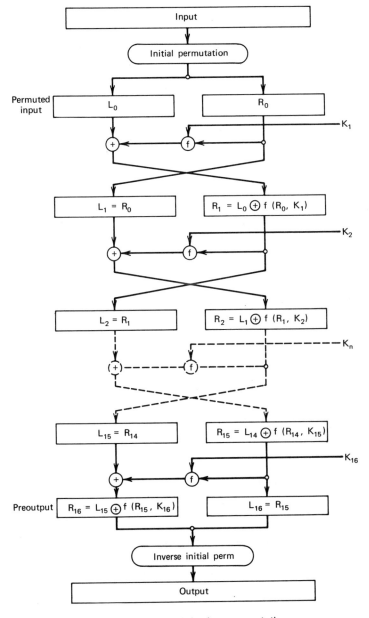

FIGURE A.2.1. Enciphering computation.

with K_n determined by the bits in 48 distinct bit positions of KEY. *KS* is called the key schedule because the block K used in the nth iteration of (1) is the block K_n determined by (2).

As before, let the permuted input block be *LR*. Finally, let L_0 and R_0 be, respectively, *L* and *R* and let L_n and R_n be, respectively, L' and R' of (1) when *L* and *R* are, respectively, L_{n-1} and R_{n-1} and *K* is K_n—that is, when *n* is in the range from 1 to 16.

$$\begin{aligned} L_n &= R_{n-1} \\ R_n &= L_{n-1} \oplus f(R_{n-1}, K_n) \end{aligned} \tag{3}$$

The preoutput block is then $R_{16}L_{16}$.

The key schedule *KS* of the algorithm is described in detail in Appendix Three. The key schedule produces the 16 K_n, which are required for the algorithm.

DECIPHERING

The permutation IP^{-1} applied to the preoutput block is the inverse of the initial permutation *IP* applied to the input. Further, from (1) it follows that:

$$\begin{aligned} R &= L' \\ L &= R' \oplus f(L', K) \end{aligned} \tag{4}$$

Consequently, to *decipher* it is only necessary to apply the *very same algorithm* to an *enciphered message block*, taking care that at each iteration of the computation *the same block of key bits* K *is used* during decipherment as was used during the encipherment of the block. Using the notation of the previous section, this can be expressed by the equations:

$$\begin{aligned} R_{n-1} &= L_n \\ L_{n-1} &= R_n \oplus f(L_n, K_n) \end{aligned} \tag{5}$$

where now $R_{16}L_{16}$ is the permuted input block for the deciphering calculation and L_1R_1 is the preoutput block—that is, for the decipherment calculation with $R_{16}L_{16}$ as the permuted input, K_{16} is used in the first iteration, K_{15} in the second, and so on, with K_1 used in the 16th iteration.

THE CIPHER FUNCTION *f*

A sketch of the calculation of $f(R, K)$ is given in Figure A2.2.

Let *E* denote a function that takes a block of 32 bits as input and yields a block of 48 bits as output. Let *E* be such that the 48 bits of its output, written as eight blocks of six bits each, are obtained by selecting the bits in its inputs in order according to the following table:

32	1	2	3	4	5
4	5	6	7	8	9
8	9	10	11	12	13
12	13	14	15	16	17
16	17	18	19	20	21
20	21	22	23	24	25
24	25	26	27	28	29
28	29	30	31	32	1

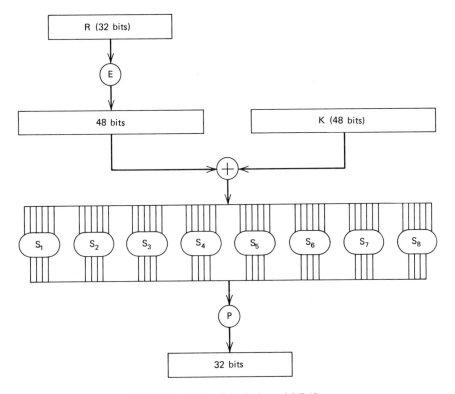

FIGURE A.2.2.   Calculation of $f(R,K)$.

Thus the first three bits of $E(R)$ are the bits in positions 32, 1, and 2 of R while the last two bits of $E(R)$ are the bits in positions 32 and 1.

Each of the unique selection functions $S_1, S_2, \ldots, S_8$, takes a six-bit block as input and yields a four-bit block as output and is illustrated by using a table containing the recommended S_1:

$$S_1$$

Row								Column Number								
No.	0	1	2	3	4	5	6	7	8	9	10	11	12	13	14	15
0	14	4	13	1	2	15	11	8	3	10	6	12	5	9	0	7
1	0	15	7	4	14	2	13	1	10	6	12	11	9	5	3	8
2	4	1	14	8	13	6	2	11	15	12	9	7	3	10	5	0
3	15	12	8	2	4	9	1	7	5	11	3	14	10	0	6	13

If S_1 is the function defined in this table and B is a block of six bits, then $S_1(B)$ is determined as follows: The first and last bits of B represent in base 2 a number in the range 0 to 3. Let that number be i. The middle four bits of B represent in base 2 a number in the range 0 to 15. Let that number be j. Find in the table the number in the i row and j column. It is a number in the range 0 to 15 and is uniquely represented by a four-bit block. That block is the output $S_1(B)$ of S_1 for the input B. For example, for input 011011 the row is 01—that is, row 1—and the column is determined by 1101—that is, column 13. In row 1, column 13, appears 5 so that the output is 0101. Selection functions $S_1, S_2, \ldots, S_8$ of the algorithm appear in Appendix 3.

The permutation function P yields a 32-bit output from a 32-bit input by permuting the bits of the input block. Such a function is defined by the following table:

$$P$$

16	7	20	21
29	12	28	17
1	15	23	26
5	18	31	10
2	8	24	14
32	27	3	9
19	13	30	6
22	11	4	25

The output $P(L)$ for the function P defined by this table is obtained from the input L by taking the 16th bit of L as the first bit of $P(L)$, the seventh bit as the second bit of $P(L)$, and so on until the 25th bit of L is taken as the 32nd bit of $P(L)$. The permutation function P of the algorithm is repeated in Appendix 3.

Now let $S_1, \ldots, S_8$ be eight distinct selection functions, let P be the permutation function, and let E be the function defined above.

To define $f(R,K)$ we first define $B_1, \ldots, B_8$ to be blocks of six bits each for which

(6) $$B_1B_2 \ldots B_8 = K \oplus E(R)$$

The block $f(R,K)$ is then defined to be

(7) $$P[S_1(B_1)S_2(B_2) \ldots S_8(B_8)]$$

Thus $K \oplus E(R)$ is first divided into the eight blocks as indicated in (6). Then each B_i is taken as an input to S_i, and the eight blocks $S_1(B_1), S_2(B_2), \ldots, S_8(B_8)$ of four bits each are consolidated into a single block of 32 bits, which forms the input to P. The output (7) is then the output of the function f for the inputs R and K.

appendix three
PRIMITIVE FUNCTIONS FOR THE DATA ENCRYPTION ALGORITHM

The choice of the primitive functions KS, S_1, . . . , S_8, and P is critical to the strength of an encipherment resulting from the algorithm. Specified below is the recommended set of functions, describing S_1, . . . , S_8 and P in the same way they are described in the algorithm. For the interpretation of the tables describing these functions, see the discussion in the body of the algorithm.

The primitive functions S_1, . . . , S_8, are

S_1

14	4	13	1	2	15	11	8	3	10	6	12	5	9	0	7
0	15	7	4	14	2	13	1	10	6	12	11	9	5	3	8
4	1	14	8	13	6	2	11	15	12	9	7	3	10	5	0
15	12	8	2	4	9	1	7	5	11	3	14	10	0	6	13

S_2

15	1	8	14	6	11	3	4	9	7	2	13	12	0	5	10
3	13	4	7	15	2	8	14	12	0	1	10	6	9	11	5
0	14	7	11	10	4	13	1	5	8	12	6	9	3	2	15
13	8	10	1	3	15	4	2	11	6	7	12	0	5	14	9

S_3

10	0	9	14	6	3	15	5	1	13	12	7	11	4	2	8
13	7	0	9	3	4	6	10	2	8	5	14	12	11	15	1
13	6	4	9	8	15	3	0	11	1	2	12	5	10	14	7
1	10	13	0	6	9	8	7	4	15	14	3	11	5	2	12

$$S_4$$

7	13	14	3	0	6	9	10	1	2	8	5	11	12	4	15
13	8	11	5	6	15	0	3	4	7	2	12	1	10	14	9
10	6	9	0	12	11	7	13	15	1	3	14	5	2	8	4
3	15	0	6	10	1	13	8	9	4	5	11	12	7	2	14

$$S_5$$

2	12	4	1	7	10	11	6	8	5	3	15	13	0	14	9
14	11	2	12	4	7	13	1	5	0	15	10	3	9	8	6
4	2	1	11	10	13	7	8	15	9	12	5	6	3	0	14
11	8	12	7	1	14	2	13	6	15	0	9	10	4	5	3

$$S_6$$

12	1	10	15	9	2	6	8	0	13	3	4	14	7	5	11
10	15	4	2	7	12	9	5	6	1	13	14	0	11	3	8
9	14	15	5	2	8	12	3	7	0	4	10	1	13	11	6
4	3	2	12	9	5	15	10	11	14	1	7	6	0	8	13

$$S_7$$

4	11	2	14	15	0	8	13	3	12	9	7	5	10	6	1
13	0	11	7	4	9	1	10	14	3	5	12	2	15	8	6
1	4	11	13	12	3	7	14	10	15	6	8	0	5	9	2
6	11	13	8	1	4	10	7	9	5	0	15	14	2	3	12

$$S_8$$

13	2	8	4	6	15	11	1	10	9	3	14	5	0	12	7
1	15	13	8	10	3	7	4	12	5	6	11	0	14	9	2
7	11	4	1	9	12	14	2	0	6	10	13	15	3	5	8
2	1	14	7	4	10	8	13	15	12	9	0	3	5	6	11

The primitive function P is

16	7	20	21
29	12	28	17
1	15	23	26
5	18	31	10
2	8	24	14
32	27	3	9
19	13	30	6
22	11	4	25

Recall that K_n, for $1 \leq n \leq 16$, is the block of 48 bits in (2) of the algorithm. Hence, to describe KS, it is sufficient to describe the calculation of K_n from KEY for $n = 1, 2, \ldots$, 16. That calculation is illustrated in Figure A3.1. To complete the definition of KS it is therefore sufficient to describe the two permuted choices, as well as the schedule of left shifts. One bit in each eight-bit byte of the KEY may be utilized for error detection in key generation, distribution, and storage. Bits 8, 16, . . . , 64 are for use in assuring that each byte is of odd parity.

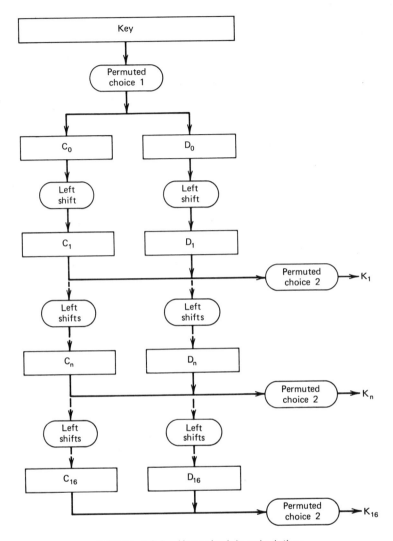

FIGURE A.3.1. Key schedule calculation.

Permuted choice (PC) 1 is determined by the following table:

PC-1

57	49	41	33	25	17	9
1	58	50	42	34	26	18
10	2	59	51	43	35	27
19	11	3	60	52	44	36
63	55	47	39	31	23	15
7	62	54	46	38	30	22
14	6	61	53	45	37	29
21	13	5	28	20	12	4

The table has been divided into two parts: the first part determines how the bits of C_0 are chosen, and the second part determines how the bits of D_0 are chosen. The bits of KEY are numbered 1 through 64. The bits of C_0 are, respectively, bits 57, 49, 41, . . . , 44, and 36 of KEY, with the bits of D_0 being bits 63, 55, 47, . . . , 12, and 4 of KEY.

With C_0 and D_0 defined, we now define how the blocks C_n and D_n are obtained from the blocks C_{n-1} and D_{n-1}, respectively, for $n = 1, 2, . . . , 16$. That is accomplished by adhering to the following schedule of left shifts of the individual blocks:

Iteration Number	Number of Left Shifts
1	1
2	1
3	2
4	2
5	2
6	2
7	2
8	2
9	1
10	2
11	2
12	2
13	2
14	2
15	2
16	1

For example, C_3 and D_3 are obtained from C_2 and D_2, respectively, by two left shifts, and C_{16} and D_{16} are obtained from C_{15} and D_{15}, respectively, by one left shift. In all cases, by a single left shift is meant a rotation of the bits one place to the left, so that after one left shift the bits in the 28 positions are the bits that were previously in positions 2, 3, . . . , 28, 1.

Permuted choice 2 is determined by the following table:

PC-2

14	17	11	24	1	5
3	28	15	6	21	10
23	19	12	4	26	8
16	7	27	20	13	2
41	52	31	37	47	55
30	40	51	45	33	48
44	49	39	56	34	53
46	42	50	36	29	32

Therefore, the first bit of K_n is the 14th bit of C_nD_n, the second bit the 17th, and so on with the 47th bit the 29th, and the 48th bit the 32nd.

bibliography

Books

Abramson, N., and Kuo, F. F. (Eds.), *Computer-Communications Networks*, Prentice-Hall, Englewood Cliffs, N.J., 1973.

Bennett, W., and Davey, J., *Data Transmission*, McGraw-Hill, New York, 1965.

Clark, A. P., *Principles of Digital Data Transmission*, Wiley-Interscience, New York, 1976.

Davidsson, L. D., and Gray, R. M., *Data Compression*, Wiley-Interscience, New York, 1976.

Davies, D. W., and Barber, D., *Communication Networks for Computers*, Wiley, New York, 1973.

Down, P. J., and Taylor, F. E., *Why Distributed Computing*, Hayden, Rochelle Park, 1977.

Galloway, J. F., *The Politics and Technology of Satellite Communications*, D. C. Heath, Lexington, 1972.

Glasgal, R., *Advanced Techniques in Data Communications*, Artech, Dedham, 1976.

Kildow, J. T., *INTELSAT: Policy Makers Dilemma*, D. C. Heath, Lexington, 1973.

Kleinrock, L., *Queuing Systems: Vol. II, Computer Applications*, Wiley-Interscience, New York, 1976.

Martin, J., *Systems Analysis for Data Transmission*, Prentice-Hall, Englewood Cliffs, N.J., 1972.

Martin, J., *Teleprocessing Network Organization*, Prentice-Hall, Englewood Cliffs, N.J., 1970.

Schwartz, M., *Computer-Communication Network Design and Analysis*, Prentice-Hall, Englewood Cliffs, N.J., 1977.

Article Collections

Abrams, M., Blanc, R., and Cotton, I., *Computer Networks*, IEEE Computer Society, Long Beach, 1975.

Chu, W. W., *Advances in Computer Communications*, Artech, Dedham, 1974.

Green, P. E., and Lucky, R. W., *Computer Communications*, IEEE, New York, 1976.

Karp, H. R. (Ed.), *Basics of Data Communications*, McGraw-Hill, New York, 1976.

Periodicals

Bell Laboratories Record

Computer Decisions

Computer Networks

Data Communications
Datamation
IEEE Transactions on Communications
Networks
Telecommunications

Articles

Beare, C. T., and Coutts, R. P., "Simulation of Data Communication Systems," *Instn. Engrs.*, pp. 83–88 (1976).

Bocker, P., "Data Transmission in Telecommunication Networks," *Rev. FITCE,* **14**(3), pp. 42–47 (1975).

Bright, R. D., "Experimental Packet Switching Project of the U. K. Post Office I. Facilities and Customer Participation," in R. L. Grimsdale and F. F. Kuo (Eds.), *Computer Communication Networks*, Noordhoff International Publishing, Groningen, The Netherlands, 1975.

"Data ARQ System for Satellite Links," *Commun. Int.*, **2**(9), p. 20 (1976).

"Data Security Using 'Telekrypt'," *Funschau*, **48**(24), p. 1080 (1976).

David, A. G., "The Legislative Implications of Setting Up a State Corporation to Manage Telecommunication Services," *Telecommun. J. (Engl. Ed.),* **42**(9), pp. 531–541 (1975).

"Digital Net to Link California State Colleges," *Digital Des.*, **6**(6), p. 24, 29 (1976).

Eckl, J., Frank, H., Frisch, I., Gerla, M., and Gitman, I., "Large Scale Computer Communication Network Architectures: Issues, Trends and Tradeoffs," *Proc. of 1976 National Telecommunications Conference, Pt. 1, Dallas, Texas, IEEE,* p. 16 (1975).

Evans, R., "Multiplexing Techniques to Save the Costs of Networks," *Comput. Wkly.,* **19**(463), pp. 14–15, 18 (1975).

Feistel, H., Notz, W. A., and Smith, J. L., "Some Cryptographic Techniques for Machine-to-Machine Data Communications," *Proc. IEEE.,* **63**(11), pp. 1545–1554 (1975).

Gitman, I., "Comparison of Hop-by-Hop and End-to-End Acknowledgement Schemes in Computer Communication Networks," *IEEE Trans. Commun.,* **COM-24**(11), pp. 1258–1262 (1976).

Grange, J. L., "CIGALE: The Packet Switching Subnetwork of CYCLADES," *Proceedings of an International Symposium on Medical Data Processing, March 2–5, 1976,* pp. 257–262.

Hajek, J., "Data Communications System of Burroughs B6700 and SATCOM Software for Connecting of Satellite Computers," *Tijdschn. Ned. Elektron & Radiogenoot.,* **40**(3), pp. 58–68 (1975).

Iimura, J., and Takatsuki, T., "Digital Data Network Field Trial," *Jap. Telecommun. Rev.,* **18**(4), pp. 230–237 (1976).

Jullien, A., and Mainguenaud, M., "'Teleinformatics' and the Transmission of Scientific and Technical Information, Status and Future Outlook," *Inf. & Doc.*, **3**, pp. 11–28 (1976).

Kallenbach, P. A., "Introduction to Data Transmission for Information Retrieval," *Inf. Process, & Manage.*, **11**(5–7), pp. 137–145 (1975).

Kelly, P. T. F., and Lee, E. J. B., "Scientific 'Hot Line' for Europe," *Post. Off. Telecommun. J.*, **28**(2), pp. 2, 4 (1976).

Kimbleton, S. R., and Schneider, G. M., "Computer Communication Networks: Approaches, Objectives and Performance Considerations," *Compt. Surv.*, **7**(3), pp. 129–173 (1975).

Kleinrock, L., "On Communications and Networks," *IEEE Trans. Comput.*, **C-25**(12), pp. 1326–1335 (1976).

Kleinrock, L., and Kamoun, F., "Hierarchical Routing for Large Networks-Performance Evaluation and Optimization," *Computer Networks*, **1**(3), pp. 155–174 (1977).

Kormendi, Z., and Lipp, I., "Economic Planning of Telecommunication Networks," *Budavox Telecommun. Rev.*, **1**, pp. 12–18 (1975).

Kovarovic, L. J., "Data Diagnostics: The Modern Approach," *Commun. Int.*, **3**(9), p. 48 (1976).

Kunz, H., "Decentralised Data Acquisition and Processing," *Neue Tech.*, **7**(11), pp. 681–689 (1975).

Larsson, T., "Completion of the Eurodata Investigation," *Rev. Telecomun.*, **30**(17), pp. 42–45 (1974).

Misra, V. K., "Data Switching Techniques for Realising the Desired Computer Communication Network Characteristics," *Electron. Inf. & Plann.*, **3**(12), pp. 947–953 (1976).

Nakano, Y., and Morino, K., "On the Performance of High-Level Data Link Control Procedures," *Electr. Commun. Lab. Tech. J.*, **24**(5), pp. 1005–1011 (1975).

"New Concept in Data Communication," *Elektro-Anz.*, **30**(6), pp. 22–23 (1977).

Nowicki, T., and Wesolowski, J., "Tasks, Organization and Kinds of Contemporary Computer Networks," *Prezegl. Telekomun.*, **49**(12), pp. 356–358 (1976).

"Packet Switching is Basis of National Network." *Can. Electron. Eng.*, **20**(12), pp. 24–26 (1976).

Pamm, L. R., "Transaction Network Data Communications for Metropolitan Areas," *Bell Lab. Rec.*, **55**(1), pp. 8–14 (1977).

Rewo, L., "Optimization of the Data Transmission Speed," *Informatyka*, **12**(9), pp. 4–7 (1976).

Rudin, H., "On Routing and 'Delta Routing': A Taxonomy and Performance Comparison of Techniques for Packet-Switched Networks," *IEEE Trans. Commun.*, **COM-24**(1), pp. 43–59 (1976).

Rudin, H., "Instantaneous Proportional Routing: A Technique for Packet-Switched Networks," *IBM Tech. Disclosure Bull.*, **17**(12), p. 3744 (1975).

Sarbinowski, H., "X25—The Packet Interface Between Data Terminal Equipment and Public Data Networks," *Online*, **14**(9), pp. 557–560 (1976).

Schutzer, D. M., and Ricci, F. J., "Design and Implementation of a PAC-SWITCH Network," in *Trends and Applications: 1976: Computer Networks, IEEE*, pp. 182–186 (1976).

Shamin, A. A., Majithia, J. C., and Mark, J. W., "Study of Overheads in Packet-Switched Data Networks," *Proc. Inst. Electr. Eng.*, **122**(11), pp. 1203–1206 (1975).

Snow, N. E., and Knapp, N., Jr., "Digital Data System: System Overview," *Bell Sys. Tech.*, **54**(5), pp. 811–832 (1975).

Sunshine, C. A., "Efficiency of Interprocess Communication Protocols for Computer Networks," *IEEE Trans. Commun.*, **COM-25**(2), pp. 287–293 (1977).

Sunshine, C. A., "Interconnection of Computer Networks," *Comput. Networks* **1**(3), pp. 175–195 (1977).

Thompson, G. B., "Towards a Clever Data Network," *Telesis* **4**(2), pp. 34–40 (1975).

Wu, W. W., "Bidirectional Data Translation Arrays," *IBM Tech. Disclosure Bull.*, **18**(3), pp. 817–819 (1975).

Zaiko, V. D., "Device for Transmission and Reception of Digital Information with High Reliability," *Mekh & Avtom. Upr.*, **5**, pp. 65–68 (1976).

Zimmermann, H., "CYCLADES: A General Purpose Computer Network," *Proceedings of an International Symposium on Medical Data Processing, March 2–5, 1976*, pp. 245–255.

glossary

This glossary defines the terms, acronyms, and abbreviations that are important in data communications and distributed processing systems. Acknowledgment is made to Digital Equipment Corporation for permission to reprint definitions from publications of that company.

Absolute Program. A program that incorporates absolute addresses, and therefore must occupy the same area of memory each time it is executed.

Access Control. The tasks imposed on a network or any of its components—performed by hardware, software, and administrative controls—to control usage of the system. Included are monitoring of system operation, insuring of data integrity, user identification, recording system access and changes, and methods for granting users access.

Access Method. A data management technique for transferring data between memory and an I/O device (e.g., direct, indexed, keyed, queued, or sequential access). Also called Communications Access Method.

Access Time. The time required for a storage unit or device to receive or transmit data after it receives a command to do so.

ACK 0, ACK 1 (Affirmative Acknowledgment). These replies (DLE sequences in Binary Synchronous Communications) indicate that the previous transmission block was accepted by the receiver and that it is ready to accept the next block of the transmission. Use of ACK 0 and ACK 1 alternately provides sequential checking control for a series of replies. ACK 0 is also an affirmative (ready to receive) reply to a station selection (multipoint), or to an initialization sequence (line bid) in point-to-point operation.

Acoustic Coupler. A device that converts electrical signals into audio signals, enabling data to be transmitted over the public telephone network via a conventional telephone handset.

Address. (1) A label, name, or number identifying a register, location, or unit where information is stored. (2) The operand part of an instruction.

Allocation. Assigning a resource (e.g., allocating an area of main storage to a task or allocating an I/O device to a job).

Alternate Route. A secondary path used to reach a destination if the primary path is unavailable.

Amplitude Modulation (AM). A method of transmission whereby the amplitude of the carrier wave is modified in accordance with the amplitude of the signal wave.

ARQ (Automatic-Repeat Request). A technique of error control in which the transmitter is requested to repeat transmissions of data segments believed to contain errors. Compare **FEC.**

ASCII. American Standard Code for Information Interchange. This is a seven-bit-plus-parity code established by the American National Standards Institute (formerly American Standards Association) to achieve compatibility between data services. Also called USASCII.

Assembler. A program that translates symbolic instructions into a machine language.

Asynchronous. Without regular time or clocked relationship (opposite of synchronous).

Asynchronous Transmission. Transmission in which time intervals between transmitted characters may be of unequal length. Transmission is controlled by start and stop elements at the beginning and end of each character. Also called Start-Stop Transmission.

Attenuation. A decrease in decibels (db) of power in a transmission signal.

Audio Frequencies. Frequencies that can be heard by the human ear (usually between 15 and 20,000 cycles per second).

Automatic Calling Unit (ACU). A dialing device supplied by the communications common carrier. This device permits a business machine to dial automatically calls over the communications network.

Availability. A system attribute that means that the system is operable and available to the user even though certain system components may have failed.

Background Processing. The automatic execution of a low-priority computer program when higher priority programs are not using the system resources.

Bandwidth. The range of frequencies assigned to a channel or system. The difference expressed in Hertz between the highest and lowest frequencies of a band.

Baseband Signalling. Transmission of a signal at its original frequencies, that is, unmodulated.

Batch Processing. A technique of data processing in which jobs are collected and grouped before processing. Data thus are normally processed in a deferred mode.

Baud. A unit of signalling speed equal to the number of discrete conditions or signal events per second. In asynchronous transmission, the unit of signalling speed corresponding to one unit interval per second; that is, if the duration of the unit interval is 20 milliseconds, the signalling speed is 50 Baud. Baud is the same as "bits per second" only if each signal event represents exactly one bit.

Baudot Code. A code for the transmission of data in which five bits represent one character. It is named for Emile Baudot, a pioneer in printing telegraphy. The name is usually applied to the code used in many teleprinter systems, which was first used by Murray, a contemporary of Baudot.

Binary Digit (Bit). In the binary notation either of the characters 0 or 1. "Bit" is the commonly used abbreviation for Binary Digit.

Binary Synchronous Communications (BSC). A uniform discipline, using a defined set of control characters and control character sequences, for synchronized transmission of binary coded data between stations in a data communications system. Also called BISYNC.

Bit. Abbreviation for Binary Digit.

Bit Transfer Rate. The number of bits transferred per unit time, usually expressed in Bits Per Second (BPS).

Block. A group of digits transmitted as a unit, over which a coding procedure is usually applied for synchronization or error control purposes. See also **Packet.**

Block Character Check (BCC). The result of a transmission verification algorithm accumulated over a transmission block and normally appended at the end (e.g., CRC, LRC).

BPS. Bits per second.

Broadband. See **Wideband.**

Broadband Exchange (BEX). Public switched communication system of Western Union featuring various bandwidth full-duplex connections.

BTAM (Basic Telecommunications Access Method). An access method for controlling the transfer of data between main storage and local or remote terminals with simple macro instructions.

Buffer. A storage device used to compensate for a difference in the rate of data flow when transmitting data from one device to another.

Byte. A binary element string operated upon as a unit and usually shorter than a computer word (e.g., six-bit, eight-bit, or nine-bit bytes).

Carrier. A continuous frequency capable of being modulated or impressed with a signal.

Carrier System. A means of obtaining a number of channels over a single path by modulating each channel upon a different "carrier" frequency and demodulating at the receiving point to restore the signals to their original form.

Cathode-Ray Tube (CRT). A television-like picture tube used in visual display terminals.

CCITT. Comité Consultatif Internationale de Telegraphie et Telephonie. An international consultative committee that sets international communications usage standards.

Centralized (Computer) Network. A computer network configuration in which a central node provides computing power, control, or other services. Compare **Decentralized Network.**

Channel. That part of a communications system that connects a message source to a message sink. See also **Information (Transfer) Channel.**

Channel Capacity. A term that expresses the maximum bit rate that can be handled by the channel.

Circuit. In communications, the complete electrical path providing one or two-way communication between two points comprising associated go and return channels. Compare **Channel.**

Circuit Switching. A method of communications in which an electrical connection between calling and called stations is established on demand for exclusive use of the circuit until the connection is released. See also **Packet Switching, Message Switching.**

Clock. A generator of precisely defined timing pulses.

Coaxial Cable. A cable consisting of an outer conductor concentric with an inner conductor and separated therefrom by insulating material.

Code. (1) A set of unambiguous rules specifying the way in which data may be represented (e.g., the set of correspondences in the Standard Code for Information Interchange). (2) In data communications, a system of rules and conventions according to which the signals representing data can be formed, transmitted, received, and processed. (3) In data processing, to represent data or a computer program in a symbolic form that can be accepted by a data processor.

Common Carrier.   In data communications, a public utility company that is recognized by an appropriate regulatory agency as having a vested interest and responsibility in furnishing communication services to the general public (e.g., Western Union, The Bell System). See also **Specialized Common Carrier, Value Added Service.**

Communications Computer.   A computer that acts as the interface between another computer or terminal and a network, or a computer controlling data flow in a network. See also **Front-End Processor, Concentrator.**

Communications Access Method.   A data management technique for transferring data between memory and a communications device.

Communications Control Character.   A functional character intended to control or facilitate transmission over data networks. There are 10 control characters specified in ASCII that form the basis for character-oriented communications control procedures. See also **Control Character.**

Compandor.   A device that is placed on a telephone circuit for compressing or expanding the signal amplitude to achieve improved signal-to-noise ratio.

Computer Network.   An interconnection of assemblies of computer systems, terminals, and communications facilities.

Concentrator.   A communications device that provides communications capability between many low-speed, usually asynchronous channels and one or more high-speed, usually synchronous channels. Usually, different speeds, codes, and protocols can be accommodated on the low-speed side. The low-speed channels usually operate in contention requiring buffering. The concentrator may have the capability to be polled by a computer, and may in turn poll terminals.

Conditioning.   The addition of equipment to leased voice-grade lines to provide specified minimum values of line characteristics (e.g., equalization and echo suppression) required for data transmission.

Connect Time.   A measure of system usage by a user, usually the time interval during which the user terminal was on line during a session. See also **CPU Time.**

Console.   (1) A part of a computer used for communication between operator or maintenance engineer and the computer. (2) Part of a terminal providing user input and output capability.

Contention.   A condition on a communications channel when two or more stations try to transmit at the same time.

Control Character.   (1) A character whose occurrence in a particular context initiates, modifies, or stops a control function. (2) In the ASCII code, any of the 32 characters in the first two columns of the standard code table. See also **Communications Control Character.**

Control Procedure.   The means used to control the orderly communication of information between stations on a data link. Syn: Line Discipline. See also **Protocol.**

Control Station.   The station on a network that supervises the network control procedures such as polling, selecting, and recovery. It is also responsible for establishing order on the line in the event of contention, or any other abnormal situation, arising between any stations on the network. Compare **Tributary Station.**

Conversational. Pertaining to a mode of processing that involves step-by-step interaction between the user at a terminal by means of keyboard and display and a computer. See also **Interactive.**

CPU Time. Central Processing Unit Time. A measure of system usage by a user, based on the total amount of computer processing time used. See also **Connect Time.**

Cross Talk. The unwanted transfer of energy from one circuit, called the disturbing circuit, to another circuit, called the disturbed circuit.

Cyclic Redundancy Check (CRC). An error detection scheme in which the check character is generated by taking the remainder after dividing all the serialized bits in a block of data by a predetermined binary number.

Data Access Arrangement (DAA). Data communication equipment furnished by a common carrier, permitting attachment of privately owned data terminal and data communication equipment to the common carrier network.

Data Acquisition. The retrieval of data from remote sites initiated by a central computer system (e.g., retrieving data during off-hours processing from a previously mounted magnetic tape at an unattended terminal or taking periodic readings from an unattended real-time station).

Data Base. (1) The entire collection of information available to a computer system. (2) A structured collection of information as an entity or collection of related files treated as an entity.

Data Base Management System (DBMS). Facilities for creating and maintaining a large, organized, structured collection of data and providing means for producing various types of predetermined reports based upon interrogation of the data base.

Data Collection. The act of bringing data from one or more points to a central point.

Data Compression. A technique whereby a repetitive string of data (usually on a byte basis) is transmitted as a count plus a string value.

Data Communication. The interchange of data messages from one point to another over communications channels. See also **Data Transmission.**

Data Communication Equipment. The equipment that provides the functions required to establish, maintain, and terminate a connection, the signal conversion, and coding required for communication between data terminal equipment and data circuit. The data communication equipment may or may not be an integral part of a computer (e.g., a modem). See also **Terminal Installation, Data Link.**

Data Concentration. Collection of data at an intermediate point from several low- and medium-speed lines for retransmission across high-speed lines.

Data Integrity. A performance measure based on the rate of undetected errors.

Data Link. An assembly of terminal installations and the interconnecting circuits operating according to a particular method that permits information to be exchanged between terminal installations. NOTE: The method of operation is defined by particular transmission codes, transmission modes, direction, and control.

Data Management. Facilities for supporting programmed access to the data files in a system by either the executing application program or direct user access.

Data Management System. See **Data Base Management System.**

Data Origination. The earliest stage at which the source material is first put into machine-readable form or directly into electrical signals.

Data-Phone Digital Service (DDS). A communications service of the Bell System in which data is transmitted in digital rather than analog form, thus eliminating the need for modems.

Data-Phone 50. A public-switched communications service of the Bell System featuring high-speed data communications at 50 kbps.

Data-Phone Set/Service. The data sets or modems manufactured and supplied by the Bell System for use in the transmission of data over the regular telephone network. The service mark of the Bell System for the transmission of data over the regular telephone network.

Data Set. (1) A modem. (2) A collection of data records, with a logical relation of one to another. See also **Data-Phone Set, Modem.**

Data Sharing. The ability of users or computer processes at several nodes to access data at a single node.

Data Terminal Equipment (DTE). (1) The equipment comprising the data source, the data sink, or both. (2) Equipment usually comprising the following functional units: control logic, buffer store, and one or more input or output devices or computers. It may also contain error control, synchronization, and station identification capability. See also **Data Communication Equipment, Data Link, Terminal Installation.**

Data Transmission. The sending of data from one place for reception elsewhere. Compare **Data Communication.**

DBM. Decibels referenced to 1 milliwatt as a measure of power. Zero dbm equals 1 milliwatt.

DDCMP. Digital Data Communications Message Protocol. A uniform discipline for the transmission of data between stations in a point-to-point or multipoint data communications system. The method of physical data transfer used may be parallel, serial synchronous, or serial asynchronous.

DDS. Data Phone Digital Service, a trademark of the American Telephone and Telegraph Company for identifying the private-line, interstate service for digital data communications.

Decentralized (Computer) Network. A computer network in which some of the network control functions are distributed over several network nodes. Compare **Centralized Network.**

Delay Distortion. Distortion resulting from nonuniform speed of transmission of the various frequency components of a signal through a transmission medium.

Delimiter. A character that separates and organizes elements of data.

Demodulation. The process of retrieving an original signal from a modulated carrier wave. This technique is used in data sets to make communication signals compatible with computer signals.

Dial-Up Line. A communications circuit that is established by a switched circuit connection.

Direct Distance Dialing (DDD). A telephone exchange service that enables a user to dial telephones outside his local area directly without operator assistance.

Direct Memory Access (DMA). A facility that permits I/O transfers directly into or out of memory without passing through the processor's general registers; performed either independently of the processor or on a cycle-stealing basis.

Distributed Network.   A network configuration in which all node pairs are connected either directly or through redundant paths through intermediate nodes. Compare **Fully Connected Network.**

DLE (Data Link Escape).   A control character used exclusively to provide supplementary line-control signals (control character sequences or DLE sequences). These are two-character sequences where the first character is DLE. The second character varies according to the function desired and the code used.

Drop.   A connection that is available for a terminal on a transmission line.

Duplex.   Simultaneous two-way independent transmission in both directions. Also referred to as Full-Duplex.

EBCDIC.   Extended Binary Coded-Decimal Interchange Code. An eight-bit character code used primarily in IBM equipment. The code provides for 256 different bit patterns.

Echo.   A portion of the transmitted signal returned from the distant point to the source with sufficient magnitude and delay so as to cause interference.

Echo Check.   A method of checking the accuracy of transmission of data in which the received data are returned to the sending end for comparison with the original data.

Echo Suppressor.   A device used to suppress the effects of an echo.

Effectiveness.   A system attribute that measures the level or degree to which the system is attaining predetermined goals.

Efficiency.   A system attribute that measures whether the system is making optimum use of the system *resources*.

Electronic Industries Association (EIA).   A standards organization specializing in the electrical and functional characteristics of interface equipment.

Electronic Switching System (ESS).   The common-carrier communications switching system which uses solid state devices and other computer-type equipment and principles.

ENQ (Enquiry).   Used as a request for response to obtain identification and/or an indication of station status. In Binary Synchronous (BSC) transmission ENQ is transmitted as part of an initialization sequence (line bid) in point-to-point operation and as the final character of a selection or polling sequence in multipoint operation.

EOT (End of Transmission).   Indicates the end of a transmission (which may include one or more messages) and resets all stations on the line to control mode (unless it erroneously occurs within a transmission block).

Equalization.   Compensation for the increase of attenuation with frequency. Its purpose is to produce a flat frequency response.

Error Control.   An arrangement or technique for the detection of errors, and often correction of errors as well, by operations on the received data or retransmission from the source. See also **ARQ, FEC.**

Error Correction Code.   A code in which the data signals conform to specific code rules so that departures in these rules at the receiving station can be automatically detected and corrected (e.g., cyclic block codes, convolutional codes).

Error Rate.   The ratio of the number of bits or other message units incorrectly received to the total number of bits of message units transmitted.

ETX (End of Text).   Indicates the end of a message. If multiple transmission blocks are contained in a message in BSC systems, ETX terminates the last block of the message.

(ETB is used to terminate preceding blocks.) The block check character is sent immediately following ETX. ETX requires a reply indicating the receiving station's status.

Extensibility. A system attribute that permits the addition of new, user-defined functions to the system.

FEC (Forward Error Correction). A technique of error control in which errors in a transmitted message are corrected through the use of redundant information at the receiving station.

Foreground Processing. High-priority processing, usually resulting from real-time entries, given precedence by means of interrupts, over lower-priority "background" processing.

Foreign Exchange Line. A line offered by a common carrier in which a termination in one central office is assigned a number belonging to a remote central office.

Forward Channel. A data transmission channel in which the direction of transmission coincides with that in which information is being transferred. Compare **Reverse Channel.**

Forward Supervision. Use of supervisory sequences sent from the primary to a secondary station or node.

Frame. See **Block.**

Frequency-Division Multiplexing (FDM). Dividing the available transmission frequency range into narrower bands each of which is used for a separate channel.

Frequency Modulation (FM). A method of transmission whereby the frequency of the carrier wave is changed to correspond to changes in the signal wave.

Frequency Shift Keying (FSK). Also called frequency shift signalling. A method of frequency modulation in which frequency is made to vary at significant instants by smooth as well as abrupt transitions.

Front-End Processor. A communications computer associated with a host computer. It may perform line control, message handling, code conversion, error control, and applications functions such as control and operation of special-purpose terminals. See also **Communications Computer.**

Full Duplex. See **Duplex.**

Fully Connected Network. A network in which each node is directly connected with every other node.

Half Duplex. A circuit designed for transmission in either direction but not both directions simultaneously.

Handshaking. The exchange of predetermined signals when a connection is established between two stations for the purpose of control and synchronization.

Hardware. Physical equipment, as opposed to a computer program or method of use (e.g., mechanical, electrical, magnetic, or electronic devices).

Hashing. A technique of calculating the address of data in memory from its value.

HASP. Houston Automatic Spooling Program. An IBM 360/370 OS software front-end that performs job spooling and controls communications between local and remote processors and Remote Job Entry (RJE) stations.

Header. The control information prefixed in a message text (e.g., source or destination code, priority, or message type). Syn: Heading, Leader.

Hertz. A unit of frequency equal to one cycle per second. Cycles are referred to as Hertz in honor of the experimenter Heinrich Hertz. Abbreviated Hz.

Heterogeneous (Computer) Network. A network of dissimilar host computers, such as those of different manufacturers. Compare **Homogeneous Network.**

Hierarchical (Computer) Network. A computer network in which processing and control functions are performed at several levels by computers specially suited for the functions performed, for example, in factory or laboratory automation.

Homogeneous (Computer) Network. A network of similar host computers such as those of one model of one manufacturer. Compare **Heterogeneous Network.**

Host Computer. A computer attached to a network providing primarily services such as computation, data base access, or special programs or programming languages.

Host Interface. The interface between a communications processor and a host computer.

Identification. (1) The process of providing personal, equipment, or organizational characteristics or codes to gain access to computer programs, processes, files, or data. (2) The process of determining personal, equipment, or organizational characteristics or codes to permit access to computer programs, processes, files, or data.

Information Bit. A bit that is generated by the data source and is not used for error control by the data transmission system. Compare **Overhead Bit.**

Information Path. The functional route by which information is transferred in a one-way direction from a single data source to a single data sink.

Information (Transfer) Channel. (1) The functional connection between the source and the sink data terminal equipments. It includes the circuit and the associated data communications equipments. (2) The assembly of data communications and circuits, including a reverse channel if it exists.

Interactive. Pertaining to exchange of information and control between a user and a computer process, or between computer processes. See also **Conversational.**

Interchange Point. A location where interface signals are transmitted between equipments by means of electrical interconnections. See also **Interface.**

Interface. (1) A shared boundary defined by common physical interconnection characteristics, signal characteristics, and meanings of interchanged signals. (2) A device or equipment making possible interoperation between two systems (e.g., a hardware component or a common storage register). (3) A shared logical boundary between two software components.

Interface Standard. A standardized method for establishing an interface (e.g., the Electronic Industries Association (EIA) RS-232C, the Department of Defense MIL STD 188B, or the CCITT standard).

ITB (Intermediate Text Block). In Binary Synchronous Communications, a control character used to terminate an intermediate block of characters. The block check character is sent immediately following ITB, but no line turnaround occurs. The response following ETB or ETX also applies to all of the ITB checks immediately preceding the block terminated by ETB or ETX.

Leased Line. A line reserved for the exclusive use of a leasing customer without interexchange switching arrangements. Also called Private Line.

Line. (1) The portion of a circuit external to the apparatus, consisting of the conductors connecting a telegraph or telephone set to the exchange or connecting two exchanges. (2) The group of conductors on the same overhead route in the same cable.

Line Hit.   A spurious signal that appears on a communication line due to electrical interference.

Link.   (1) Any specified relationship between two nodes in a network. (2) A communications path between two nodes. (3) A Data Link. See also **Line, Circuit, Virtual Circuit.**

Link Redundancy Level.   The ratio of actual number of links to the minimum number of links required to connect all nodes of a network. See also **Fully Connected Network.**

Load Sharing.   The distribution of a given load among several computers on a network.

Local Exchange.   An exchange in which subscribers' lines terminate. Also called "End Office."

Login.   A user access procedure to a system involving identification, access control, and exchange of network information between user and system. Syn: Logon.

Logout.   A user exit procedure from a system, often providing usage statistics to the user. Syn: Logoff.

Longitudinal Redundancy Check (LRC).   An error-checking technique based on an accumulated exclusive OR of transmitted characters. An LRC character is accumulated at both the sending and receiving stations during the transmission of a block. This accumulation is called the Block Check Character (BCC), and is transmitted as the last character in the block. The transmitted BCC is compared with the accumulated BCC character at the receiving station for an equal condition. An equal comparison indicates a good transmission of the previous block.

Mark.   Presence of a signal. In telegraphy, mark represents the closed condition or current flowing. Equivalent to a binary one condition.

Mask.   To suspend recognition of a signal.

Master Station.   See **Primary Station.**

Message Switching.   A method of handling messages over communications networks. The entire message is transmitted to an intermediate point (i.e., a switching computer), stored for a period of time, perhaps very short, and then transmitted again towards its destination. The destination of each message is indicated by an address integral to the message. Also called Store-and-Forward Switching. Compare **Circuit Switching.**

Modem.   Modulator-Demodulator. A device that modulates signals transmitted over communications circuits. Syn: Data Set.

Modulation.   The process of varying a specific characteristic of a *carrier* in accordance with the instantaneous value of the signal to be transmitted [e.g., amplitude modulation (AM), frequency modulation (FM), phase modulation (PM), pulse amplitude modulation (PAM), pulse code modulation (PCM)].

Multileaving.   A technique that allows simultaneous bidirectional communications traffic; for example, output from a previous remote batch job may be received while a new job is being transmitted.

Multiplexer.   A device used for multiplexing. It may or may not be a stored program computer.

Multiplexing.   A division of a transmission facility into two or more channels. See also **Frequency-Division Multiplexing, Time-Division Multiplexing.**

Multipoint Line.   A single communications line to which more than one terminal is attached. Use of this type of line normally requires some kind of polling mechanism, addressing each terminal with a unique ID. Also called "Multi-Drop." Compare: Point-to-point connection.

Narrowband Channels. Sub-voice grade channels characterized by a speed range of 100 to 200 bits per second.

Negative Acknowledgment (NAK). Indicates that the previous transmission block was in error and the receiver is ready to accept a retransmission of the erroneous block. NAK is also the "not ready" reply to a station selection (multipoint) or to an initialization sequence (line bid) in point-to-point operation.

NETWORK. (1) An interconnected or interrelated group of nodes. (2) In connection with a disciplinary or problem-oriented qualifier, the combination of material, documentation, and human resources that are united by design to achieve certain objectives (e.g., a social science network, a science information network). See also **Computer Network.**

Network Control Program. That module of an operating system in a host computer which establishes and breaks logical connections, communicating with the network on one side and with user processes within the host computer on the other.

Network Operations Center. A specialized network installation that assists in reliable network operations. Typical activities are monitoring of network status, supervision and coordination of network maintenance, accumulation of accounting and usage data, and user support.

Network Redundancy. The property of a network to have additional links beyond the minimum number necessary to connect all nodes. See also **Link Redundancy Level.**

Network Security. The totality of measures taken to protect a network from an unauthorized access, accidental or willful interference with normal operations, or destruction. This includes protection of physical facilities, software, and personnel security. See also **Privacy.**

Network Topology. The geometric arrangement of links and nodes of a network.

Node. An end point of any branch of a network, or a junction common to two or more branches of a network.

Noise. Undesirable disturbances in a communications system. Noise can generate errors in transmission.

Nonswitched Line. A communications link that is permanently installed between two points.

Nontransparent Mode. Transmission of characters in a defined character format (e.g., ASCII or EBCDIC) in which all defined control characters and control character sequences are recognized and treated as such.

Null Modem. A device that interfaces between a local peripheral that normally requires a modem and the computer near it that expects to drive a modem to interface to that device. An imitation modem in both directions.

Off-Line. Pertaining to equipment or devices not under control of the central processing unit.

One-Way Only Operation. A mode of operation of a data link in which data are transmitted in a preassigned direction over one channel. Syn: Simplex Operation.

On-Line. (1) Pertaining to equipment or devices under control of the central processing unit. (2) Pertaining to a user's ability to interact with a computer.

Operating System. Software that controls the execution of computer programs and may provide scheduling, debugging, input and output control, accounting, storage assignment, data management, and related service. Sometimes called Supervisor, Executive, Monitor, or Master Control Program depending on the computer manufacturer.

Overhead Bit. A bit other than an information bit (e.g., check bit, framing bit).

Packet. A group of bits, including data and control elements, that is switched and transmitted as a composite whole. The data and control elements and possibly error control information are arranged in a specified format.

Packet Switching. A data transmission process utilizing addressed packets, whereby a channel is occupied only for the duration of transmission of the packet. NOTE: In certain data communication networks the data may be formatted into a packet or divided and then formatted into a number of packets (either by the data terminal equipment or by equipment within the network) for transmission and multiplexing purposes. See also **Circuit Switching, Message Switching.**

Paging. The division of data or programs into fixed-size blocks or "pages" which are loaded into main memory only as required.

Parallel Transmission. Method of data transfer in which all bits of a character or byte are transmitted simultaneously either over separate communication lines or on different carrier frequencies on the same communication line.

Parity Check. Addition of noninformation bits to data, making the number of ones in each grouping of bits either always odd for odd parity or always even for even parity. This permits single error detection in each group.

Partition. A subdivision of main storage into fixed or variable regions or "partitions" which is allocated to a job or system task.

Password. A word or string of characters that is recognizable by automatic means and that permits a user access to protected storage, files, or input or output devices.

Peripheral Device. Any device that is not part of the central processing unit (CPU) in a computer system or network.

Phase Jitter. An unwanted random distortion of signals that changes their duration in time.

Phase Modulation (PM). A method of transmission whereby the angle of phase of the carrier wave is varied in accordance with the signal.

Point-to-Point Connection. (1) A network configuration in which a connection is established between two, and only two, terminal installations. The connection may include switching facilities. (2) A circuit connecting two points without the use of any intermediate terminal or computer. Compare **Multipoint Line.**

Polling. The process of inviting another station or node to transmit data. Compare **Selecting.**

Primary Station. (1) The station that at any given instant has the right to select and to transmit information to a secondary station and the responsibility to insure information transfer. There should be only one primary station on a data link at one time. (2) A station that has control of a data link at a given instant. The assignment of primary status to a given station is temporary and is governed by standardized control procedures. Primary status is normally conferred upon a station so that it may transmit a message, but a station need not have a message to be nominated primary station.

Priority Queue. A queue that is maintained in priority sequence.

Privacy. The right of an individual to the control of information about himself. Compare **Network Security.**

Process. (1) A systematic sequence of operations to produce a specified result. (2) A set of related procedures and data undergoing execution and manipulation by one or more computer processing units.

Program Sharing. The ability for several users or computers to utilize a program at another node.

Protocol. A format set of conventions governing the format and relative timing of message exchange between two communicating processes. See also **Control Procedure.**

Pulse Code Modulation (PCM). Modulation of a pulse train in accordance with a code.

QTAM (Queued Telecommunications Access Method). An access method which provides the capabilities of Basic Telecommunications Access Method (BTAM) together with the capability of queuing messages on direct-access storage devices.

Queue. An ordered listing of items. Queues may be ordered according to a simple first-in first-out (FIFO) basis or a more complex Queuing Discipline.

Queuing Discipline. A rule for providing insertions and deletions in a *queue* (e.g., Priority Queue, FIFO, yo-yo).

Random Access. Pertaining to a storage device where data or blocks of data can be read in any particular order (e.g., disk or tape). In random access devices you do not have to read from the beginning to find what you want as you do with paper tape and industry-compatible magnetic tape.

Real Time System. A system performing computation during the actual time the related physical process transpires, so that the results of the computation can be used in guiding the process.

Redundancy. In a protocol, the portion of the total characters or bits that can be eliminated without any loss of information.

Regional (Computer) Network. (1) A computer network whose nodes provide access to a defined geographical area. (2) A network whose nodes provide access to a specified class of users.

Regulatory Agency. In data communications, an agency controlling common and specialized carrier tariffs (e.g., the Federal Communications Commission, the state Public Utility Commissions).

Remote Job Entry. (1) Submission of jobs through an input device that has access to a computer through a communications link. (2) The mode of operation that allows input of a batch job by a card reader at a remote site and receipt of the output via a line printer or card punch at a remote site. Abbr: RJE.

Remote Station. (1) In a multipoint system, synonymous with tributary station. (2) In a point-to-point switched network, a station that can be called by the central station or can call the central station if it has a message to send.

Repeater. A communication system component that receives a signal, amplifies it, and retransmits it to a further or different destination.

Resource. Any means available to network users, such as computational power, programs, data files, storage capacity, or a combination of these.

Resource Allocation. The assignment of a system resource for the use of a program, partition, job, or task.

Resource Sharing. The joint use of resources available on a network by a number of dispersed users.

Response Time. The elapsed time between the generation of the last character of a message at a terminal and the receipt of the first character of the reply. It includes terminal delay, network delay, and service node delay.

Reverse Channel. A channel used for transmission of supervisory or error-control signals. The direction of flow of these signals is opposite to that in which information is being transferred. The bandwidth of this channel is usually less than that of the Forward Channel (i.e., the Information Channel).

Reverse Interrupt (RVI). In Binary Synchronous Communications, a control character sequence (DLE sequence) sent by a receiving station instead of ACK1 or ACK0 to request premature termination of the transmission in progress.

Ring Network. A computer network where each computer is connected to adjacent computers.

SDLC (Synchronous Data Link Control). A uniform discipline for the transfer of data between stations in a point-to-point, multipoint, or loop arrangement, using synchronous data transmission techniques.

Secondary Station. A station that has been selected to receive a transmission from the primary station. The assignment of secondary status is temporary, under control of the primary station, and continues for the duration of a transmission. Compare **Primary Station.**

Selecting. A process of inviting another station or node to receive data. Compare **Polling.**

Serial Transmission. A method of transmission in which each bit of information is sent sequentially on a single channel rather than simultaneously as in parallel transmission.

Signal Element. Each of the parts of a digital signal, distinguished from others by its duration, position and sense, or by some of these features only. In start-stop operation a signal element has a minimum duration of one unit interval. If several unit intervals of the same sense run together, a signal element of duration of more than one unit element may be formed. Signal elements may be start elements, information elements, or stop elements.

Signal-to-Noise Ratio (SNR). Relative power of the signal to the noise in a channel, usually measured in decibels.

Simplex Mode. Operation of a channel in one direction only with no capability of reversing.

Sink. (1) The point of usage data in a network. (2) A data terminal installation that receives and processes data from a connected channel.

Slave. A remote system or terminal whose functions are controlled by a central "master" system. It is similar in concept to a Host system in that it responds to remotely generated requests, but unlike a Host system it is usually capable of performing a limited range of operations.

Software. A set of computer programs, procedures, rules, and associated documentation concerned with the operation of network computers (e.g., compilers, monitors, editors, utility programs). Compare **Hardware.**

Source. (1) The point of entry of data in a network. (2) A data terminal installation that enters data into a connected channel. Data entry may be under operator or machine control.

Specialized Common Carrier. A company that provides private line communications services, e.g., voice teleprinter, data, facsimile transmission. See also **Common Carrier, Value Added Service.**

Spooling. An input/output technique utilizing fast intermediate storage to handle I/O operation for slower devices to make more efficient use of the system.

Stack. A queue or list of items ordered on a last-in first-out (LIFO) basis.

Star Network. A computer network with peripheral nodes all connected to one or more computers at a centrally located facility. See also **Centralized Network.**

Start Element. In Start-Stop Transmission, the first element in each character, which serves to prepare the receiving equipment for the reception and registration of the character.

Start-of-Header (SOH). A communication control character used at the beginning of a sequence of characters which constitute a machine-sensible address or routing information. Such a sequence is referred to as the *heading*.

Start-of-Text (STX). A communication control character that precedes a sequence of characters that is to be treated as an entity and entirely transmitted through to the ultimate destination. Such a sequence is referred to as *text*. STX may be used to terminate a sequence of characters (heading) started by SOH.

Start-Stop Transmission. Asynchronous transmission in which a group of code elements corresponding to a character signal is preceded by a start element and is followed by a stop element.

Station. That independently controllable configuration of data terminal equipment from or to which messages are transmitted on a data link. It includes those elements that serve as sources or sinks for the messages, as well as those elements that control the message flow on the link by means of data communication control procedures. See also **Terminal Installation.**

Stop Element. In Start-Stop Transmission, the last element in each character, to which is assigned a minimum duration, during which the receiving equipment is returned to its rest condition in preparation for the reception of the next character.

Supervisory Programs. Computer programs that have the primary function of scheduling, allocating, and controlling system resources rather than processing data to produce results.

Supervisory Sequence. In data communication, a sequence of communication control characters, and possibly other characters, that perform a defined control function.

Swapping. The technique of storing low priority programs or data in secondary storage and exchanging or "swapping" such data with data in main storage when necessary.

Switched Line. A communications link for which the physical path may vary with each usage (e.g., the dial-up telephone network).

Synchronous Idle (SYN). Character used as a time-fill in the absence of any data or control character to maintain synchronization. The sequence of two continuous SYN's is used to establish synchronization (character phase) following each line turnaround.

Synchronous Transmission. Transmission in which the data characters and bits are transmitted at a fixed rate with the transmitter and receiver synchronized. This eliminates the need for Start and Stop Elements, thus providing greater efficiency. Compare **Asynchronous Transmission.**

Tariff. (1) A published rate for services provided by a common or specialized carrier. (2) The means by which regulatory agencies approve such services. The tariff is a part of a contract between customer and carrier.

TCAM (Telecommunications Access Method). An access method that controls the transfer of messages between the application program and the remote terminals.

Teleprocessing. The general concept of data transmission and processing by a computer system and remotely located devices.

Teletype. Trademark of Teletype Corporation. Usually refers to one of their series of teleprinters.

Teletypewriter Exchange Service (TWX). A public teletypewriter exchange (switched) service in the United States and Canada formerly belonging to AT&T Company but now owned by the Western Union Telegraph Company. Both Baudot- and ASCII-coded machines are used.

Telex Service. A Western Union worldwide teletypewriter exchange service that uses the public telegraph network. Baudot equipment is used.

Telpak. The name given to the pricing arrangement by AT&T in which many voice-grade telephone lines are leased as a group between two points.

Temporary Text Delay (TTD). In Binary Synchronous Communications, a control character sequence (STX . . . ENQ) sent by a transmitting station either to indicate a delay in transmission or to initiate an abort of the transmission in progress.

Terminal. A device or computer that may be connected to a local or remote Host system, and for which the Host system provides computational and data access services. Two common types of terminals are time-sharing (typically interactive keyboard terminals) and remote-batch (e.g., the IBM 2780).

Terminal Installation. (1) The totality of equipment at a user's installation, including data terminal equipment, data communication equipment, and necessary support facilities. See also **Terminal, Station.** (2) A set composed of data terminal, a signal converter, and possibly intermediate equipment. This set may be connected to a data processing machine or may be part of it.

Text. (1) A sequence of characters, forming part of a transmission, which is sent from the data source to the data sink and contains the information to be conveyed. It may be preceded by a header and followed by an "End-of-Text" signal. (2) In ASCII and communications, a sequence of characters. Treated as an entity if preceded by a "Start of Text" and followed by an "End of Text" control character.

Throughput. A measure of system or network efficiency as a function of the amount of data handled compared with the theoretical maximal data handling capacity.

Tie Line. A private-line communications channel of the type provided by communications common carriers for linking two or more points together.

Time-Division Multiplexing. A system of multiplexing in which channels are established by connecting terminals one-at-a-time at regular intervals by means of an automatic distribution.

Time-Sharing. A method of operation in which a computer facility is shared by several users for different purposes at (apparently) the same time. Although the computer actually services each user in sequence, the high speed of the computer makes it appear that the users are all handled simultaneously.

Time-Slicing. The allocation of specific time intervals or "slices" to programs or jobs contending for CPU time.

Torn-Tape Switching Center. A location where operators tear off incoming printed and punched paper tape and transfer it manually to the proper outgoing circuit.

Touch-Tone Device. AT&T device for pushbutton dialing. The signaling form is multiple tones.

Transparent Mode. Transmission of binary data with the recognition of most control characters suppressed. In Binary Synchronous Communications, entry to and exit from the transparent mode is indicated by a sequence beginning with a special Data Link Escape (DLE) character.

Tributary Station. A station (other than the control station) on a centralized multipoint data communications system, which can communicate only with the control station when polled or selected by the control station.

Trunk. A single circuit between two points, both of which are switching centers or individual distribution points.

Turnaround Time. (1) The elapsed time between submission of a job to a computing center and the return of results. (2) In communications, the actual time required to reverse the direction of transmission from sender to receiver or vice versa when using a two-way alternate circuit. Time is required by line propagation effects, modem timing, and computer reaction.

Two-Way Alternate Operation. A mode of operation of a data link in which data may be transmitted in both directions, one way at a time. Syn: Half-Duplex Operation (US).

Two-Way Simultaneous Operation. A mode of operation of a data link in which data may be transmitted simultaneously in both directions over two channels. NOTE: One of the channels is equipped for transmission in one direction, while the other is equipped for transmission in the opposite direction. Syn: Full-Duplex, Duplex.

Unattended Operation. The automatic features of a station's operation that permit the transmission and reception of messages on an unattended basis.

Unibus. The single, asynchronous, high-speed bus structure shared by the PDP-11 processor, its memory, and all of its peripherals.

Unit Element. A signal element of one-unit element duration.

Unit Interval. The duration of the shortest nominal signal element. It is the longest interval of time such that the nominal durations of the signal elements in a synchronous system or the start and information elements in a start-stop system are whole multiples of this interval. The duration of the unit interval (in seconds) is the reciprocal of the telegraph speed expressed in Baud.

USASCII. See **ASCII**.

Usability. A system attribute that means that the system hardware and software interfaces to the user are simple, convenient, and easy to use.

User Exit. An external reference to which a user program may be linked (e.g., a user procedure for processing RJE batch job output).

Value Added Service. A communication service utilizing communications common carrier networks for transmission and providing added data services with separate additional equipment. Such added service features may be store-and-forward message switching, terminal interfacing, and host interfacing.

Vertical Redundancy Check (VRC). A check or parity bit added to each character in a message such that the number of bits in each character, including the parity bit, is odd (odd parity) or even (even parity).

Virtual Address. A relative location in main or secondary storage which must be converted to a real address before use.

Virtual Circuit. A connection between a source and a sink in a network that may be realized by different circuit configurations during transmission of a message. Syn: Logical Circuit.

Voice-Grade Channel. A channel used for speech transmission usually with an audio frequency range of 300 to 3400 Hertz. It is also used for transmission of analog and digital data. Up to 10,000 bits per second can be transmitted on a voice-grade channel.

WACK (Wait Before Transmitting Positive Acknowledgment). In Binary Synchronous Communications, this DLE sequence is sent by a receiving station to indicate that it is temporarily not ready to receive.

WATS (Wide Area Telephone Service). A service provided by telephone companies in the United States that permits a customer to make calls to or from telephones in specific zones for a flat monthly charge. The monthly charges are based on size of the zone instead of number of calls. WATS may be used on a measured-time or full-time basis.

Wideband. A communications channel having a bandwidth greater than a voice-grade channel, characterized by a data transmission speed of 10,000 to 500,000 bits per second.

index